M

DATE DUE

SEP 2 9 2007	
NOV - 9 2007	
DEC 2 6 2007	

DEMCO, INC. 38-2931

AUG 0 8 2007

HOUSE
OF STONE

*The True Story of a Family Divided
in War-Torn Zimbabwe*

Christina Lamb

Lawrence Hill Books

Library of Congress Cataloging-in-Publication Data
Lamb, Christina.
  House of stone : the true story of a family divided in war-torn
Zimbabwe / Christina Lamb.
        p. cm.
  ISBN-13: 978-1-55652-735-7
  ISBN-10: 1-55652-735-7
  1. Hough, Nigel. 2. Aqui, 1962- 3. Land tenure—Zimbabwe—
Case studies. 4. Whites—Relocation—Zimbabwe. 5. Farmers—
Violence against—Zimbabwe. 6. Zimbabwe—Race relations—
Case studies. 7. Zimbabwe—Politics and government—1980- 8.
Zimbabwe—Social conditions—1980- 9. Zimbabwe—History—
Chimurenga War, 1966-1980. I. Title.
  HD992.Z63L35 2007
  968.91051—dc22

                                                    2007019814

Map by Leslie Robinson

Published by arrangement with HarperCollins Publishers Ltd.

This U.S. edition published in 2007 by
Lawrence Hill Books
An imprint of Chicago Review Press, Incorporated
814 North Franklin Street
Chicago, Illinois 60610
ISBN-13: 978-1-55652-735-7
ISBN-10: 1-55652-735-7
Printed in the United States of America
5 4 3 2 1

*To my parents
who taught me there are always
at least two sides to a story*

CONTENTS

ILLUSTRATIONS

ACKNOWLEDGEMENTS

There are two people without whom writing this book really would not have been possible and they are of course Nigel and Aqui, for this is their story.

I would also like to thank their families, in particular Nigel's wife Claire and their children Jess, Christian, Emma, Megan and Ollie, his mother Mary and sister Tess; as well as Aqui's daughter Heather and her mother Chipo Tamari. Among Nigel's friends, Barry and Rosanne Percival, Pete Moore and Larry Norton were all extremely helpful as were Felipe Noguera, Tom Claytor, and Geoffrey Atkinson, the headmaster of Prince Edwards School.

As I write this, Zimbabwe has once again been named the most unhappy country in the world by Holland's Erasmus University which compiles an annual World Happiness Index. They may be the unhappiest but Zimbabweans are high up on my list of the friendliest people I have ever met.

Even war vets, I discovered, have their nice side. One of the most notorious, Wilfred Marimo in Hwedza, politely offered me tea at a farm he had just taken over, and war vets came to my rescue and towed me out when my car got stuck in the sand at night in a remote part of the Zambezi Valley during the height of the brutality.

Only once did I really feel threatened – in 2000 during the violent run-up to parliamentary elections when I went on the campaign trail with opposition activists in the lakeside town of Kariba. The candidate had fled after a coffin was prepared for him in the centre of town, and the only time his workers could stick up posters was late at night. Unfortunately just after midnight we rounded a corner to come face to face with a band of axe-wielding thugs from the ruling party. They surrounded myself and photographer Chris Cox and took us to the Zambezi Valley motel where they had raped and tortured a number of women a few days earlier. For three hours they harangued us, accusing Britain of being behind petrol shortages and poisoning the fish in Lake Kariba, in between asking the latest news about David Beckham. We were sat in a courtyard opposite rooms 3 and 4 where the rapes had taken place and it was hard not to think about the battered victims we had interviewed earlier in the day. Then for no reason at all they suddenly released us.

Over the last few years I have gone back and forth to Zimbabwe, particularly since the first white farm was invaded in 1999. In the last five years since British journalists have been mostly banned (in 2004 the government introduced the penalty of two years imprisonment), I have made twelve undercover trips. These would have been impossible were it not for the brave help of those who have to stay living in the country long after I am on a plane home.

Because Zimbabwe remains under brutal dictatorship where dissenters disappear in the night, many cannot be mentioned but I hope they know who they are and how much I appreciate their assistance.

In particular I would like to thank Henry, Fredi and Rita, Ian and Sue, Mr Pishai, John N. and Simon Spooner, and, outside the country, James Mushore and Georgina Godwin and also Algy Cluff for letting me stay in his beautiful house.

Those trips would have been a lot less fun were it not for Firle Davis; Loki and Lucy for providing a wonderful safe haven; Andrew and Julia; and Rob and Nicky to whom I also owe thanks for rescuing me when I ran out of petrol.

I would also like to thank Justin Sutcliffe and Paul Hackett, both talented photographers as well as friends, and Paul Salopek, one of the best reporters I know. All of them were at times travelling companions in difficult circumstances which involved cars breaking down in the middle of nowhere, secretly interviewing rape victims, sneaking into camps of the Green-bombers and hiding from secret police.

Back in London, writing this book would have been impossible were it not for the support and encouragement of my editor at the *Sunday Times* John Witherow and foreign editor Sean Ryan.

As always, huge thanks to my agent David Godwin and editor Arabella Pike who somehow managed to turn my manuscript round in record time in between moving house, looking after a new baby and taking on a new job.

Most of all, my wonderful husband Paulo and son Lourenço, both of whom were incredibly patient about a neglectful wife and mother.

Last but not least, a special mention to The Corrs for getting me safely through numerous police checkpoints throughout Zimbabwe. I have no explanation for this but the only times I was ever stopped and questioned were on the few occasions that I had forgotten to put my *Talk on Corners* tape on the car stereo.

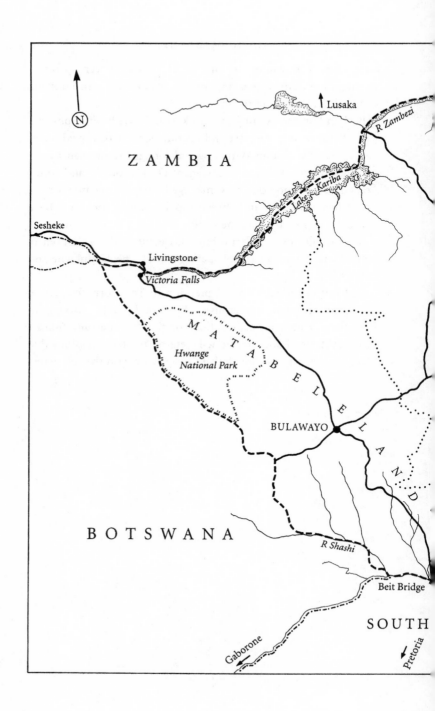

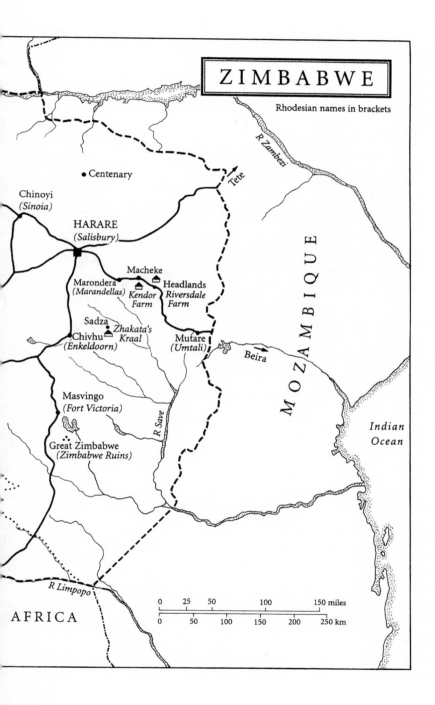

ZIMBABWE

Rhodesian names in brackets

• Centenary

Chinoyi
(Sinoia)

HARARE
(Salisbury)

R Zambezi

Tete

MOZAMBIQUE

Macheke
Marondera   Headlands
(Marandellas) Riversdale
  Kendor   Farm
  Farm

Sadza
Chivhu   Zhakata's
(Enkeldoorn) Kraal

Mutare
(Umtali)

Beira

Masvingo
(Fort Victoria)

R Save

Great Zimbabwe
(Zimbabwe Ruins)

Indian
Ocean

R Limpopo

AFRICA

| 0 | 25 | 50 | | 100 | | 150 miles |

| 0 | 50 | 100 | 150 | 200 | 250 km |

The mysterious tower of Great Zimbabwe

Among the gold mines of the inland plains between the Limpopo and Zambezi rivers [there is a] . . . fortress built of stones of marvellous size, and there appears to be no mortar joining them . . . This edifice is almost surrounded by hills, upon which are others resembling it in the fashioning of stone and the absence of mortar and one of them is a tower more than 12 fathoms high.

> VICENTE PEGADO, captain at the Portuguese garrison of Sofala,
> on seeing the ruins of Great Zimbabwe,
> *dzimba dza mabwe*, House of Stone, 1531

I have one great fear in my heart – that one day when they are turned to loving they will find we are turned to hating.

> ALAN PATON, *Cry, the Beloved Country* (1948)

Prologue

THE WAR VETERANS had been living at the bottom of the garden for months. Every afternoon the family would take tea on the terrace and stare beyond the swimming pool and children's tree house to the plumes of smoke rising from the round thatched huts that the squatters had built. Every night the family tossed and turned to their drumming and chanting. The next morning the farmer would find the carcasses of the cattle that the intruders had slaughtered.

Kendor Farm was in Wenimbi Valley in the rich tobacco-growing district of Marondera. Tobacco was Zimbabwe's main export, and for the previous two and a half years neighbouring farms all around them had endured similar invasions. The first murder of a white farmer had happened only a few miles away on 15 April 2000. Since then many farmers had been badly beaten; some had been hacked to death. Most had been either kicked off or fled. By August 2002 the morning roll call over the radio, started to check on the safety of local farmers, had stopped because Kendor was the only white farm left in the valley.

The Hough family had thought about leaving. But the 1,400-acre ostrich and tobacco farm and eight-bedroom house with its sweeping view over the balancing rocks and floaty canopy of msasa trees was their dream. They had worked hard for the farm and sunk all their money into it. They wanted their children to grow up as they had and could not imagine starting all over again. Other white farmers who had moved abroad to England or Australia had ended up driving minicabs and living in poky council flats. Besides, it was not only them. On the land they had a factory producing bags and shoes from ostrich leather and they employed 300 people as well as running an orphanage for children whose parents had died in the AIDS pandemic.

One morning, Claire Hough had gone to take the children to school and her husband Nigel had left for a meeting in town when their manager called in a panic. A crowd of people had arrived at the gate waving a letter demanding the farm. Nigel grabbed a friend and rushed back in his pick-up. By the time they got there, the mob had started a fire in his driveway, taunting him and barring their way with sticks and shamboks. '*Hondo, hondo,*' they chanted, Shona for 'war'. He could see that some of his furniture had been taken out of the house and piled up in front of the terrace.

Nigel telephoned the police but they refused to come, saying they did not involve themselves in 'domestic matters'. By now the crowd had surrounded him, dragging him off, nostrils flaring as they scented blood. 'This is not Rhodesia any more!' shouted one man. 'Go back to your own people.' As they pulled him towards an outhouse, Nigel noticed that some of the women had draped themselves in his wife's scarves and dresses and were tossing around his children's stuffed animals. Then he noticed something else.

In the front was Aqui Shamvi, the woman who had worked as their maid and much-loved nanny to their children since their first baby had been born six years earlier. To the Houghs she was almost part of the family. Now she was transformed. 'Get out or we'll kill you!' she spat at him, eyes rolling with hatred. 'There is no place for whites in this country!'

*   *   *

I first met the Houghs (pronounced Huff) and their maid Aqui (Ack-we) in August 2002 when they were all still living on Kendor Farm. Their relationship seemed different to me from any other I had seen between white farmers and black servants in Zimbabwe, and rather uplifting at a time when Robert Mugabe's government was promoting racist hate-speak in the state media.

The Houghs encouraged me to talk to Aqui and she was refreshingly candid as well as stunning in her red and white polka-dot uniform and green headscarf, and with her great big laugh. The setting was both sinister and surreal – we all sat on the terrace chatting and taking tea and Madeira cake trying to ignore the wood-smoke rising from the huts of war vets at the end of the lawn. To get to the farm had involved negotiating a series of roadblocks manned by youth militia adorned with Mugabe bandannas, their eyes bloodshot from smoking weed. Marondera was only an hour's drive outside Harare and its rich red soil had made the area one of the main targets of the government's land grab.

I wrote an article about the farm in the *Sunday Telegraph*, for which I was then diplomatic correspondent. In it, I described Nigel Hough as 'a model white farmer' for all his involvement with the local community and pointed out that to take his farm would expose the fact that the government was clearly not interested in helping its people.

A week later, to my horror, the farm was seized.

At that time, like many, I could not believe that Mugabe was really serious about seizing all the white-owned farms. The land distribution was undoubtedly unfair, with most of the productive land still in white hands. But the 5,000 commercial farms produced most of the food for the nation, were the country's biggest employer and responsible for 40 per cent of its export earnings.

Three years on, fewer than 300 white farmers remain on their farms. Yet it was never really a racial issue. Those of us in the Western media played into Mugabe's hands by initially portraying it as such, focusing on white farmers like the Houghs, perhaps because they seemed people like us. But the real victims were the hundreds of thousands of farm workers like Aqui who lost their homes and jobs. Many of them were beaten by marauding youth brigades who accused them of supporting the opposition and raped their wives or daughters while forcing them to sing pro-Mugabe songs. With nowhere else to go, they fled to the rural areas where they struggle to survive on wild fruits and fried termites.

My first visit to Zimbabwe was in 1994 when I was living in neighbouring South Africa. I was so taken with its beautiful scenery and friendly people that a few months later I went back on holiday with my husband-to-be. In those days, it was one of the most prosperous countries in Africa. We got giggling-drenched in the spray from Victoria Falls, drank gin-and-tonics as the sun set over the Zambezi and laughed at road signs warning 'Elephants Crossing'. We sat awed by the silent grandeur of the Matopos Hills, burial place of Cecil Rhodes, empire builder after whom the country was originally named and a man who said, 'I would annex the planets if I could.'

We also marvelled at an African nation with traffic lights that worked (even if they did call them robots), the pothole-free roads, neat brick schools everywhere, cappuccino bars and book cafés. It seemed a true Garden of Eden and the roads on which we travelled passed through a patchwork of lush green fields of tobacco, cotton and maize. They looked like model farms with combine harvesters gathering up neat bundles, long greenhouses full of neatly spaced roses, and rainbows playing through the water sprinkling from sophisticated irrigation systems.

Today Zimbabwe looks as if a terrible scourge has swept through. Some of the most advanced farms in the world have been reduced to slash and burn. The fields are charred and spiked with dead maize stalks or overgrown with weeds; the equipment has been plundered and stripped; and what little ploughing still goes on is by oxen or donkey. The country, which used to export large amounts of food, cannot even feed its own people. The destruction of the farms has left more than half of Zimbabwe's 12 million population on the edge of starvation and life expectancy has plummeted to around 30. The money is so worthless, with a loaf of bread costing 90,000 Zim dollars, that the country is returning to a barter economy.

In 2005, Mugabe switched his attention to the cities, targeting the urban population who had dared vote against him in successive elections. In the last week of May, I watched in shock as police bulldozers demolished thousands of homes, market stalls and small businesses. Operation Murambatswina or 'Clean Up the Filth' turned the country into an apocalyptic landscape wreathed with plumes of smoke and scattered with fleeing refugees clutching the scant belongings they had managed to salvage in bundles or on their heads. The few lucky ones had wardrobes or iron beds strapped onto wheelbarrows.

I have seen many dreadful things in my nineteen years of foreign reporting but nothing has affected me so profoundly as wandering through the smoking ruins of Mbare, the southern suburb of Harare that sprawls around Zimbabwe's oldest and largest market. My Lonely Planet guidebook recommends it as one of its five highlights of Harare and the place to see 'colourful crowded scenes typical of Africa'. Instead, it looked as if a tsunami had passed through, reducing the famous market into drift-piles of smashed wood, twisted metal and broken bricks. The ground was awash with fruit and tomatoes trampled by the boots of Mugabe's henchmen, the ultimate indignity in a country where so many were starving.

Sirens wailed and newly acquired Chinese warplanes roared overhead to add to the fear. I walked around, careless of the fact that I was illegally in the country and that my white skin and fair hair were acting like a beacon to my presence, so stunned was I that a country's leader could do this to his own people.

A few figures were picking among the debris like vultures while

Harare after Operation Murambatswina

others crouched in small dazed groups by the roadside. It was winter and the ground was hard and cold. The ubiquitous face of Robert Mugabe stared impassively up through the broken glass of a smashed picture. Ten or so women, two of them breastfeeding babies, squatted amid the rubble of what they told me had been the country's oldest chicken cooperative, founded in 1945. Further on, next to a pile of pink concrete and some torn magazine photos of celebrities, sat a large woman with elaborately beaded hair and a face that was crumpling inward. She tonelessly explained that the scattered debris was all that remained of her beauty salon, Glory's Hair Palace, which she had built up over many years. Glory was an extremely ample woman, jokingly known in the neighbourhood as Miss Universe. Her reputation for nimble weaving of hair, all the time dispensing sound advice about the male species (with frequent references to her own long-departed husband 'the useless Blessing'), had enabled her to feed and educate her children.

A little further was a small fire around which huddled a terrified family with a daughter in a wheelchair. The mother, Memory, had the white flaking skin common among those who are HIV positive. 'When they came with the bulldozers we told the police we have a disabled child, so please don't knock down our house,' she said. 'They just said we don't care about the disabled and bulldozed our house and my husband's carpentry workshop and all his tools.' Since then they had been sleeping in the open, and she showed me a seeping wound on her daughter's leg where she had been bitten by a rat.

None of these people were beggars or criminals. They had all been working for years to provide their families a decent life, only to find their homes and workplaces crushed to rubble in the name of 'urban beautification'.

Along the railway line, past the National Foods factory, I came to Kambu Zuma suburb where police and militia had just arrived on their trucks and bulldozers. I stared aghast as people sat and did nothing while police took axes to their homes. Some of the houses were not shacks but two-storey concrete houses that took the bulldozers an hour to demolish.

Impatient with their slow progress, the police started ordering residents to destroy their own homes. Large fires were lit and people told to throw on their possessions. I watched hundreds of Zimbabweans, one of Africa's most educated populations, obediently smash and burn all they had ever worked for, leaving them with nowhere to live, no means to feed their children or pay their school fees.

I had made repeated trips to report on Zimbabwe since 1999 when the first farm invasion took place. Throughout the subsequent intimidation of the population and rigging of three elections, I had never understood why Zimbabweans did not rise up against their leader as people had in Yugoslavia or Ukraine. It irritated me that they kept asking why the outside world did nothing, when it seemed they were unwilling to help themselves. But at that moment in Kambu Zuma, watching people meekly burn their own belongings, I realized for the first time just how much twenty-five years of Mugabe's rule had oppressed the population. The next morning I had coffee with Nelson Chamisa, the youth leader of the opposition Movement for Democratic Change. Usually something of a firebrand, he stared into his cup, looking utterly defeated. 'The people will never rise up now,' he said, 'Mugabe can do anything he likes to them.'

Afterwards when I returned home to London, I found myself waking in the middle of the night seeing those blank faces watching the bulldozers. I went to see *Macbeth* at the magical Wilton Music Hall in the East End and found Shakespeare's tragic hero portrayed as an African dictator as if to haunt me further.

'Where will it stop?' had been the plaintive cry of a friend from one of the United Nations agencies in Harare. 'It's just so unnecessary.' His organization, like all foreign aid agencies, had been banned by Mugabe from assisting the hundreds of thousands made homeless because the President insisted there was 'no humanitarian crisis'. Later, Mugabe refused to let the UN supply tents to those still sleeping in the open, saying 'there is no tradition of tents' in Zimbabwe, and his bulldozers destroyed a model settlement built by the UN in Headlands. I wasn't surprised to read the latest World Bank statistics revealing that 70 per cent of Zimbabweans are living below the poverty line and describing its fall in living standards from 1999 to 2005 as 'unprecedented for a country not at war'.

The tragedy of Zimbabwe, as my friend from the UN said, is that it is just so unnecessary. But to this African Macbeth it is very necessary indeed. For Mugabe is a man who, in a quarter of a century, has gone from liberation hero and darling of the left to tyrant with much blood on his hands. Staying in power has become synonymous with survival.

This is a story then about two people who have lived through all this, from a brutal civil war to the elation of becoming the last British colony in Africa to win independence; the early optimism and international acclaim, with Mugabe even receiving an honorary knighthood; and then the descent into madness. It is a story of two people, from completely different backgrounds, one rich, one poor, one white, one black, yet it is not about race. Rather it is about power and one violent man trying to save his skin even if he destroys the whole country in the process.

Ethnic cleansing is a loaded term and not quite accurate for what Mugabe has done, though the Ndebeles have been targeted most and he has increasingly surrounded himself with members of his own Zezuru clan whom he has known since the days of the liberation war. Perhaps it should be called political cleansing or class cleansing, for Mugabe's Marxist ideology and loathing of the bourgeoisie underpin many of his actions. Anyone with a different point of view is forced to conform or flee. In the last five years, at least a quarter of the population have left the country – more than 3 million people, including many of Zimbabwe's brightest, such as doctors, nurses, journalists and teachers. Those who remain are enfeebled by fear and hunger, and many are sick. Around a third of the adult population are infected with the HIV virus, and few of those are able to access drugs. Mugabe has even banned church feeding programmes. By 2006 Zimbabwe had the world's lowest life expectancy – just 37 for men and 34 for women. People were so desperate in Zimbabwe's brutalised society that the United Nations Children's Fund reported one child abused every hour partly because of a myth that AIDS could be cured by having sex with a virgin.

Back in 2001, on one of the last times I was actually allowed

into the country as a journalist, I went with a group of colleagues
to attend a press conference of Didymus Mutasa, hardline Mugabe
loyalist and Politburo member. 'We would be better off with
only six million people, with our own people who support the
liberation struggle,' he told us in his soft voice. 'We don't want
these extra people.' He spoke extremely politely and at the time I
thought this was just crazed talk. But Mutasa then became State
Security Minister in charge of secret police and it was he who
headed Operation Murambatswina. For in the violence-filled
years since his threat was made, Zimbabweans have learnt to their
cost that Mugabe and his henchmen mean exactly what they say.

London, November 2006

1

Zhakata's Kraal, 1970

IT WAS ONLY WHEN Aquinata crossed the second of the three rivers where her two brothers lay buried that she felt safe. Her way back from the Catholic mission school went up and down through yellow elephant grass and over rocky kopjes or hills dotted with spiky acacia trees where green mambas lurked. If she walked quickly she could just do it in an hour.

The teachers would always keep back two or three of the girls after school to cook their supper. Aqui hated that. She had never fainted in lessons like some of her friends but most days she had been up since four or five, collecting water and firewood before school, and had eaten nothing since tea in the morning. *I would be so hungry in my belly that it hurt just to look into that pot of fine white sadza. Sometimes it would even be fortified with lumps of meat. Yet they wouldn't even give me a scrap.*

It also meant she would be walking home as the shadows turned crimson and the sun swelled like an elephant's bottom then suddenly slunk from the sky. That was the hour when trees turned to dark murmuring shapes where spirits or *tokoloshis* might hide and bad men and animals came out. On what Aqui thought of as the Wrong Side of the rivers, warthogs and vicious dogs might dart from the bush, and once she even saw a cobra lying like a stick across the path, its skin shiny as if coated with dew. In the rivers were crocodiles that occasionally ate people from the village, though that did not stop Aqui and the other children from swimming.

But once she had navigated the log over the middle river, a crossing she could now do in five steps, she would finally be relieved of the fist that clutched at her chest and forced her breathing into an asthmatic wheeze. *Then I could walk head high, for I was back in my territory, crossing the lands where the ancestors lay buried.* The wood-smoke on the wind came from the fires of her people, a subclan of the Zezuru, one of the biggest Shona tribes, and the thump-thump she could hear was the pounding of millet by their women.

Aqui lived among the prickly cactus trees in the so-called Remote Areas of Mashonaland. Her village was named Zhakata's Kraal, after a former headman, and it lay on the highveld in the stony shadow of the Daramombe Mountains behind which the birds chased the disappearing sun every evening. It was not on any map or road and was a long day's walk from the nearest town of Chivhu, a small cattle-ranching settlement that the whites called Enkeldoorn after the Dutch for 'single thorn', about 90 miles south of their capital, Salisbury. Zhakata's Kraal was in one of the Native Reserves, communal lands into which blacks had been shunted when the whites came, and it was a desolate place, the surrounding trees all having been shorn of limbs for firewood. The village consisted of a line of round mud-and-pole huts with thatched roofs all facing east and dotted amid large rocks and thorn trees. Chickens scratched in the dust and a stray dog with a withered leg scooted about on its bottom. The headman's place stood on the other side, and a little away was the house of the witchdoctor or *nganga* near the sacred muchakata tree under which the elders would hold their meetings and lay offerings to appease the ancestral spirits.

Aqui was proud that her parents were very clever and, unlike most of the villagers, did not believe in ghosts or *tokoloshis* that could possess you, poison your food or bewitch your enemies,

A cactus tree

but that did not stop her quickening her step as she passed by. Sometimes lightning could turn itself into a ball and chase a person round a hut to strike him dead, as had happened to her father's cousin who let his mombes trample his neighbour's fields and she wasn't sure what that was if not witchcraft. 'Better to be safe than late [as in dead],' said her grandmother who saw faces in the fire and was a *mhondoro*, which meant she had the spirit of a lion and could act as a medium to talk to the ancestors.

Aqui was the eldest of five children. There had been eight of them but two of her younger brothers and a sister had died as infants. Such deaths were common in the village. *I think one brother and sister died of dehydration from diarrhoea and one brother from jaundice but my mother said it was because the spirits were not happy. The first boy was almost two when he died and my mother said it was because she had met another mother whose child had muti on his head to protect him.* The weeping after the death of the first son had gone on for days and he had been buried in the banks of the first river Aqui crossed on the way to school. The elders had explained that children could not be buried in dry places like older people because they are weak and their souls not yet formed so had to be buried in the soft clay of the riverbanks.

Their home was a small compound comprising three *rondavels*, round windowless huts, inside a fence of jagged branches. Like all the huts in the village, theirs were made from mud from anthills that the women would mix up with water from the river to form sticky dough then plaster it on with their hands. *I loved watching them doing it and longed for the day I would have my own hut.* Some of the more artistic women used sticks to decorate them with swirls or a sharp stone to cut a diamond pattern, but her mother left theirs plain. The roof was made of dried elephant grass that the women carried on their heads in bundles from the river, and for the floor they mixed cowpats with water, which set as solid as concrete.

The biggest hut in their compound was the bedroom hut where her mother, father and surviving baby brother slept and their few belongings were kept. The only decor was a small cracked mirror and a yellowing 1966 calendar advertising tractor parts that her father had brought back from a job; there was a thin lumpy mattress on the ground and a tin trunk held clothes and a Bible.

The second hut was on stilts with a ladder of crooked logs leading up to it. That was the storeroom for mealie meal to dry, safe from the white ants that got everywhere and the rats that kept Aqui awake with their scrabbling at night as they tried to tunnel under the hut walls. The third and last hut was the kitchen hut in which they cooked the meals and Aqui and her sisters would sleep. The kitchen hut also served as the sitting room and as the female members of the family entered they would squat on the ground on the left while the men veered right to sit on a raised bench that ran all along the side. It was always smoky inside, but once a visitor grew accustomed to the gloom they would see shelves at the back moulded from the wall. On these were arranged the family's few cooking utensils and tin cups as well as two green enamel plates decorated with red flowers that her father had brought from town. The back of the hut was considered the sacred abode of the *mudzimu*, the ancestral spirits that protect the family, and when Aqui's siblings died they were laid on one of the shelves before being buried to help them cross the boundary to the spirit world.

In the centre of the floor was a fire in a round hearth where her mother would cook *sadza*. Sometimes they would eat it spiced up with relish from her mother's garden or wild fruits like marula or chakata that the chief had forbidden the villagers from selling because he believed that would cause lightning.

Zhakata's Kraal

If the mealies were ready in the field they would roast them brown and crispy, and this was Aqui's favourite food. She thought there was nothing better than blowing off the ash and biting into the crunchy sweetness. Apart, perhaps, from the first rain when the children would all run outside and dance about, holding their hands out to try and catch the little liquid rocks which burst all around them and would turn the brown land green overnight and wash away the red dust that coated their feet and shins. *In winter the cooking meant the hut would be nice and cosy to sleep in but in summer it was like an oven and horrid.*

The happiest days were those when she arrived home to a yeasty smell in the air and a large oil-drum bubbling away on a fire. This would mean her mother was making Seven Days, a homemade beer of maize and rapoko millet mixed with well water, so named because it took seven days to be ready. It was this that paid for Aqui's school fees and the uniform of blue and white striped dress that she always kept immaculate.

Her mother's beer was renowned in the village. On the first day of brewing, beer drinkers would pass by and give a long sniff then say, 'Eh, eh, that smells good, I am looking forward to drinking this one.' After a day of simmering, the drum would be left to cool in the hut for two days and on the fourth day more rapoko added until the mixture was of porridge consistency. It was then repeatedly boiled and simmered to reduce it and more water added from the well. When the beer was ready it had a thick froth which had to be poured off through a sieve.

On the seventh day if the beer drinkers did not automatically return to the hut, Aqui would climb an anthill or rock and shout, 'Seven Day is ready!' Her mother would then sit by the big drum, her wide skirt arranged around her considerable girth, and ladle out the lumpy yellow liquid with a cup hooked to a long stick. *She usually told me to give the first cup to the biggest beer-drinker because if he pronounced it good then others would flock in. People gave ten cents a cup if they had money, otherwise they paid in kind with cobs of corn or cabbage heads, and would sit there from morning till night, talking, drinking, playing tsoro [a kind of backgammon* with bottle-tops] and fighting. The customers were almost all men but there was one married couple who would arrive early in the morning holding hands nicely, and, by the evening, be fighting like dogs.

Aqui hated fighting. Her full name Aquinata meant peacemaker and she was the family's firstborn in a land where everyone wanted a son. She also had a Shona name – Wadzanai – which her mother said meant 'Don't shout at each other'. It was only later that Aqui would ponder the circumstances that on the long night of her birth in August 1962 had led to her parents choosing such a name rather than Precious, Blessing or Joy like her friends, or Chipo, which means Gift, like her mother.

Aquinata was the name she was christened by the Irish missionary with the shaky hands who downed her in the bowl of water and let slip. It was a story she never tired of hearing from her mother. She particularly liked the bit where for a moment there was complete silence in the room that served as a church and the congregation all held their breath wide-eyed. Her mother usually paused in the telling at that point. Then baby Aqui was retrieved and borne aloft dripping, and to everyone's astonishment she did not cry. Father Walter said she was named after a saint who was a man of peace and renounced all things. She did not really have anything to renounce, apart from her school uniform, but she liked having a distinguished name even if everyone in the village shortened it to Aqui, pronounced ack-we.

On days that Aqui had not been kept at school late to cook, when she got home, she would go to their stand or field and tend the cattle and goats. This meant swatting away the clouds of flies that hovered over their hides and picking the ticks from their skin as the animals pulled and chewed at the grass, then herding them back to their compound before the first stars lit in the sky. Her *mhondoro* grandmother was so wealthy from selling clay pots that she owned six cows that Aqui was sometimes allowed to milk. She loved to drink the thick yellow cream off the top.

The thing I really didn't like was ploughing. As the eldest I was
expected to learn but the mombes [cows] never stopped moving and
would always pull away as I tried to yoke them to the plough. The
task she dreaded most of all was trying to attach the scotch-cart.
This was a trailer fashioned from planks of wood set on an axle
and two wheels purloined from a car that had crashed on the
road. *We used the scotch-cart to collect the crops after they had been*
reaped and placed in lots of heaps, ready to take to the village store.
I was small and the log to join the cart had to be held high up while
all the time the cows would be moving.

She knew they were lucky to have cows and not just a small
hoe to plough with manually like many of the villagers, but the
mombes were obdurate creatures and she hated the boys laughing
at her as she tried over and over again to yoke them. All the
villages ploughed down the hills rather than across like the white
man because it was easier. No land was ever left fallow as it was
all needed for the cattle and growing maize, particularly in those
years when the maize grew no higher than her waist.

She had never been to Chivhu where the whites had their farms but she had heard villagers say that the fields there had special machines for spraying water for times when the rains did not come, and long golden corn, not at all like the stunted brown stalks that grew in their fields and often withered away. *They told of cows fatter than huts and chickens that laid giant eggs. My father said that the bones of our ancestors and cattle were under those fields and one day we would get them back from the whites.*

Land had not been the main aim of the first white settlers when they left Cape Town for Mafeking in April 1890 to gather in a long line of ox-wagons behind a Union Jack and head off across the Limpopo or Crocodile River for Mashonaland. Stories of hills of gold, even more dazzling than the Rand, the great gold ridge of Johannesburg then making many fortunes, had spread through the Cape Colony and Europe. It was known that there had been gold mines in Mashonaland in the time of the kings of Monomatapa, the African rulers who had traded with the Portuguese who settled on the Mozambique coast in the sixteenth and seventeenth centuries. But the kingdom had mysteriously collapsed, leaving nothing but the ruins of a vast granite fortress at Great Zimbabwe. Rumours abounded that Mashonaland was the site of King Solomon's mines or the fabled land of Ophir referred to in the Bible, and the 200 members of Cecil Rhodes's Pioneer Column had each been promised fifteen gold claims.

Mashonaland was located on the Great Central African plateau between two mighty rivers, the Limpopo to the south and the Zambezi to the north. It was next to Matabeleland, which was ruled over by Lobengula, King of the Ndebele, whose father Mzilikazi had led his people north to escape the spears of Shaka Zulu and the guns of the Boers. Almost as warlike as their Zulu cousins, the Ndebele considered the Mashona their subjects and sent frequent raiding parties to steal their cows.

Aqui, like all Mashona children, knew that Lobengula had been

Pioneer wagons

tricked by Rhodes into granting British rights for mining and colonization of these lands. Rhodes was already fabulously wealthy from his control of the diamond mining industry in Kimberley and gold mines in Johannesburg but believed that even greater riches lay further north. He also dreamed of one day extending Anglo-Saxon control to all the land from the Cape to Cairo. He saw that Bismarck's Germany and the Portuguese throne which controlled territory to the west and east were already casting covetous eyes the same way, as were the Boers to the south. So, in 1888, he sent three emissaries led by Charles Rudd to King Lobengula's kraal in Matabeleland to request a monopoly on prospecting rights.

The Ndebele king must have presented a bizarre sight. Six feet tall and weighing perhaps twenty stone, he was naked apart from a modest loincloth and spread his massive bulk on a throne made of packing cases for condensed milk tins. On the wall hung a painting of Queen Victoria of whom he was a great admirer. But the name of his kraal was Gu-Bulawayo, which meant 'Place of slaughter', and behind its high palisade of wood he maintained one of the most powerful armies of any African kingdom.

Lobengula was illiterate but highly intelligent and wavered over Rudd's request. He was finally persuaded by the arrival of Rhodes's special emissary, Dr Leander Starr Jameson, who had alleviated the king's gout with morphine injections. Encouraged by Dr Jim, as he was known, Lobengula put his mark to the so-called Rudd Concession in return for a pension of £100 a month, 10,000 rifles, 100,000 rounds of ammunition and a gunboat on the Zambezi. Similar deals were made with chiefs further north in what would become Zambia and Malawi.

The king later claimed the document had been deliberately mistranslated. The missionary who read it to him had assured him that the British would not bring more than ten white men and 'would abide by his laws and be as his people'. Even so the story made Aqui angry. *Lobengula was given sugar and he gave away the country – they have that weakness, the Ndebele.* Lobengula sent two envoys to London with a letter of protest to Queen Victoria, all to no avail. Despite the method by which the concession was obtained, Rhodes was granted a royal charter to make treaties, promulgate laws, establish a police force, and award land throughout Mashonaland and Matabeleland, an area of 175,000 square miles – about three times the size of England.

Initially known as Zambezia, the name was changed to Rhodesia in his honour, while the land north of the Zambezi became Northern Rhodesia. *In the picture in our schoolbook he looked like a very small man to have two whole countries named after him. I couldn't think of anyone else who did, even the Queen of Britain who we used to sing asking God to save every morning. I thought she must have done something very bad to need so many children so far away asking God to save her.*

With the charter granted, the Pioneers had set off on horseback or in their covered wagons through the British Protectorate of Bechuanaland, skirting the edge of Matabeleland with its Ndebele warriors, toward the unknown land of the msasa tree. Their guide was the big game hunter Frederick Selous whose bestseller *A Hunter's Wanderings in Africa* had made him a hero in Britain. To protect them they had been assigned 300 paramilitary police from Rhodes's new British South Africa or Charter Company who were armed with Martini-Henry rifles and a steam-powered naval searchlight that would sweep the plains at night.

It was hard work hacking their way through the wilderness even though they had taken hundreds of African labourers to cut and dig. The dryness of the season meant the column spent much of its time enveloped in a huge dust cloud and their boots 'rotted like paper'. Several Pioneers fell sick and died, keeping the Jesuit priests who had accompanied them busy with funerals. Many oxen succumbed to tsetse fly and almost 100 horses died of horse sickness while several wagons of supplies had been washed away in crocodile-infested rivers or jammed on stony stream-beds. Their perilous journey would inspire Rudyard Kipling to write in 'The Elephant's Child', one of his *Just So Stories*, of the 'great grey-green greasy Limpopo all set about with fever trees'.

The natives laughed at these strange arrivals in their unsuitable thick clothes even though the *ngangas* were warning of bad times ahead. The white men were undeterred and pitched their canvas tents in Masvingo, which they renamed Fort Victoria after their Queen. From there they rode off to see Great Zimbabwe and were astonished by its soaring walls made of 'even shaped blocks of granite fitted so closely that a blade of a knife could not be inserted'. Although it was overgrown they saw 'enough to realise that their extent and importance had not been overstated', and excitement mounted.

They continued north, past Chivhu or Enkeldoorn, up to a marshy spot they named Fort Salisbury, after the Prime Minister. A 21-gun salute boomed out over the plains as on 13 September 1890, five months after setting off, they hoisted the Union Jack on a hill called Harare after a local chief.

Raising the Union flag on Harare Hill

A year later their women started arriving, first nuns and ladies of the night, a strange vision in all their petticoats, then wives. There were gold rushes all over the land, including in the hills around Chivhu, but instead of the imagined quartz reefs studded with lumps of gold they found malaria and famine. So they turned to the next available prize – land.

Each settler was awarded 3,000 acres for just sixpence – the price of a British South Africa Company revenue stamp – and farms were pegged out regardless of whether there were people living there. The Jesuits were rewarded for their services with 12,000 acres for a mission station. Soon the whites had taken the best land on the Mashonaland plateau, chasing away the area's previous inhabitants, stealing their cattle and forcing them to flee to stony ground. *When you went there you couldn't think you were going to visit a person but a baboon climbing in all those mountains and bush.* To pay the hut tax of ten shillings a year that the whites charged them, many of the men had to go and work in the mines in South Africa or the farms of the settlers.

Aqui's father said their own people were fortunate to have been granted communal land which might not have been grassy like that of the whites in Chivhu, and was away from the places with rain, but at least some things grew, when there was no locust or drought. He said they were lucky too not to have been moved again after the Big Wars in Europe when new whites came and land had to be found for them, given commemorative names like Victory Block. More than 400,000 people, almost a third of the black population, were evicted from their villages between 1945 and 1955. Nothing but mounds of red mud remained of their huts and homes.

Hut tax had been replaced by cattle tax, which was supposed to pay for dipping the cows against tick fever. But to Aqui it seemed that the land was running out. *In the old days when a man got married he would go to the headman and ask for a stand for himself, but now all the land was already allocated so as sons married they were having to divide up their parents' land. It didn't seem fair to me that it was the women who did all the work but only the men who got given land. My brother would get land but not me.*

The headman of Zhakata's Kraal had a bicycle and late one afternoon he came cycling back, a black Homburg on his head and his withered knees pedalling furiously, carrying a large cream and red Bakelite box with a big dial and lots of knobs. Her father explained it was a radio. *Everyone gathered round to listen. They tried to shoo us children away but I crept near.* Through the crackle she heard a voice come out of the box to slowly announce: 'This is the News from the Rhodesian Broadcasting Corporation', and she jumped as if there were a frog in her pants.

It was from this magic box that in 1969, when she was seven, they heard the nasal voice of the Prime Minister Ian Douglas Smith announce the Land Tenure Act so that the division of land – good to the whites and bad to the blacks – would be fixed for all time. *God bless you all*, he ended and the elders snorted. Aqui knew from listening to the Seven Day drinkers that Ian Smith was *a Bad Man* and what he said meant there would never be land for her and her children, *not in a thousand years*, but there were some people fighting against this. Pamphlets sometimes appeared in the nearby township with names like Ndabaningi Sithole, Robert Mugabe and Joshua Nkomo, nationalist leaders who had been in jail since 1963. They were always quickly burnt.

Mostly though we were all too busy with the small things of life to think about these matters. Apart from all the work in the fields, we had to go to collect firewood and water at the well. The elders had built a protection of logs around to stop cows defecating in it but sometimes it was a brownish colour.

Every morning the women and girls went to the well, which was forty-five minutes' walk away. To Aqui, trying hard not to splash any precious water, they looked like ghostly figures walking through the mists balancing clay jars on their heads, every so often a hand fluttering upwards to support the weight. In the summer they went again in the evening, but not in the winter when the nights were too dark to wash the cooking pots because they could not see if there were any snakes lurking inside. *We village children would all gather after supper. The moon was our electricity, and we would play games like Hide and Seek, Spot Spot or Hwaai hwaai which meant 'Sheep, sheep, come here'. That was my favourite where we took turns being sheep and someone was the hyena and had to try and catch us.*

Twice a week the choirmaster blew his whistle, the signal for those in the choir to meet under the forked tree. People said Aqui had a honey-sweet voice and she loved singing in the choir, the bare hills echoing the music. Sometimes there were competitions against other villages and once their choir won a cup, but only as runner-up. Everyone knew this was because of the choirmaster's wife who *sang like a dog whose tail had been stepped on*.

Another kind of singing was often to be heard in the village and that was from members of the Apostolic Church of Africa, which would later become the Zion Church with clothes and capes like nurses' uniforms and coloured ribbons on brass pins.

Dressed in white robes they would dance about to a drummer faster and faster until one of them started speaking in tongues and frothing at the mouth as if possessed by a spirit. Their eyes would roll back so only the whites were visible. Aqui didn't like them at all. *I thought they were scary.*

Aqui was proud of being a Catholic praying in a proper church or at least a hall with a painted white cross outside. *People would say you can't take that path because of the tokolosh or the bus broke down because of the tokolosh but I never thought I'd get possessed. They would warn you can't say that or the dead will be unhappy but I didn't believe in spirits. If I said that, though, they would laugh at me and say, 'You think you're a murungu,' a white person. I'd reply, 'I'm not a fool,' and they would point their fingers menacingly and say, 'One day you'll see.'*

One day she came home from school to hear wailing so agonized as to rival the hyenas in the hills. It was Priscilla, one of the white-robed Apostolics who always had her nose pointed towards the sky because her husband Lovemore had a full-time job on a tobacco farm and sent back regular money. She had used this to buy a sewing machine from which she made children's clothes from scraps of material. She had no children herself, though – Aqui once heard her father say, 'That woman is as dry and barren as the earth after two seasons of drought.'

Priscilla's husband worked as a night watchman in the tobacco barn and his duty was to keep the fires burning so that the tobacco dried at the correct temperature. But Lovemore was always falling asleep at his post, and one day the *baas* had come in and found him snoozing. It was not the first occasion and usually the farmer would cuff him awake. Once he had spray-painted Lovemore's hair completely white to make him the laughing stock of all the workers. This time, though, the farmer was in an angry temper, perhaps because the crop was poor or his wife was becoming bitter-tongued, and he threw Priscilla's husband on the fire and left him to burn.

Now he was the late Lovemore and Priscilla was distraught. 'Not even a body to bury,' she sobbed. 'How will his spirit settle?' The wag-wags in the village said that not only had she lost her monthly stipend but no one else would marry her, because they all knew no seed would ripen in her womb.

Aqui's mother was always scolding her daughter for her vivid imagination which kept her awake with thoughts of the unformed souls of the dead children escaping the riverbanks, or remembering the day the locust cloud came and turned day into night. She had cowered in the hut fearing something terrible while the other children ran to pick the insects off the thorn trees to fry for supper. The burning of Lovemore gave Aqui something new to think about.

Whites didn't often venture into Native Reserves. The only white people I had ever seen were Father Walter, the Irish missionary at the church, and the white policeman. It was very important in those days for a white person to talk to you, you would be so happy, but most of them didn't. When they did they spoke loudly as if we were many miles away.

All I knew was that our skins were different and that being white somehow gave you a special power and my grandfather didn't like them. He was very cheeky and refused to pay tax on his cattle, and when the black policemen came on a motorbike to collect it he told them off for doing the dirty work of whites and took out his shambok to chase them away. Although Aqui knew that the nuns at school said it was wrong to hate, they also said they were all God's creatures and she didn't understand why having a white skin should make them different. She thought about Priscilla's husband toasting on the fire and how his skin would have crackled and burnt like the mealie cobs, and began to hate them.

2

Riversdale Farm, Headlands, 1971

NIGEL THOUGHT there was no better feeling than that of arriving home for the beginning of the long school holidays, weeks of freedom stretching ahead. Like most Rhodesian farm children he had been dispatched to boarding school at the age of seven, so young that many of them still wet their beds. An early photograph shows him in his uniform looking into the camera and trying to affect a jaunty pose while struggling not to let his lower lip wobble. *We were all bundled off on the train and we would cry like mad. We wouldn't come home again for three months. It was tough but you got used to it.*

For Rhodesian farming families, child-rearing was kind of like a lottery – you sent your children away at an early age and just hoped they turned out all right and would one day be able to run your farm.

His first school was Chancellor Junior School in Umtali, which was reached by climbing Christmas Pass where the blue gums gave way to the eucalyptus and pine-scented firs of the Vumba hills. Umtali sounded like an African name but was actually the white way of saying Mutare, the easternmost city in Rhodesia, not far from the border with Mozambique. War had been raging just across the mountains since 1964 as Frelimo (Frente de Libertação de Moçambique) guerrillas led by Samora Machel fought to oust the Portuguese colonists. *Our hostel was right on the border and sometimes mortars would go over the top of us and land inside the compound. It was a phenomenally loud noise and we would hide under the blankets.*

Chancellor was an 'A' school which meant it was all-white and the day began with an assembly thanking God for all their blessings and a shrill chorus of 'Morning has broken'. The school had extensive grounds, a swimming pool and even a roller-skating rink, but Nigel counted the days to the holidays when he could run free with his brothers and sisters. *Although even at an early age I was aware of tension when there was drought and farming seemed a lot of work, I could not imagine a better lifestyle, the outdoors and the space. We were little kings.*

As the car turned off the main road from Umtali to Headlands and onto the winding red track signposted 'Riversdale Farm', he thought excitedly about the swimming, hunting, biking and cricket ahead of him. Rustling gum trees lined the way, and after a couple of miles a twin-towered anthill marked a fork in the road. The other turn-off led to their nearest neighbour, an old Afrikaner doctor they called Oom Jannie. It was to Oom Jannie's clinic that farm workers and their families went when they were sick. Nigel was slightly scared of him. *He used to say, 'The bleks come with runny noses and leave with itchy scrotums,' then laugh, 'Heh heh heh.' We were too young to understand what he meant but his patients never became fathers again after that. It was his way of reducing the black population.*

Beyond Oom Jannie's turn-off was a big hump in the road that Nigel and his siblings called Danger Hill. *Dad would go fast over it so the car would sort of lift off, you know that kind of feeling where your tummy drops, and we'd all beg, 'Again, again, please can we do it again?'* Then it was through the gate with the Riversdale sign and into lush peach orchards, beyond which opened out a green and yellow tapestry of tobacco and maize fields spread across a series of hills. At the top of the track were the farm buildings, a cluster of white-painted stores and barns, and then

an exuberant garden of palm trees, jacaranda, honeysuckle and
African tulip trees with their bulbous red blossoms. The tiled roof
of the one-storey house was just visible through the trees and
the dogs would run out jumping and barking whenever a car
drew up.

As Nigel got out, his mother Mary would come down the steps
and greet him with a brisk hug, then quickly return to her jam
or pickle making. Born in 1962, Nigel was the fifth child, with
two older brothers and two older sisters, and as the house filled
with the sound of all the children shouting and bickering Mary
Hough would shake her head in amused despair.

On the first day of holidays, the children would be allowed to
stay up late as a special treat with a tray of her home-made
lemonade and cookies on the terrace. As on most Rhodesian
farms, this was where much of life took place and where tea
turned to sundowners brought by servants. Mary and John Hough
always sat there at dusk with cold beers, the dogs curled at their
feet barely stirring as the couple clinked glasses and looked out
over their lands. Often John would be tending a wounded bird
he had found in the fields or reading Blake's poetry to Mr Ponsonby, his pet crow. 'Mr Ponsonby never answers back,' he joked
to neighbouring farmers with a nod to his talkative wife.

At 1,000 acres, Riversdale Farm was small by Rhodesian standards. But everyone agreed that the view was hard to beat. An
open veranda ran all along the back of the house, looking across
lawns kept brilliant green by sprinklers. Beyond lay the fields of
crops leading towards a smudge of mountains that changed colour
with the seasons. Yellow-green in summer when eagles circled
their peaks, in winter they were purple-blue and dawned draped
with strange mists known as gutis.

As a chorus of crickets heralded nightfall with growing insist-
ence, the five freshly scrubbed Hough children in pyjamas would
be paraded out by Faith, the nanny, to say good night. Another
maid brought out the Tilly lamps, and, if there were visitors,

Mary might suggest a hand of canasta or bridge. Light switched suddenly to dark with just the tiniest swivel of the earth, and someone could usually be relied upon to mutter that it was the best climate in the world and perhaps the best landscape too, and they nodded and felt blessed to have been born in such a place.

Such reassurances had taken on a more urgent note since Ian Smith's Unilateral Declaration of Independence from Britain (UDI) on 11 November 1965. Finding themselves the first white settlers to rebel since the Boston Tea Party in 1776 had come as a shock for the Houghs, like most Rhodesians. Although the colony had been self-governing since control was transferred from Rhodes' British South African Company to Whitehall in 1923, its formal occasions were always opened with the national anthem; its army and air force had been integrated with the British in the war; and Smith once boasted it had more Union Jacks than Britain. Even the names of farms and settlements reflected nostalgia for what was seen as the motherland. Typical examples were Surrey, Arundel and Dorset farms, the small towns of Plumtree and Bromley, the lake of Loch Moodie, Essex Valley and Brighton Beach, while the capital Salisbury had suburbs of Kensington and Belgravia.

But the region was undergoing enormous change. Apart from Portuguese Mozambique to the east and South Africa-controlled Namibia to the west beyond Botswana, all the other surrounding colonies had been given independence under constitutions granting majority rule. The independence of Ghana in 1957 had been followed by Nigeria and Belgian Congo in 1960, then Tanzania, Uganda, Kenya, Malawi and Zambia in quick succession.

Smith had no doubt that black-run government was a bad thing. 'The story was always the same,' he later wrote in his autobiography. 'Tribal violence and massacres, political opponents imprisoned, coups, streams of white refugees who had been dispossessed of their property, rampant corruption and the establishment of external bank accounts by their leaders.' In particular, he commented, the white refugees fleeing from the newly independent Belgian Congo 'left an indelible impression on our people'.

When he was elected Prime Minister in 1964, Smith had no intention of being the next victim of what Harold Macmillan called the 'winds of change' sweeping through the continent. Rhodesia was more complicated because although the whites numbered only 220,000 compared to almost 5 million blacks and went back at most three generations, they considered themselves just as indigenous. The Rhodesian leader also pointed out that, unlike other African colonies, his country had a sophisticated economy based on mining and agriculture with its own merchant banks and stock exchange. If it was to be independent, he wanted it under continued white minority rule to safeguard all this.

But Wilson's Labour government insisted that independence must come with a constitution entrenching universal suffrage, and negotiations ended in stalemate. After taking the precaution of moving the country's gold and other assets out of the Bank of England, Smith took a vote of his cabinet, placed a crack SAS unit on standby and drove to the studios of the Rhodesian Broadcasting Company. There he recorded a message to the nation in which he accused the British of shattering years of loyalty 'on the rocks of expediency' and proclaimed independence. Smith was no orator, but even in his flat nasal monotone it was dramatic.

After the initial shockwaves, the white community rallied round, generally agreeing with their Prime Minister's assessment of Rhodesia as 'an oasis of peace in an otherwise turbulent continent'. Some African states called for a British invasion, but this was ignored, and although an international trade embargo was imposed, Rhodesians soon developed ways to circumvent it, helped by Portugal and South Africa on whom they depended for ports. Alone among the European colonial powers, Portugal's fascist regime refused to grant independence to its African possessions and fought a bitter war in Mozambique, which borders

Smith signing his Unilateral Declaration of Independence

Rhodesia. South Africa's apartheid regime was a natural ally of Smith, and extended considerable military and economic assistance as well as allowing Rhodesian gold and other minerals to be passed off as of South African origin. Farmers like the Houghs were urged to increase production to feed the nation.

Nigel's mother was a staunch supporter of Smith and would come back from shopping with locally produced cornflakes and teabags in plastic bags stamped with the words *'Rhodesia is SUPER'*. Nigel wore T-shirts bearing similar patriotic slogans. *Smith was quite a dour man but he did have a presence and, especially for a country that was basically farming-based, he was kind of one of the boys.*

Mary had been born in Rhodesia on the farm her father Jerry had pegged out in 1919 when he arrived from England. Jerry

Mary being carried as a baby

Timms was from a cricketing family in Syresham in Northamp-
tonshire and his wife was from Yorkshire. Nobody talked much
about it but, from what Nigel understood, his grandfather had
been the black sheep of the family who had been sent as far
away as possible after the First World War for some unspecified
misdeed. Sending wayward sons off to far corners of the empire
was common in those days. Timms had travelled by ship to Cape
Town, and there picked up a horse, which he rode across the
country to Rhodesia where he had heard there were plenty of
opportunities. He had pegged out some land and become a
farmer, eventually prospering enough to be able to send his
daughters back to finishing school in England.

   John Hough had also been born on a farm, but in England, in
the affluent stockbroker belt of Surrey. His father was not a farmer
but a director of Lloyds of London who had purchased Jordans
Farm because he happened to like the country life, and John grew
up a dreamer, always up trees bird-watching or tending fledglings
that had fallen from their nests. After such freedom, it was a

shock for John and his twin brother to be sent to Repton public school in Derbyshire. Repton was a strict establishment which instilled in him both a love of Beethoven and Blake and a lifelong hatred of pomposity. One of his classmates was Roald Dahl, and the school had an unusual saving grace, which John believed must have inspired his schoolfellow's famous literary confectioner Willie Wonka. Every so often boxes would arrive from the Cadbury's chocolate company of prototype bars for the boys to test out and award ratings.

Apart from ornithology, John Hough's great passion was flying. After leaving Repton, he had been a Spitfire pilot in the Second World War, along with Roald Dahl and also Ian Smith. The future Rhodesian leader was seriously injured when he crashed in North Africa, but recovered to be based in Corsica where he was shot down and helped by Partisani resistance fighters to escape through enemy lines. While Smith liked to be seen as a wartime hero, Nigel's father rarely talked about his own experiences. *He would be the first to confess that his motives for joining the RAF were less the destruction of Hitler and more to imitate the flight of a peregrine falcon. The Spitfire gave him the dual pleasure of breathless flight and the thrill of being powered by a Griffin engine. He loved flight and he loved engines.*

When the war was over, John's father hoped his sons would follow him into the family insurance business. Instead both loved the outdoors and went to Africa, only their sister remaining behind. Tragically John's twin brother died shortly after, drowning while saving the life of a friend who had fallen in the Zambezi.

The twins had been inseparable, and John was distraught. Rather than return home, he found himself a job in Rhodesia, training pilots for the Rhodesian Air Force which had combined operations with the RAF. He was one of many British war veterans who turned up with handlebar moustaches and RAF badges. Like most of them, John fell in love with the country, which must have seemed like a land of plenty after the deprivations of post-war

London with its grey skies, food rationing and empty shelves. In Southern Rhodesia there were fresh eggs, ham, sausages and bacon as well as endless sunshine, golf courses and wide-open spaces, wonderful for a keen sportsman and bird-lover. There was also the luxury of maids to do the washing and cleaning.

When John finally went back to London to work at Lloyds as his father wished, he found office life suffocatingly dull and was soon hankering for the wide skies of Africa. A friend found him another position in Rhodesia, managing the Timms' farm at Inyazura near Rusape. The Timms' daughter Mary had recently returned from finishing her studies in England and was working as a matron at a local school, but John saw enough of her over the dinner table to be smitten. However, the romance seemed doomed when he lost his job on the farm because Mary's sister married a farmer who took his place, and he returned to the Rhodesian Air Force as a trainer.

John was a slightly built man in a land of hale, sporty types and had little other than his eccentric sense of humour to win the charms of a local beauty, so had to resort to other means. At times when he thought Mary would be at the farm, he would sign out his Spitfire for an hour, then make the twenty-minute flight from Harare, perform a twenty-minute aerobatic display overhead in the manner of a peacock fanning its feathers, then fly back. With him in the cockpit was his crow Mr Ponsonby. Once he flew so fast to get back within the hour after dallying over the farm that the bird lost all his feathers and John had to stick some back in.

His airborne wooing succeeded and the couple were married on 11 September 1952, Mary's 26th birthday, at Rusape. Their honeymoon was spent at Leopard Rock hotel, along with Mr Ponsonby and John's pet owl and a hawk. Leopard Rock had been built entirely of stone by Italian prisoners of war during the Second World War and looked like a castle with its lavish gardens and incredible views over the lush green Bvumba valley. It was

Mary and John's wedding

the most fashionable resort in Rhodesia and the Queen stayed there during her visit the following year. Nine months after their honeymoon, the Houghs' first son Edwin was born and they bought their own farm.

In his first year as a farmer John Hough learnt just how tough a life it could be when heavy floods washed away all his crops. The couple lost everything and for some years had to lease a farm called Ripplemead. Finally they saved enough to buy Riversdale where they could provide their growing number of children the idyllic childhood of running free that they had both enjoyed.

The Houghs made an unlikely couple, but the relationship worked. Like most Rhodesian farmers' wives, Mary was a strong, practical woman who taught all her children to read in between

John and Mary's first farm

bottling preserves, while John was a dreamer. *They were a perfect two-part harmony, John taking care of the important issues in life like crowned eagles, building bird-hides and producing a dazzling display of useless gadgets, while Mum made sure we all were fed and went to school and had a house to live in.*

Even as a young boy, Nigel was well aware that it was his mother who held the family together. *Father was a wonderful person but not a great businessman. I always felt that dealing with the rigours of a drought never held the same mental anguish for him as the disappearance of some egg from an African hawk eagle's nest.* Even with Rhodesia's cheap labour, they would not have been able to maintain their lifestyle were it not for the fact that John Hough had inherited a large sum of money from his father.

Although neither parent was at all demonstrative, the Hough brothers and sisters grew up so close that outsiders would refer to them as the Mutual Admiration Society. *Whenever a member of the family needed help we would call on the siblings – we referred to it as calling out the artillery. If more than one came out we called it heavy artillery. If my mother arrived that would be the nuclear warhead.* Childhood pranks usually involved the boys against girls. *Every evening we would all go for baths in the bathroom at the end of the corridor along which we all had our rooms. Once my elder brother told my sisters that the coast was clear for them to go back to their bedrooms then called the cook boy Maxwell so he saw them all running past naked.*

All the surrounding farms in Headlands were white-owned. Farming was a close-knit society and there were about thirty other white farming families in the district. Apart from his brothers and sisters, Nigel had a group of young friends with whom to go hunting, shooting and fishing in the dam as well as riding on motorbikes. *We were all about five or six when we started with a pellet gun, and I went on my first bird shoot with my father when I was ten.* He was given his first serious weapon – a 20-bore shotgun – at the age of 14 and mostly they shot guinea fowl and doves. *For young guys that kind of life is like a dream.*

In those days the bush seemed full of game. Leopards stalked the hills, their cries often to be heard in the night and their spoors left outside the living room windows in the mornings. It was common for the children to come across duikers with their liquid eyes or see wild pigs shooting out from under a msasa tree. Speckled francolin partridges would skit across dusty red tracks, usually in threes, and there were often snakes to dodge away from, cobras and mambas. An enormous python lived in a pile of rocks on the way to the dam and they always hurried past, though sometimes one of the boys would poke in a stick then run. *Once we saw the python just after it had swallowed a big duiker and it couldn't move it was so full.*

After checking their boots for scorpions or baboon spiders, the children would set off hunting with a retinue of black boys to carry their things, track animal spoors and collect any kills. *The blacks were good trackers and would carry whatever we shot and*

*were always keen to come because afterwards we'd give them what-
ever we'd bagged so they might get a guinea fowl or something for
their suppers. We knew so little about blacks that once, when we
were about eight years old, my cousin saw one of the black guys
doing a wee and she rushed back saying, 'Jeez, you can't believe how
big this guy's willy is!' So we asked to see it and he was quite
indignant. He charged us all a penny. I don't remember how big it
was but we felt it was worth paying.*

Nigel and his brothers and sisters were almost entirely ignorant
of the black majority all around them, even though the most
recent official census showed blacks outnumbered whites by
21 to 1.* To Nigel the blacks were just *a kind of supporting cast*
that did his family's washing and cooking or laboured in the fields
then melted away back into the bush or their kraals. He and his
siblings sometimes played pranks on them, like placing a dead
cobra on the watchman's chest when he fell asleep on duty.

When Nigel was not hunting or fishing, he spent his time
playing sport. The farm had a swimming pool and a tennis court
and at weekends the Houghs often held tennis parties with local
farming families coming over for some of Mary's lemon meringue
pie and their cook Robert's famous piripiri chicken. Robert was
very small and round and most of his cooking was stodgy and
forgettable but so good was his piripiri chicken that Nigel's father
always said he would 'put up with any amount of nonsense from
Robert' because of it. The children knew better than to interrupt
their father while eating it for his *level of concentration exceeded
a lioness honing in on her prey.*

Nigel was extremely competitive, as was his eldest sister Shirley,
and his other sister Tess often had to act as peacemaker between
the two after a showdown over tennis. If none of Nigel's siblings
or white friends were around, he would play football or cricket

---

* According to the 1969 official census the population of Rhodesia was 228,296
Europeans, 15,153 coloureds, 8,965 Asians and 4,846,930 blacks (Rhodesia Central
Statistical Office).

with the workers' children. *It was kind of one-sided because when we played cricket I would do all the batting and with soccer they would never tackle me hard and they would always let me win as I was the baas's son.*

He also developed a passion for squash. *Father had got a loan from the Land Bank to build a tobacco-grading barn, which he had built to the exact dimensions of a squash court so it was a grading shed during grading season and a squash court for the rest of the year.* Nigel played with their maid Maria. *I used to make her play me for hours and hours each day.* A large, fat woman, who would puff and sweat as Nigel made her run around, Maria was the only one of the workers who dared venture into the sweet tobacco-smelling barn. There were two owls in the rafters and most Shona are scared of owls, believing if one lands on a building and hoots, someone inside will die.

From a young age, Nigel would often trot round after his father to inspect the progress of the tobacco or maize. *I was soon aware that farming was extremely hard work and that without endless supervision the munts would do nothing.* Every morning at 5 a.m., John Hough set off for the fields in his long khaki shorts, safari shirts with folded-up sleeves, and long stockings with boots, all topped off with a grubby white floppy hat that his wife would long have liked to dispose of. A man of strict routine and firm principle, he came back to the house at 8 a.m. sharp for a cooked breakfast, often lambasting Robert for his 'miserable' eggs, and at 8.30 a.m. would disappear into the bathroom for half an hour to 'contact his stockbroker', chiding his children that 'good plumbing is the secret to good health'. He came home again at half past midday for lunch, after which he would sleep for exactly thirty minutes before returning to the fields until late afternoon.

Sometimes he would let Nigel sit with him as he distributed the fortnightly wages to the workers, entering the amounts in black ink in his big ledger. All had stories of woe, leading them to beg for an advance for the funeral of a relative or to buy

Nigel as a toddler at Beira

medicine for a sick child. *Mother said they would just fritter it on beer and that he should pay the wages to the women to make sure the children got fed, but the munts would never accept that.* But his father often gave in to their requests, admonishing Nigel not to let his mother in on the secret.

The only time John Hough ever took off was for their twice-yearly holidays. In August the family always decamped to Nyanga dam near Rhodes's old stone cottage in its English gardens, and would sleep in tents under the fir trees, while every April they spent a month in Beira on the Mozambique coast. This was usually in a group with other families, renting chalets on the beachfront, and it was Nigel's favourite time of year. *Mozambique seemed very exotic. We children would play all day in the Indian Ocean, diving through the huge rolling waves and trying to catch jellyfish on sticks.* There was a zoo where they laughed to see animals in cages instead of running free in the bush or in game reserves like back home, and a funfair. In the evening, they might go to their favourite Johnnie's Seafood Restaurant or the dads would grill fresh prawns on the barbecue and dip them in peri peri, a sauce so hot it burnt the tongue.

Nigel was aware that his father was different from other dads. It was not so much his British accent – only 40.71 per cent of whites at that time were Rhodesian-born. Around half had entered the country like John Hough since the Second World War, largely from Britain but also from former colonies in East Africa and India, as well as Greeks, Afrikaners and a considerable Jewish community. Between 1946 and 1960, the number of whites rose from 82,000 to more than 220,000 attracted by the high standard of living, sustained as it was by the inequalities between blacks and whites. Even Ian Smith was only second generation – his father had been a Scottish butcher who moved to Rhodesia in search of a better life.

But John Hough had always seemed more interested in birds than children, particularly crows, which he said had 'amazing characters'. *Paradise for Dad was listening to Beethoven's Emperor Piano Concerto while watching eagles in flight and eating a smidgen of Mum's lemon meringue pie.* As he grew older he even began to resemble a bird. Nigel's school friend Larry Norton found him alarming. 'He looked exactly like a falcon. He was balding with long grey hair round the edges, a big nose and a big moustache.'

Nigel and his elder brother Edwin would take advantage of their father's eccentricity to tease him mercilessly. Once on holiday in Ballito Bay on South Africa's northern Natal coast, John could not understand why every time he went into the local shop he was treated extremely rudely by the shopkeeper who would follow him around snatching things from him as he picked them up. The boys had whispered to the shopkeeper, 'That's our dad. He's an alcoholic and a shoplifter and often takes naughty magazines from the shelf.'

Shortly after one of their holidays, Nigel's parents purchased their first LP player, prompting great excitement when it was unloaded at the farm. The sanctions imposed by the West after UDI meant most things were locally assembled, and the 'Supersonic' radiogram was no exception. Apart from John's beloved Beethoven, the family record collection soon featured Cat Stevens, Sandy Shaw, Gary Glitter and Mick Jagger. Later they bought a television, a Philips set built in socialist Yugoslavia. The Rhodesian Broadcasting Corporation (RBC) had a monopoly and evening viewing largely consisted of old American comedy series like *The Ed Sullivan Show* and *I Love Lucy*. The Smith government was obsessed with protecting the country against encroachment of the so-called permissive society corrupting the outside world, so there was strict censorship. *Penthouse* and *Playboy* magazines were not allowed into the country, while the RBC even banned Olivia Newton-John and Gene Pitney.

Every Thursday, the family would drive to Rusape Club. It was only 30 miles away, but on unmetalled strip roads in their light green Ford Cortina station wagon that felt like a real trek. John Hough was not a gifted driver and it was a squash to fit all six children in, two always having to sit in the boot. Their parents were always telling them to keep quiet. *Once my sister Tess fell out on the way to the club. When we tried to tell Mum and Dad they told us to mind our manners and wait till they finished talking. Afterwards when they realized what had happened they were more favourably disposed to us butting in.*

Everything in the community revolved round the Club. There was cricket, tennis and golf and on weekend afternoons it would be crowded with farmers dressed in their uniform of khaki shirts with tight shorts and long socks with combs tucked in the top. They would gather for *braais*, grilling thick *boerewors* sausage and slabs of meat, and downing Lion or Castle beers from the bar as they conversed loudly in the flat vowels similar to the Boers'.

The topics were usually the same – commodity prices, the prospects of rain, hunting and guns, and complaints about workers – 'the Affs' or *munts* as they called them. It was rarely long before discussion turned to Ian Smith and the ramifications of his decision to secede from Britain. There were close relations between Smith's Rhodesian Front and the Commercial Farmers' Union and most farmers supported UDI, fearing that the British government had been about to 'sell them down the river and hand the country over to the blacks'. Before entering politics Smith had been a farmer like them, and they referred to him as 'good ol' Smithy'. Despite his long-winded speeches delivered in that nasal burr with a finger jabbing the air, he had come to be seen as the true Rhodesian, born and bred in a land he would never leave and guarding his country from an outside world full of evil. His lack of facial expression, the result of plastic surgery on his war injuries, gave him a heroic status.

The farmers liked to see themselves in the front line, feeding the nation, and finding innovative ways to keep selling their tobacco, the country's biggest foreign exchange earner. Undeterred by attempts by MI6 agents to tail the perpetrators, the Rhodesians had become adept at sanction busting and a nightly meat run flew around Africa delivering cargoes of Rhodesian beef.

The children liked the club because they could drink Coca-Colas with ice-cream floats and eat chips in greasy paper and sometimes there would be movies on the bioscope like *Jungle Book* or *Alice in Wonderland*. Every so often there were dances or gymkhanas, and at Christmas one of the farmers would dress up as Santa Claus to distribute presents. Occasionally a farmer with a plane would fly in, like their uncle Noel Waller, and might even be prevailed on to take some children up for a spin.

The whole family was in the car returning from the club one evening when they rounded a bend and found themselves heading straight into a tractor and trailer parked on the road without lights. A car was coming the other way, and as the bulk of it filled the windscreen it was too late to swerve. One minute the children were all chattering and arguing, their mother telling them to keep quiet, then there was a tremendous searing crash. The doors burst open with showers of glass as the car hit the oncoming vehicle and rolled over and over, then it was ground underneath the tractor. Nigel, who was only two at the time, was thrown straight out of the windscreen and initially presumed dead. His father was also thrown out and his mother's head smashed straight through the glass. The other driver was killed. Everyone had cuts, bruises and broken limbs, and as they started coming round groaning, his mother saw her nine-year-old son Terry lying inert on the roadside, literally cut in half. Those who heard her scream never forgot it. 'It was horrible, devastating,' she recalls, 'but it also brought us closer together as a family.'

For a long time after Terry's death, once they were all back from hospital, the farmhouse was a hushed place. Terry's bed remained made and ready from the night he had never come home. Mary stayed in her room, and the children sometimes crept up to the door and could hear muffled crying, though never in front of them. Their father spent even longer periods out in the bush or up trees with his binoculars, leaving the children to be looked after by the nanny. The nightly drinking on the terrace took on a more relentless nature. Neighbours came with home-made pies and hushed condolences and averted their eyes as they spoke. For once it was a relief for the children to go back to school.

3

Zhakata's Kraal, 1973

AQUI STOOD IMPATIENTLY, holding the donkey and shifting from foot to foot, as her mother stopped and exchanged the traditional Shona greetings with people along the way.

'*Mangwanani.*' (Good morning.)

'*Mangwanani.*'

'*Marara here?*' (How did you sleep?)

'*Ndarara kana mararawo.*' (I have slept well if you did.)

'*Ndarara.*' (I slept.)

She was eager to get to the store because for the first time she and her sisters were going to be given a share of the money from the groundnuts and allowed to buy something for themselves. Groundnuts were the only crop that was paying well in those days and her mother had divided some of their land into strips for her and her sisters each to tend their own crop. Aqui had gone to the stand every day after school to check on hers, clearing the sandy soil of weeds and keeping away kudu and *whorwe* birds. *When they were ready it was very exciting. We collected them in small mounds on the earth. My baby brother was strapped to my back in a sling and we borrowed donkeys from the headman to take the nuts to the stores in the township.*

The shopping area was ten miles away in the growth point of Sadza where the daily bus stopped for Chivhu. It was reached by a dusty path and rather grandly called the Business Centre. The

Aqui's mother

main shop, to which they were headed, was Musarurwa General Stores which stocked food and clothes. Next to that was a maize-flour mill, a butcher's with giant iron hooks from which hung fly-covered carcasses that stank in the heat, and the Come Again Bottle-store where the men would hang out drinking and making gob-shop.

Aqui's mother had kept back a few groundnuts to grind into oil to rub into the girl's skins at night but all the rest were solemnly handed over to Mr Musarurwa to be weighed and the price calculated on a scrap of paper. The money was then counted out and Aqui took her few coins and began to decide what to buy. It was hard to choose from such a treasure trove. On the floor were sacks of sugar out of which the storekeeper would scoop out a paper coneful for their mother. A large jar of coloured lollipops stood on the counter next to a tray of single cigarettes. Shelves along the back held bolts of bold-patterned cottons, thick blue cakes of laundry soap, pink plastic pots of skin-lightening cream, and dusty packets of Lobells biscuits. Pans and kettles hung on strings from the ceiling.

Aqui lingered long in front of a cupboard containing bottles of Cream Soda and Ripe'n'Ready, boxes of sweet cigarettes and bags of toffees in coloured wrappers, and wondered how they tasted. *On the way to the shops I had thought I would buy a torch so that when I came back late from school or went to the bush in the night to relieve myself, I could spy any snakes or tokoloshis. But my mother explained that these would need batteries. There was the same problem if I bought a kerosene lamp to give light to do my homework. So I bought a blanket for winter and my sister bought tackies [canvas tennis shoes].* It was the first time the nine-year-old had worn shoes; usually the village children went barefoot. *How we laughed at her, she walked like a duck.*

They returned home in festive mood that night, singing as they walked. The blanket was soft and would be cosy for sleeping, her mother had mixed up a special drink of maize and sugar, and there was even meat from the butcher's for dinner. Aqui had just taken a mouthful of the rich stew when she heard loud shouting outside. *The food which had been tasting so good turned bitter in my mouth. It was my father and he had been drinking.* Her mother pretended not to have heard and carried on chattering gaily. But the girls fell silent for they all knew he would soon drag her out to beat her, then leave her under the shivering stars. They cringed like the ownerless village dog as they waited for the sound of the stinging slaps they knew would follow.

Our African men have this problem – when they get money they use it not for their family but on their girlfriends, forgetting their wives and children, and on beer. My father would go insane when he was drunk. He would beat up my mother, be abusive and chase

*her away so she slept in the kraal with the animals even in winter
when it was cold.*

When he had finished beating his wife, he would return to the
kitchen hut where the children all sat rooted to the spot and grab
the food left untouched on their plates, smacking his lips with
lusty pleasure. If they moved, he would cuss at them and sometimes beat them too. *Once when I was about three, he picked
me up and threw me out of the hut like a ball, so hard that I still
have the scar. My grandmother, the one who was a spirit medium,
mixed a paste of herbs to rub in the wound which made it hurt even
more.* That was the year that Prime Minister Ian Smith had
illegally declared Rhodesia independent from Britain. *I didn't
know what UDI was but from the way grown-ups talked about it I
knew it was something very bad that meant that our people would
never have their own country like our brothers had got in Zambia
next door.*

The next day as always her father was very contrite and hang-
dog, tickling her under her chin and calling her his little princess.
*The evenings when he was not drunk he would tell stories. Often
they were about long-ago times when the Ndebele came and killed
our men and took our beautiful women and cows, or when the whites
came and drove out the black people to the hills and mountains and
barren land and took away the good land.*

Sometimes they were about Nehanda, the *mhondoro* woman
from Mazowe who inspired the 1896 uprising of the Shona against
the white settlers when they realized they had been cheated out
of their land by the strangers. *I loved those stories best of all. My
father said we were even descended from one of those who had led
the fight with her.*

The rebellion was known as the *Chimurenga*, a poetic Shona
word which means fight or struggle, and it was one of the most
violent and organized rebellions against white rule anywhere in
Africa. Three hundred and seventy-two whites were killed –
around 10 per cent of the settlers. Some of those scattered around

Pioneers in one of their laagers

on homesteads gathered together to form laagers such as that around the large thorn tree which eventually became the settlement of Enkeldoorn.

The Pioneers were taken by surprise by the revolt of natives they had seen as placid and submissive as the cattle they herded, and whom they had thought welcomed their arrival as protection against the raiding parties of the Ndebele. But the Shona were angry that not only had they lost their land but were also expected to pay hut tax which meant losing their menfolk to the mines and farms of the strangers. On top of that the year the white man arrived in 1890 coincided with a plague of locusts that returned again each year. By 1895 the numbers were so many that people said they blotted out the sun. On top of that, in 1894, a terrible drought had started. Lastly, in early 1896, an epidemic of rinderpest broke out among the cattle, leaving a trail of carcasses across the country. The authorities panicked and herded thousands more cows into kraals for slaughter.

To the superstitious Shona these were all signs that the spirits were angry and they were eager to take up their weapons and

Nehanda

follow Nehanda in rebellion. *Nehanda could summon up spirits and she instructed our people, 'Spread yourself through the forests and fight till the stranger leaves.' She was so strong and brave, she just thought about the country, not like Lobengula who just wanted the sugar. When the whites tried to break her spirit by offering things, she just said No. The whites were very cunning but she was also cunning.*

The Shona might have had numbers and spirits on their side but the settlers had guns and dynamite. The Shona chiefs were hunted down and the caves where they and their followers were hiding were blown up. In December 1897, Nehanda was eventually caught and taken to Salisbury. Father Richartz, the Jesuit priest from the Chishawasha Mission, was called for. He wrote in the mission records, 'Nehanda began to dance, to laugh and talk so that the warders were obliged to tie her hands and watch her continually as she threatened to kill herself.' She refused his entreaties to be taken into the Catholic faith, instead demanding to be returned to her people, and on 27 April 1898 she was hanged. Unrepentant to the last, on the scaffold she warned, 'My bones shall rise again,' then her body dropped through the trapdoor with a heavy thud.

Aqui lay on a rock in the long shadow of a tree, sucking on a chakata fruit and dreaming about becoming a nurse. She was supposed to be tending the mombes, which was an important job as cattle represented wealth in the village. But it was so hot that the heat rippled across the yellow plains and the cattle lumbered about slowly. As long as she gave them an occasional shoo to keep them away from the crops then she could drift off and let her thoughts dance away.

These days, she always thought about the same thing. A few years before, when she was about seven and her second brother had fallen ill, she had gone with her mother to the clinic in Sadza. Chipo Tamari had already lost one son and this time when rubbing him with pastes of ground bark from the *nyanga* did not work and his pupils started rolling back in their sockets, she resolved to take action, whatever the other villagers might say. She wrapped the infant in swaddling to absorb the diarrhoea, dripped some well-water on his lips which were permanently open like the beak of a small bird, and placed a knitted hat on his head to protect it from the harsh sun. Then she tied him to her back and gave Aqui a calabash of water to carry so they could keep wetting his parched mouth. By the time they had made the three-hour-long walk to the township in the blinding heat, it was too late; the child's body was limp and could not be revived. Her mother began sobbing that she would never have a son and that they must have done something to offend the spirits. But Aqui was entranced by the bustling figures in uniforms, full of purposefulness, with pens in their pockets and metal trays laid out with instruments – stethoscope, tongs and syringes. The clinic smelled of paint and disinfectant, not of death and fear, as she had imagined. It was enough for her to know she had found her dream.

I admired the nurses' uniforms, how smart they were, and saving lives, and wanted to look like them and also because being a nurse or a teacher was something very special in the community. But she knew it was impossible because her body was turning into that of a woman and her parents would soon take her out of school. It was different for boys. *Boys were so precious, more precious than girls, we were useless in their eyes.* Her young brother Tatiwa who had been born after the death of her previous two brothers was even more precious because he was the only son to survive. He would get all the land and as much schooling as the family could afford even though he was dull and slow at learning.

As for Aqui, she might have been the brightest girl in her class but she would not go to secondary school because by the age of thirteen a girl was supposed to be married. *The idea of a girl's education was just for you to be able to read the note asking for your hand, then you were fine.*

At that time there were only about 150 secondary schools in the whole country and few black children did more than six years' education. But Aqui loved school, particularly English and geography. *I did not want to marry one of the silly boys in the village or, worse, an old man who had lost his wife and would pay good lobola [bride price].* In times of drought, when the rivers and wells dried up, the land shimmered with heat, and people had nothing to eat but the small yellow fruits that baboons ate, families often sold their daughters to such men, *some such Mr Banana*, as she thought of them, who had built up good stores of crops.

I begged the missionaries to let me stay on at school with the boys

Fetching water

but I knew my father would never agree. Her mother had not gone to school at all but she could read a little and it was clear to Aqui that she did most of the work. *My father, like all the men, was just talking, talking. It was my mother who walked to the well every morning when the sun came up, a pot on her head to fetch water for tea; she who took the animals to the stand; planted and weeded the crops; mended our clothes and cooked the food. In the dry season she grew all sorts of vegetables – tomatoes, cabbages, onions and rapeseed for relish with the sadza. In the rainy season she grew maize, pumpkins and groundnuts.*

Aqui's father worked as a contractor putting up wire fences on the big white farms around Chivhu, but the jobs came few and far between. *I loved it best when he went hunting with his catapult and knobkerry and would bring back doves or guinea fowl or sometimes even a duiker which we would eat in thick rich gravy with the sadza. Then our bellies would be full and he would tell stories and life had never seemed so good.*

But those days seemed long ago. Recently she had heard him and her mother arguing about her school fees and the cost of the new uniform she needed as her body started sprouting in all directions. 'No man is going to want a wife with so much knowledge in her head,' he pronounced, and the beer-drinkers enjoying some Seven Day in the yard all nodded agreement.

The pressure to get married beat like a drum on her temples until sometimes she thought her head would explode. *I wished I was like the other girls in the village who just wanted to find a man to look after them, then life would be easier. Most of the time I could just busy myself with tasks and not think beyond. But then I remembered the books I had read at school and the nurses I had seen and I knew there was more out there than Zhakata's Kraal.*

She hated passing the Apostolics gathered for one of their sessions, their white robes flapping around. *I wasn't scared of them any more, but if they saw me one of them would point a finger and declare that I should marry this Mr Banana or that Mr Pumpkin.*

At the well or washing clothes in the river, she noticed women hushing their voices as she approached and guessed they had been discussing her marriage prospects. Sometimes one of them made pointed pronouncements like, 'An unmarried woman is a troubled woman.' At the New Year's dancing which always took place after a small portion of each crop had been left for the spirits and the babies born that year had been blessed, a wealthy widower from the next village had tried to grab her hand. So old was he that skin hung in webs from his arms and it was all Aqui could do not to curl up her lip in revulsion. But he had cows and goats and a storeroom of maize and told her he would give her the best hut in the village and take her on the bus to Chivhu to buy a shop dress.

If she married him, her father would receive a hefty *lobola* of several cows. There was a proverb in the village that 'a son-in-law is like a fruit tree; one never finishes eating from it'. *I knew as the eldest I should help my family and marry a man like that with stocks for bad times, but it did not seem fair.* Her only hope was if he shared the same totem as her, the animal spirit which all Mashona are given at birth as a way of safeguarding against incest. *Mine was impala like my father because in Shona society men are more powerful than women so the children always take the totem of the father. It would be completely taboo for me to marry another impala.*

Even Aqui's mother, who she had thought was on her side, had started saying that now she was twelve her eldest daughter should be taking more care of her appearance. One day she sat Aqui down and smeared her hair with a paste made of water and ashes from burning the dry bark of the mutsvedzabeni tree to try and tame its frizziness. *I was quite sure Nehanda never did such things.*

Aqui wondered about appealing to the headmaster of her school to see if there was some kind of scholarship that would let her study to be a nurse. She had always had glowing reports, which she read out to her mother, and she knew he liked her. At a sports

day for schools in the area they had camped on the field of
another school, St Judes, because it was too far to get back to
their homes. While she and some friends were sitting round the
fire they had made, a boy had come running with a message that
the headmaster was calling for her. *I went to him, he was standing
and I knelt down because we were always taught to kneel to big
people. He lunged at me and started groping.* Fortunately he was
so inebriated that he could hardly stand and she had managed to
run away. When she got back to her friends the fire had gone out
and they were already sleeping in their blankets. She huddled
inside hers and shivered. *I didn't sleep all night.*

Under the tree, a light rustling disturbed her reverie and she
watched a chameleon pause in the wind and lift its head before
scuttling away. The sun had already disappeared behind the Daramombe Mountains and Aqui realized she should be moving the
cattle back to their pen before the wild animals came out and she
was scolded for dreaming again. As she hurried back, flicking the
cows' haunches with a large twig, darkness fell and seemed to
grow thick and black around her until the moon took pity and
showed half its face to light her path.

4

Train to Salisbury, 1974

'LET ME, LET ME!' The white boys on the train took turns at holding the lighter flame to the pennies until they were burning hot, then placed them ready on the window ledge.

Outside the window the countryside from Umtali to Salisbury flashed by, hills and valleys, grass and streams, and strange balancing rocks that defied all notion of gravity. Unique to that part of southern Africa, the granite boulders strewn about the landscape looked like Easter Island figures tumbled on their heads by a mischievous giant. White Rhodesians often referred to their homeland as God's Own Country, and this part was the most beautiful of all.

On the racks above the seats were stacked the boys' straw boaters and black tin trunks with their surnames stencilled in white above the words 'Prince Edward School, Salisbury'.

There was a shrieking whistle and the train shuddered to a halt at Marandellas station. As usual the platform was packed with natives hoping to sell sodas and biscuits. To Nigel, the crowd of women in colourful prints resembled a cloud of butterflies that parted as the train approached. Most rushed to the whites-only carriages in the front, urgently pressing their wares and black faces against glass panes etched with the words Rhodesian Railways. The schoolboys, smart in their maroon blazers, white shirts and maroon ties, hair cut into fresh pudding bowls by heartless

mothers, stared out at the dusty children and strangely humped women with babies strapped to their backs. Then one of them wound down the windows a little to toss out the scalding pennies. They laughed uproariously as the black children jostled each other, hands outstretched, only to drop the coins in wide-eyed agony.

'Works every time!' shouted Nigel. 'The *piccanins* are so stupid.'

'Have you heard?' asked Charlie Tibbets. 'They are talking about having *munts* at our school.'

'No!'

'Ja, Freddie Wilderkamp's dad is a governor and he told me.'

'Ach, those *munts* have a hang of a smell. They don't wash, man. Imagine having them in the same dormitory.'

'They don't even know how to use a bog. I heard the ones at St Georges stand on the seats!'

'Imagine getting one of them as your fag!'

They all fell silent contemplating this prospect as the train chugged on its way. Occasionally it stopped at farms to leave mail or collect churns of milk and boys in similar school blazers who would clamber aboard with a cheery 'Howzit?'

Nigel watched as a small black boy in torn red shorts held up with a pin jumped on clutching a plastic container to fill with water from one of the train's taps, then scampered off with a delighted smile. Outside a handful of dove-white clouds chased each other across the wide blue sky and one of his friends mimicked taking aim and pulling a trigger with his fingers.

I guess we were thinking about the munts we had on our farms, recalled Nigel, *how they smelled and stole things and how our parents always said the black man couldn't be trusted. We knew that blacks were way behind in civilization.*

Just before the previous election in 1970 in which the Rhodesian Front had won every single seat for the second time since declaring UDI, Smith told a rally: 'Sixty years ago Africans here were uncivilized savages, walking around in skins. They have made tremendous progress but they have an awful long way to go.'

White boys like Nigel talked of the black population as 'they' and thought it not at all unreasonable that they should be barred from white hospitals, schools, bars, swimming pools, restaurants and shops or from voting.* After all, Smith described them as 'the happiest blacks in the world'. Besides, these were people who did things like leaving a tractor and trailer on a main road with no lights at night, which had led to his brother's tragic death.

Growing up in Rhodesia it was so easy to be drawn into generalizations. When you have all these incidents at the farm, endless theft and betrayals by servants, you have one or two ways of going. You can either rationalize and say, 'Well, that would happen with any race,' or say, 'No, they're just an inferior breed and what do you expect?'

---

* Only whites could vote in the country's elections apart from a handful of blacks who fulfilled an extraordinary combination of educational and financial criteria.

Prince Edward School

None of us could imagine them in our school. Prince Edward was one of the oldest and most prestigious schools in Rhodesia. Founded as Salisbury Public School in the early days of the Pioneers back in 1898, it was renamed after the Prince of Wales who visited Rhodesia in 1925, and even today the school prospectus states that it 'seeks to build balanced gentlemen'. The flag fluttering over the red-brick tower of the main building bore the school crest of a lion and a sable holding up a shield on which was the three-feathered coronet of the Prince of Wales. The lion carried a flag emblazoned with the English Tudor rose and both animals rested on a grassy knoll decorated with a Tudor rose, the African flame lily and the Welsh leek. Underneath was the Latin motto *Tot facienda parum factum* – So much to do, so little done, a translation of Rhodes's weary words on his deathbed in 1902.

The school was divided into eight houses named after Pioneers and heroes of the colonial era including Jameson, after Leander Starr Jameson, first administrator of the British South African Company; Baines, after Thomas Baines, the explorer; Selous, for Frederick Selous, the adventurer; and Moffat, for John Moffat, the British government emissary who first persuaded Lobengula to keep out the Boers. Nigel was in Rhodes House, where the initiation process included stealing fruit from the neighbouring convent and being woken in the middle of winter at 2 a.m. to swim in the pool and do a cross-country run. *I thought it built up camaraderie but then one year a boy died doing it because he had a weak heart that no one knew about.*

Apart from extensive rugby and cricket fields, the school had its own observatory and memorial chapel funded by the donations of old pupils. Nigel had managed to find a hiding place at the back upstairs and would sleep all the way through Sunday service. Latin and Greek were key parts of the Prince Edward curriculum and there was a set of rules such as always wearing a tie inside – maroon with the three feathers or green-striped for prefects – but never a cap. Any violations were punished with a set of cuts, beatings with a cane, sometimes six at a time, which left the victim bruised black and scarlet although of course no self-respecting boy would allow himself to cry.

The school day began somewhat brutally with a junior blowing a bugle at 6 a.m. Nigel was fagging for one of the prefects, Philip Nicholas, so had to get up even earlier to polish his shoes, run his bath and carry his books. Inspection and roll call were at 6.30 a.m. Everyone then filed over to the main school building for morning assembly which started with a rousing chorus of the school song. This opened with the lines:

> *When the lion roared of old*
> *And the sable tossed his crest*

It went on to become increasingly martial with verses such as:

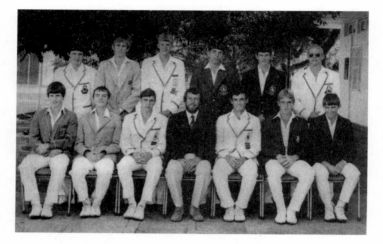

The school cricket team (Nigel is first left, bottom row)

> *When we lay aside the pen*
> *And abandon bat and ball*
> *We will acquit ourselves like men*
> *Answering our country's call*

Under Rhodesian law, no government school was permitted to have more than 6 per cent blacks, and Prince Edward had never admitted black students. But it was not the effect on traditions that concerned Nigel – Prince Edward was the country's top sporting school and he was worried about the impact a black presence might have on the performance of their teams. *I lived for sport – squash, cricket, rugby.* Although he was small for his age, within days of arriving the eleven-year-old Nigel had beaten the school tennis and squash champions and by the following year he was playing first-team cricket.

Their main rival school, St Georges, had black boys and because of that their teams were not allowed to play away games. Some schools refused to play them at all. *I was really worried that would happen to us too. Also I dreaded the idea of being in a rugby scrum with an African. I thought they were dirty and would smell. Peterhouse School used to have black guys and when we went to play against them we used to be very reluctant to eat off their plates because they seemed greasy and we thought it was because blacks had been eating off them.*

White Rhodesia was an outdoor society where sport was very much part of life and enormous value was placed on sporting achievements. The first cricket pitch was laid by the Pioneers in Salisbury in 1891, as early a priority as building a school or hospital. At Prince Edward, schooldays started with a cross-country run and there was no greater honour than being in the rugby first fifteen. Most of the national sports teams had ex-PE boys, and when Nigel joined the school, both Duncan Fletcher, the Zimbabwe cricket captain who went on to coach England to win the Ashes, and John Bredenkamp, the rugby captain (later better known as an arms dealer and one of Britain's richest men), were Old Hararians, as alumni were known. *All other schools feared playing Prince Edward,* said Nigel. *Even St Georges boys spent most of their time running away from Prince Edward men.*

The few black boys who managed to get places at white schools found life almost intolerable. James Mushore was one of the first in the 1970s, a scholarship boy at St Georges who went on to co-found Zimbabwe's largest merchant bank, NMB. 'I had a terrible time,' he said. 'The white boys did something called "ball brushing", which was pulling down my pants and painting my balls with bootblack. But worst of all was "bog washing". There was one boy in particular who would defecate in the toilet, leave his faeces there, then force my head down into the bowl and flush it over me.'

When James won a nationwide spelling bee, his parents were not allowed in the hall to watch the competition and had been forced to sit outside in the car park waiting for him to come and tell them the result. Afterwards, he watched the mother of a white boy slap the cheek of her son, the runner-up, and loudly demand, 'How could you let a *kaffir* beat you?'

Nigel admits he would have shared that mother's feelings. *I clearly remember when I was at Prince Edward that there was an article in the newspaper where some American scientist had proven that blacks were 10 per cent more stupid than whites and they didn't have the same brain capacity and I remember us discussing how they must have been further down the evolutionary scale. This was a very politically correct view then; I suppose it sort of justified the behaviour.*

At school they studied 'Builders of Rhodesia' – Rhodes, Rudd, Jameson and Alfred Beit, the diamond and gold magnate – and were left under the impression that before the Pioneers arrived the country was a no man's land. Nigel had heard adults tell the story of the border between Rhodesia and Portuguese East Africa being decided by the toss of a die. *Every white schoolboy had been taught the story of the last stand of Allan Wilson's patrol who died so bravely on the banks of the Shangani river as they were outnumbered by Lobengula's hordes. When they ran out of bullets they started singing 'God Save the Queen' until one by one they all fell.* In fact what Nigel had learnt about as 'a glorious sacrifice in the name of founding the country' had no factual basis as no survivor lived to tell the tale. The deaths of the 34 men were probably caused by a reckless blunder during Jameson's barbaric war on the Ndebele in 1893.

The war ended with Lobengula telling his people, 'Now here are your masters coming ... You will have to pull and shove wagons but under me you never did this kind of thing ... the white people are coming now, I didn't want to fight with them.' The King apparently then swallowed poison after learning that the last of his impis had surrendered, though other reports suggest that he fled across the border. *Inkosi yanyamalala*, the Ndebele say, 'The King has vanished.'

But Nigel had never heard of this, nor of Rhodes's tricking of Lobengula that had led to the creation of Rhodesia. *Even when I left school all I knew was that Lobengula was fat and primitive and that's all.*

For us the history of Rhodesia started with the arrival of whites to civilize warring kaffir tribes. At school I learned all about the two world wars and the threat of Communist advancement but I never knew anything about the Shona or Ndebele people or any local language or culture. We didn't think they had a culture. I knew how to say 'mangwanani' in Shona, which means 'good morning', and nothing else. I knew nothing about how blacks lived.

Ian Smith's description in his memoirs typified the Rhodesian view. On the Pioneers' imposition of hut tax on the natives, he wrote: 'They [the natives] were happy to have the opportunity to work and for the first time in their lives, earn money which enabled them to join in the excitement of this new adventure of purchasing and selling – something they had never previously known.' As for the white settlers taking the best land, he explained: 'Because of the primitive agricultural implements used by the black people which were wooden as opposed to the iron used by the white man, they were concentrated on the light sandy soils which they found easier to work.'

History had been rewritten to fit a white notion of Rhodesia and it did not stop with politics. Revisionism also turned to cultural artefacts. Great Zimbabwe appeared on Rhodesian maps as the Zimbabwe Ruins, the remains of a white empire in Africa built by Phoenicians, Greeks or Egyptians, because the Rhodesian government did not want to believe that black Africans could have built such a place. In the 1960s the Smith regime even commissioned a history promoting that view despite the complete lack of supporting evidence. Postcards were sold showing it as the possible palace of the Queen of Sheba, the view propounded by the first Europeans to come across it.

Nigel's dislike of authority made it hard for him to settle at school and he always felt in the shadow of his bright elder brother Edwin. Although his sporting prowess made him popular, he had also

Postcard showing the Queen of Sheba
at Great Zimbabwe

inherited his father's eccentric sense of humour, which led him into all sorts of trouble. One of his masters, George Armstrong, who was partial to a drink, owned a lime green Vauxhall. Nigel managed to acquire a Corgi model of the exact car and one night, when they had seen the master coming back more than a little unsteady on his feet, they moved his car from the car park and replaced it with the tiny replica. As the master stood there, blinking in confusion, they fell about laughing.

Rhodesia was an extremely rigid society and its boarding

schools, based on the English model, highly disciplinarian. Nigel was soon notching up large numbers of cuts. Although he quickly learnt to wear extra underpants as protection, he never got used to the pain and would stand nervously, waiting for the crack of the Irish housemaster's stick on his backside that would leave him with such a set of red welts that he was barely able to sit down.

His bad behaviour was always a source of tension when his parents drove up for sports days and afterwards took him for tea and scones in Meikles Hotel. There they sat in the cane chairs among the potted palms of the colonnaded coffee lounge, sipping their drinks and trying to talk over the sound of the band.

Nigel's parents were not sure what to make of their sports-mad son. He was in almost every school team yet at the same time was steadily building up a school record for the highest number of cuts or canings, usually for being cheeky to teachers.

But they had other things to worry about. In December 1972 the Houghs had been spending the Christmas holiday in Centenary with their cousins the Wallers, when the farm radio suddenly crackled into action. An urgent voice called for all men to get their guns and help. A nearby white farmhouse had been attacked, that of farmer Marc de Borchgrave, and his two young daughters asleep in their parents' main bedroom had narrowly escaped death. The shaken family moved to a neighbouring homestead where two nights later they were woken by rocket and grenade fire. Again they had a lucky escape, de Borchgrave and his eight-year-old daughter suffering shrapnel wounds. The next morning when an army patrol went to investigate, their vehicle hit a landmine and a white officer was killed.

For Rhodesia's white population, the audacious raid on Altena Farm would be seen as the start of the civil war. The black resistance fighters dated it from six years earlier, to 28 April 1966, when they clashed with Rhodesian Security Forces in the town of Chinhoyi, north of Salisbury. A group of seven guerrillas had tried to destroy power pylons with no success and had then killed a farmer, Hendrik Viljoen, and his wife, just 50 miles outside the capital. Within days the fighters had all been killed by Rhodesian security forces; they would be remembered as the Chinhoyi Seven.

For the next six years the guerrillas made so little headway that few Rhodesians took much notice. Their camps were far away in Tanzania and Zambia, from where their attacks were launched, and a lack of arms and training made them little threat. Like most of the country, the area around the Houghs' farm in Headlands had not been affected at all.

However, in late 1972 the Mozambican province of Tete, which bordered Rhodesia's long north-eastern frontier, had come under the control of Samora Machel's Frelimo forces fighting against the Portuguese colonial government. This enabled Rhodesia's free-dom fighters to set up camps in Tete from where they could cross the Zambezi and infiltrate the north-east of the country around Centenary and Mount Darwin, starting with the attack on Altena Farm. The raid was led by a commander called Solomon Mujuru, though like most of the guerrillas he used a *nom de guerre* – his was Rex Nhongo. Mujuru's men started making bases in villages and the bush from which they attacked white farmers, laid mines and set ambushes on the roads.

The war, which until then had seemed no more than a low-level annoyance, suddenly intensified. By 1974, Smith had introduced blanket conscription and Nigel's elder brother Edwin was one of those called up. Recruits were told they were like Peter in the Dutch fable holding a finger in the dyke, stopping the guerrillas pouring over the borders to bring down all they stood for. Brought up on the myth of the Shangani patrol, whether it was right to be fighting for white supremacy and against universal suffrage was not something they questioned.

5

Zhakata's Kraal, 1974

AQUI WOULD REMEMBER the year that the Bush War came to her village for a number of reasons. It was the year that she finally managed to join the scotch-cart to the cows first off without any help. Not that there were many cows left. *That was the summer of the cows dying. First snot started running from their nostrils and that turned to pus and there was diarrhoea running from their bottoms, and it was like someone was squeezing all the liquids out of them until they could no longer stand and fell down.* The disease was probably rinderpest from not dipping the cattle, but some of the villagers said it was poison of the white man.

The bad things had started with one of the *ngangas* seeing a secretary bird roaming the skies above a lightning-struck tree, a sign to the Shona forewarning death. Although Aqui pooh-poohed such talk, knowing what Father Walter would think of it, she had to admit there had been so little rain that the maize shrivelled and died, and the crocodiles left the river, all in a line. The heat throbbed until the land cried out for moisture but the sun had no pity and the sky remained defiantly cloudless. Her mother had taken to sitting on the beer drum, scouring the heavens for storks or grasshoppers, anything that might be taken as indicators of rain. *Then the headmaster told us there was to be something called curfew. He said if it is six o'clock and you are not at home you better stay where you are because it is curfew and you could be shot.*

A few days later he called Aqui into his room and asked her to remain behind that afternoon to get her results. *I was surprised because he had just told us about the curfew and how we must hurry home and not dally. Then I thought maybe he had found a way for me to stay on at school so I could study to become a nurse and I was quite excited.*

But she had not forgotten his behaviour at the sports day so she asked two other girls to stay behind with her. After the day's final lesson, they all went to the headmaster's office, feeling nervous. He said, 'I'm still busy,' *and kept us waiting and waiting. First it was two o'clock, then three, then four, finally it was 5.30 p.m. Then he said it's wartime and it will soon be curfew so you can't go home, because if anything happens to you, soldiers shoot you, it will be my responsibility. You will have to come with me.*

The three girls followed him to the teachers' compound. Two teachers were waiting at the headmaster's house and took the two other girls away. Aqui did not know what to do but the headmaster beckoned her in with a smile. She tried not to look at his sticking-out eyeballs and one blackened front tooth that reminded her of the eagles that sometimes circled the Daramombe Mountains because she knew that would be rude. Once inside he told her, 'You a very nice girl, Aquinata.' He used her whole name, something only Father Walter did when he greeted her after mass on Sunday.

The headmaster lived in a small brick shack with a corrugated iron door and roof and a partition in the centre. One side had a bed and some clothes strewn around; the other had a small brown sofa with the stuffing leaking out, a gilt plastic clock and a picture of waves crashing on a rocky shore. Rhodesia was a landlocked country and Aqui did not know anyone who had seen the sea. Even the men who went to work in the goldmines in South Africa and came back again had not seen the sea on their travels.

The headmaster patted a place on the small sofa and told her to sit there, then he locked the door. Aqui began to tremble.

'Sir, please can I have my results now, I have to be home before curfew and I have a long walk back,' she said.

He said not to trouble about that. Then he told me to lift my skirt.

'I want to have a look at you, see what kind of shape you are in, you a big girl now,' he said, reaching forward. She noticed that his hands were hairy and his fingers flabby like the butcher's in the township. The headmaster was the only black man she knew who wore a watch.

Then I saw his trousers were open and his jigga jagga out. His knob was purple and shiny at the end like the damba fruit. He said, 'I'm going to undress and you also undress.' I told him I can't do that but he insisted. 'No, it's just a small thing, everyone does it.' I knew that was not true and I said, 'No, only when people are married do they do it.'

But before she knew what was happening he had thrown her to the ground and her face was full of his stale smell, his head bald like a lizard thrusting back and forth. *I couldn't even catch breath, he was dashing me down, tugging at my panties. I heard my skirt tearing and I was scared my dress was going to be destroyed.*

I even forgot that as he hurt me, thrusting himself inside me so it felt like he was ripping me apart. I pushed and kicked and tried to scream but he slapped my face hard then stuffed his hand in my mouth.

Aqui was only twelve but she was a strong girl. That year at school she had been Netball Player of the Year. She tossed and struggled but that only seemed to excite him more. Finally he shuddered to a climax, yanking himself out so that his juice sprayed in a sticky white fountain over her thighs and skirt.

She tried to pull away but the headmaster grabbed her back down.

'Where do you think you are going?' he laughed. 'You must stay with me.'

Aqui could only think of one thing.

'Sir, I need to pee!' she shouted.

'Ah, do you think I am so stupid?'

'Believe me, sir, I am not playing with you. I really need it!'

'All right then, do it out of there if you must,' he said, opening the window. 'But I will hold onto your legs.'

Aqui sat on the ledge and the headmaster grabbed her ankles.

'Sir, I need to shift back or it will come inside!'

As he loosened his grip, she swung her legs round and jumped out of the window, then ran and hid in the bush. The night was still and quiet and she could hear him cursing and fiddling with the lock.

The door flung open and she could see the red eye of a cigarette and a torch beam swinging around. Aqui ran and ran, her torn skirt flapping around, tears stinging her eyes. The air blew inside where her panties should be. Only when she could see the torch no more did she pause to catch her breath. The moon had come out from behind the clouds and as she caught sight of the shiny snail's trail across the blue and white fabric of her school skirt, she retched. There was nothing to come up, as she had not taken anything since tea that morning. She did not start to feel safe until after she had crossed the middle river and stopped at the last where her dead sister and brothers were trapped for ever in the clay. Careless of crocodiles, she scooped water in her hand over and over to dab away the stain.

At home, she explained away the torn clothes and marks on her arms and face, saying that she had tripped over some stones on the way back. Her mother ticked her off for being 'slovenly' but in those days everyone was distracted by the falling cows and buzzing heat.

That night after washing and mending her skirt, Aqui's dreams were filled with giant one-toothed lizards forcing their long tongues down her throat. She tossed and turned so much that her sisters complained she was kicking them.

The next morning instead of leaping up as usual to assist her mother as she came into the hut at first light to make the fire for the morning tea, she pretended an urgent bowel motion and wandered off outside to the bush. She jumped at a scuffing sound, then saw it was one of the goats mounting another in the dust. Aqui did not see how she could go to school. She thought about feigning a sore tummy but that would mean taking one of her grandmother's foul potions of ground tree-bark and herbs, and besides, in those days everyone had that hollow feeling inside.

So she set off early as usual and crossed the second river and climbed the first kopje. But instead of continuing on the path, she turned behind some rocks. She was going to what she thought of as her own Special Place. In an African village, privacy was a rare commodity. Most villagers would go through life without ever having spent a single day or a night alone.

Aqui had stumbled on the place one day when she was playing hide and seek on the way home with some of her schoolmates. A strange grassy mound caught her eye as a good place to hide, but as she jumped behind it she felt the ground giving way and herself falling.

For a moment she panicked, thinking she had landed in the den of a wild pig. But then she realized there was stone either side of the hole, forming a kind of gateway. As her eyes accustomed to the gloom she could see she was in a cave and there was a sliver of light at the other end. It was already late to be going home and she was about to climb out and call her friends, then something stopped her. *I had never had anything that was just mine before.*

The passage was just wide enough for one and the stone either side was marked in a herringbone pattern. Aqui edged her way through, coming out at the end as if through a keyhole to an area of flat stones almost like a platform. She slid her way forward on her stomach. The stone was cool and soothing to lie on and looked out over shimmering plains dotted with glowing yellow rocks and low thorn trees. The shadows stretched longer and

longer. Everything was still as if awaiting a signal. Then the cicadas began their crazed chirping, and as she watched the late afternoon sun dissolve in a display of pinks and crimsons in the sky, it felt as if she were on top of the world, close to some Great Power like the God of creation that Father Walter talked about and she wondered who had built such a thing.

Aqui may have stumbled across one of the caves used as hiding places by the Shona chiefs during the Chimurenga, though most were blown up by the whites with their dynamite, even with women and children inside. She had heard the stories of how the country-side had echoed for weeks with the screams of the dying and rotting bodies strewn around for jackals and vultures to feed on.

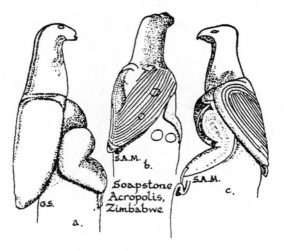

Soapstone Acropolis, Zimbabwe

The central Zimbabwe plateau, on which lay Zhakata's Kraal, has many such mysterious ruins. By far the most famous and extensive is Great Zimbabwe from which the independence move-ment had taken its name. Zimbabwe or *dzimba dza mabwe* is Shona for House of Stone and Great Zimbabwe was a massive stone fortress for a king with walls some 36 feet high and 17 feet thick yet with no plaster or cement to hold the stones together. The walls were decorated with great birds carved of soapstone that looked down over the plains and giant circular enclosures in which lived the king's wives and his subjects. Cecil Rhodes was so taken with the bird sculptures that he made copies to put on the gateposts of his home in Cambridgeshire. When the ruins were first encountered by Portuguese traders in the sixteenth

Great Zimbabwe

century, they believed they had found the fabled palace of the Queen of Sheba. To this day it remains shrouded in mystery. Dating back to the eleventh century, it was the greatest medieval city in sub-Saharan Africa and evidence of a great African civilization. But its inhabitants – thought to have numbered at least 10,000 people – disappeared without trace and left no written history.

It was to her own House of Stone that Aqui went the day after the headmaster attacked her – she could not bring herself to use the word rape. She lay on the stone platform chewing a msasa twig. Apart from the red mark where he had slapped her, she was quite sure what had happened must show on her face. It was impossible that she could look the same as she had the previous day. Hungry baboons jeered at her and even the morning songs of the birds sounded mocking. She wondered if she had committed a sin and should confess. She knew the skirt of her school dress had become short for her and the blouse was so tight that she had several times had to re-sew on the buttons. But she could not tell anyone, particularly Father Walter; there would be too much shame and no one would marry her. *It was bad enough that I was tall and thin instead of plump peach-bottomed and breasted like our African men liked.*

She had no doubt she would have to stop school now. She could not bear to face the headmaster again. Later she would discover that he had impregnated two other pupils. At least her parents would be happy; she could work in the fields all day and cook and sew until she found a husband of her own.

While Aqui was sitting there, her mind tossing with all of these things, she heard a strange rumbling that seemed to be coming from within the earth. From her hidden platform, she saw clouds of red dust rising down below as a column of green-painted vehicles appeared on the track. 'Soldiers!' She caught her breath. The metal of their guns glinted in the sun. Aqui had never seen soldiers before.

She ran home like the wind to tell the news but it was already all round the village. The soldiers had been through the village warning everyone to beware of terrorists – 'terrs', they called them, but no one knew what they meant – and to give information if they saw anything.

Over the coming months and years, the soldiers' Land Rovers and Bedford trucks, bristling with radio antennae like strange insects, would become part of life, moving up and down the track either early in the morning or late in the day as the sky bled crimson. Aqui learnt to live with them though she always kept them in her sight and felt relieved when they had moved on.

Zanla fighters – the Comrades

Shortly after we saw Smith's soldiers, guys from the bush, Mugabe's recruits, began to appear, vanamukoma – the boys. They referred to the war as the Second Chimurenga after the unsuccessful 1896 uprising of the Shona against the white settlers, prompting Aqui to recall the stories she had heard of Nehanda and wonder if again a woman might emerge to inspire the forces. *When the vanamukoma came, we were very excited. Our mothers made food and we girls took pots of it into the bush. We had to be careful*

*Smith's soldiers didn't see us. Lots of the boys ran away to the bush
to join them, younger than me even. I wished I could learn to fight
too.*

Her brother was only eight and too young to fight but he ran
around excitedly mimicking gunfire and collecting bullets. Every
evening the men gathered at the headman's hut to listen to
news of the war on Mozambique radio at 8 p.m. *which was very
illegal.*

*To start with it was fun, a kind of secret war. We knew all
the places to hide in the caves and culverts and could follow the
paths of the ancestors by the stars while the white man needed
torches and maps.*

Sometimes the Comrades, as they called themselves, would
descend on the village after dark and summon everyone to a
pungwe, a meeting through the night which they all had to
attend. The Comrades made endless speeches about Marxism,
neo-colonialism and the War against Imperialism which no one
understood. Aqui tried to keep awake by looking up at the sky
and making pictures from the limpid stars. But there were always
cheers at the end when the Comrades recalled the pledge of
Nehanda on the hangman's block and promised, 'We will give
you back the white man's land!' *We would sigh with pleasure for
we all imagined having farms of rich red fields like those in Chivhu
and brick houses like those where the whites lived.* They then led
the villagers in chanting slogans for something called ZANU,
which stood for Zimbabwe African National Union.

Their leader was a man called Reverend Ndabaningi Sithole,
who had been in Salisbury Maximum Security Prison since 1963.
Locked up with him were the movement's founder Joshua Nkomo,
a Methodist lay preacher and leader of the railway workers,
renowned as a firebrand orator, and the ZANU secretary-general
Robert Gabriel Mugabe who had come late to the nationalist
cause but was highly ambitious.

Mugabe was the son of a carpenter who had left his family for work and never returned, apparently taking another wife. His mother was left to bring up their four children, the eldest of whom died after eating poisoned maize. Like Aqui, Mugabe had gone to a Catholic mission school, then he had trained as a teacher at Fort Hare University, the only all-black university on the Cape, where Nelson Mandela had studied law. It was there that Mugabe had been introduced to Marxism, sending off for copies of *Das Kapital* and Engels' *Conditions of the Working Class*. He had gone on to teach in Northern Rhodesia and then Ghana which in 1957 had just become the first black African colony to get independence. Mugabe was inspired by what he saw, and also fell in love with a fellow teacher, Sally Hayfron, a Ghanaian who shared his political ideals. Together they returned to Rhodesia and married in February 1961 and joined Nkomo's National Democratic Party. Within two years, he had been arrested.

Mugabe used his eleven years of incarceration, rather like Mandela in South Africa's notorious Robben Island, to dedicate himself to study. As he neither drank nor smoked, and was described by associates as 'something of a cold fish', he found prison life easier to adjust to than most of his fellow prisoners. His wife Sally, in exile in London, spent all her spare time copying passages from library books to send him. So hard did he work for his correspondence courses with London University that one of his tutors referred to him as 'the Japanese'. But in between completing the last of seven degrees, he was plotting to become the independence movement's leader.

We didn't really know anything about any of these people but Mugabe was a Zezuru like us, so we felt happy with him, whereas Nkomo was an Ndebele, like Lobengula and those who had stolen our women and cows and given away our country, and the others like Sithole were from the Karanga tribe.

The *pungwes* usually ended with the rebel commander demanding that the villagers belt out songs such as:

'*Pamberi ne Chimurenga*' – 'Up with the Chimurenga'
'*Pasi na Smith*' – 'Down with Smith'
'*NeZvimba sungata zwake*' – 'And the dogs that follow him'
'*A luta continua*' – 'The struggle continues'

Aqui quite liked singing the songs at first. Her choir had
stopped meeting because of the danger of being out at night when
the sound of gun firing and mortars had replaced the hoot of
owls, scrabbling of rats and grunts from inside the huts. It was
nice to sing again and she felt like part of something. The Comrades had *ngoma* drums, pounding the skins in a frenzied rhythm,
and old Josiah played along on the *mbira*, the thumb piano of tiny
keys set in a pumpkin gourd or calabash. To Aqui, its mournful
twanging sounded like the weeping of the spirits, luring the
sleep-starved villagers into a far-away trance.

One of her favourites was:

> *Oh grandmothers*
> *Oh mothers, oh boys*
> *There's a snake in the forest*
> *Mothers take hoes*
> *Grandmothers take hoes*
> *Boys take axes*

But she was shocked by the way the Comrades beat people who
did not participate with sufficient enthusiasm. *I would like to have
told them that the choirmaster had just used a whistle and that had
been enough.*

Things were changing in the village. *You could see it with the
beer. People did not want to wait for seven days any more. They
started thinking, you can't brew beer for seven days, so they would
mix yeast, sugar, millet, maize, anything they could find, even car
battery fluid, and ferment it just for 24 hours. They called it One
Day and it was too dangerous.*

*   *   *

In what was turning into one of the continent's most brutal civil wars, villagers suffered more than anyone because they would be punished by both sides for helping the other. But they had little choice other than to aid whichever soldiers turned up. *We girls would go into the bush and carry pots of food and tea to the Comrades but they became more and more demanding. They didn't just want sadza with vegetables, they wanted meat. My parents gave the freedom fighters our goats and roosters and blankets and clothes. If there was food in the huts they would take it. Cows and goats disappeared. They would just say, 'I want that' and take anything, even my two dresses for their girlfriends. When there was no more meat left in the village, they made our people go to farms to steal cattle.*

Then Smith's soldiers would come and harass or whip you, accusing us of looking after bush fighters. They came in our huts and eh, if you had meat you were in for it, even if it was from your own beasts. They could kill you for that. 'Put your head down,' they would say, then they would put the head of a cow on top and squash and squash until the person was dead.

The stores in the township were all destroyed and the government forces had set up sandbagged machine-gun posts on the hills. Aqui was scared when Rhodesian soldiers came through. Their faces were greased black and green, giving them a terrifying appearance, and they wore green bandannas round their heads, while their jackets were slung with heavy belts of ammunition.

Everyone had heard the stories of women with babies on their backs being gunned down and their babies' throats slit; of their helicopters which came from the sky and sprayed bullets everywhere, and of people being penned into camps.

Sometimes the white soldiers would grab a villager at gunpoint to travel in the front vehicle of their convoy so that if the rebels had laid any mines or set ambushes they would be warned. But as far as Aqui was aware mostly the villagers did not have such information, and whoever was picked to ride would quiver with fear.

One day Aqui's uncle, her father's brother, left the house around
dawn to walk to a funeral in another village. *You were not supposed
to leave the house in the early morning so they stopped him and
said, 'Where are you going?' and demanded he went over to them.
He just walked so they ordered him, 'Run over here,' and he said,
'No, I'm walking,' so they just opened fire and killed him. I was very
angry.*

Over time the villagers became almost as scared of the Comrades. They seemed convinced that people were collaborating with
the Rhodesian soldiers and appointed what they called Political
Commissars as their eyes and ears. People were being killed as
sell-outs, found in the morning with their throats cut or entire
families burned to death in their huts.

'It was common for us to come into a village and find villagers
whose legs had been broken or incinerated in their huts by the
terrs,' said Barry Percival, a teacher who served in the Rhodesian
Security Forces and, like most veterans of that war, was left
haunted by the atrocities he witnessed.

The war developed into a kind of cycle with the guerrillas
preferring to launch their operations during the rainy season
between December and February when there was foliage to give
cover. Aqui longed for those times because the rest of the year
the fighters would mostly be in their camps in the bush with
plenty of time to harass the villagers.

Aqui thought it was all very confusing. First of all some of
Smith's soldiers were black, not white. And the fighting was not
just between the Rhodesian security forces and the freedom
fighters. Sometimes the Comrades fought each other.

Most of the Shona fighters were in Zanla, the Zimbabwe African
National Liberation Army, which was the military wing of ZANU,
the party of Sithole and Mugabe. Their bases were in Mozambique
and they were funded and armed by China. Then there was Zipra,
the Zimbabwe People's Revolutionary Army, the military wing
of ZAPU led by Joshua Nkomo, the original founder of the

independence movement and also in jail. Nkomo was from the minority Ndebele tribe, as were most of his fighters, and their bases were in Zambia while they were mainly armed and financed by the Soviet Union.

Initially all these leaders had been in the same group, the National Democratic Party (NDP) which had started life as the African National Congress that Nkomo had founded in the 1950s until it was banned. But the NDP was also outlawed by the Rhodesian government in 1961 and two years later the movement had split into ZANU and ZAPU on tribal lines.

The two groups shared a slogan, 'Land for the People', and an objective – independence and reclaiming the land from the white man. But their tribal rivalry went back to long before the white man, and when they came into contact they often fought each other. While the Mashona tended to be of docile nature, busying themselves as cattle breeders, the Ndebele were once respected according to the number of Mashonas they had killed.

We never trusted the Ndebele, and we listened to many mouths, but what we knew was we were fighting for our freedom. We thought it was right because of all this racism we had grown up with and we knew that the land should be ours. I felt white people were very bad. If one fish is rotten, so is the whole pond.

For as long as Aqui could remember, she had heard the elders explain that their blood and sweat – and the bones of their dead – were in the land and they must get it back. *The white man who jumped from place to place and could not even name his ancestors would never understand that.*

By 1976 Mugabe had taken control of ZANU after organizing a vote of no confidence in Sithole while in prison – which Mozambique's President Samora Machel referred to sceptically as 'Mugabe's coup in jail'. It was to newly independent Mozambique that Mugabe had fled across the mountains after being released and where the Zanla guerrillas had moved most of their bases. For a while Machel kept him under virtual house arrest, not trusting this aloof academic who he feared was an agent for Ian Smith. He believed that the leader should come from the fighting forces in the bush as he had. But within six months of leaving Rhodesia, around 10,000 guerrillas had followed Mugabe to fight and Machel finally recognized him as leader.

For Mugabe, politicizing the masses was as much a part of the liberation struggle as fighting the enemy. Chinese instructors taught his forces the methods of indoctrination used by Mao Zedong during the Cultural Revolution. Summary trials were held in the bush, modelled on the purges of the Communists, with people hanged or shot for 'treason'.

In the villages the *pungwes* were becoming more demanding. *They would make us sing for the entire night until we were dropping with tiredness.* Anyone not showing sufficient enthusiasm would be beaten with sticks or clubs studded with nails. The freedom fighters had taken names like Comrade Double-Danger or Comrade Instant Death. Sometimes a comrade would denounce someone as a collaborator and drag that person forward to be tortured to death in front of everyone as an example.

In the villages people already have grudges. They hate each other or are jealous because you have many cattle because you are working hard at your place, you are growing vegetables in your garden, you have lots of goats, your children are going to school and you can feed your family nicely, whereas this one he is lazy and can't do what are you doing. There is a lot of jealousy in our race, even your own brother can be jealous about you, it's very common. So when war started, those who were jealous started saying bad things about others and they would be beaten up. They might say one is a witch and the comrades would go after that person and kill him.

Crops withered and died as women stopped going to their stands or gardens in case they were abducted. At night people were afraid to sleep because the thatch over their head might be set alight. Nobody trusted anyone any more. People whom Aqui's parents had known since childhood had become spies. *It was frightening how easy it was for anyone to become violent or to turn on each other if their own survival was at stake as if it was something ugly inside all of us just waiting to be unlocked.* Boys as young as ten started disappearing into the bush and emerging clutching bazookas.

It was particularly dangerous being a pretty girl to whom a commander might take a fancy and pick up to take to the bush. Teenage girls were the most vulnerable.

Because of this risk, Aqui and her sisters were not supposed to go on their own to the fields or to fetch water. But after days and days of eating nothing but plain sadza, Aqui had a deep yearning for some rapeseed for a relish so she decided to risk going down to their stand to see if there was anything to be picked. As she crossed the first river, she suddenly heard a rustling in the bushes. A group of khaki-clad figures emerged, and before she knew it four Rhodesian soldiers had surrounded her and pushed her into a pit.

'Dance for us!' they demanded, prodding her with their rifles.

Aqui's heart was pounding so hard that she could hardly breathe. One of them pushed her skirt up with the end of his rifle.

'She's a cutie,' he said, leaning so close that she could smell the tobacco on his breath. As she pulled away he spat at her and called her bad words. Aqui could feel the spittle running thickly down her cheek.

'We've seen you monkeys taking pots of food to your gook friends in the bush,' said another, jabbing at her with his rifle so she had to jump.

'Not me.' She shook her head vigorously. She was really scared now, her heart banging wildly against her ribs. Everyone had heard the stories of white soldiers raping girls or sticking burning pokers up their vaginas until their wombs sizzled like burnt porridge.

'Suppose you were taking sadza to Granny,' snorted one. 'And stew too. We see everything that goes on here. We know about your father stealing meat from the farms and we've watched you feeding the terrorists.'

'I don't know what you mean,' she said.

'Don't give me that shit! You know we watch the way they come to your village and make you sing at night and fuck you girls.'

All of them were jabbing at her crotch and circling the pit like predators and she jumped this way and that like a cornered deer to try and avoid being poked.

'Enough playing around. Either the monkey tells us where the gooks are hiding or we let her have it!' ordered a tall man with pocked skin who seemed to be in charge.

Tears were starting to stain Aqui's cheeks when she heard the distinct noise of a twig snap and people coming. Within moments the soldiers had spread out across the path and were demanding the villagers' *situpas* or identity cards. As they scrabbled to produce them, Aqui scrambled out of the pit and began to run, trying not to think about what would have happened had no one passed near. Her legs were coated in red dust.

Eventually my uncle came and said, 'You can't leave your daughter here at such a ripe age or she'll get killed or raped by one side or the other.' Just hearing the word made beads of sweat break out on Aqui's forehead. Soon her mother was deep in discussions with her uncle about where she could go and how they would pay. Her father had disappeared again after turning up reeking of beer a few days earlier.

Aqui's uncle and his second wife lived in Marondera, the town the whites called Marandellas, some 100 miles to the north. He suggested that he take her back there with him and she could look after his house in return for her keep. So, in 1976, at the height of the war, aged just 14, Aqui left the village for the first time, much to the envy of her three younger sisters.

'Be careful, Aquinata, there are lots of bad men in the city,' warned her mother the night before her departure. *My uncle explained that there were certain areas in Marondera blacks should not go or the whites would set their dogs on you. For example, the road of the White Hospital.* He told her there were separate queues for whites and blacks at shops.

The sun was only a palest shadow and the moon not yet departed from the sky when they set off for the long walk to Chivhu where they would board a bus. It was unlikely they would get all the way before curfew so they would have to stop at another village where her uncle had a friend. Aqui's mother held her in an awkward hug, her daughter breathing in her familiar woodsmoke and groundnut oil smell, then pushed her away. 'Take this,' she said, giving her the New Testament, 'for you will need God in the city'. She pressed a few precious pennies into her hand for the bus fare. Apart from the Bible and her few clothes, Aqui had carefully placed her school uniform in the small bag. *I took my school uniform because I still wanted to go to school. It was very silly because of course there was no school in Marondera with uniform like that.* She picked up the bag and walked through the thorn bushes, past the *nganga*'s hut and the *muchakata* tree and out of the village. The few things did not seem much of a life, but her spirit was big.

6

Salisbury, 1976

FOR NIGEL AT THE AGE OF 14, life had suddenly become very exciting. *The war was all we talked about and I desperately envied the older boys who became soldiers and my elder brother Edwin in intelligence in the Special Branch.*

He and a few friends had dug a secret tunnel from behind the seniors' prep room under the fence to come out the other side, and at night they would escape from school and go to bars where soldiers hung out. *Because I had been playing first-team cricket, tennis and squash since second form, I knew a lot of older guys who had finished school and got their call-up papers. Many of them were in the SAS.* He loved to hear their stories about *gooks* or CTs (Communist terrorists) as they called them in the Vietnam-speak they often employed, though they rarely talked about actual contacts with the enemy.

Nigel could not wait until he was 18 and could be out in the bush like them, head shaved, face smeared with camouflage cream, and killing *gooks* or *terrs*. *I was like any other Rhodesian boy at that time. I really wanted to get involved and I would have pulled the trigger on a black as quickly as anyone.*

A favourite hang-out was the bar of The George Hotel in central Salisbury where Nigel and his schoolmates would often be thrown out by the manager for being under age. Whenever that happened they would sit in the garden outside and their army friends would pass them beers out of the window. One day Nigel noticed that across the road was a butcher's shop with some biltong in the window. *We worked out if we slid wire through the door we could get it so we would give the army guys biltong and they would give us Castles.*

Sometimes the soldiers took them to the bar at the SAS barracks near Salisbury airport which would give the boys a real swagger. *All of us were so desperate to get into the war; it was always presented as so glamorous. There was no question we wouldn't join up. I wanted to be in the SAS and even trained to make sure I was ready.*

There was a real recklessness about life. Some nights we would go to bars such as the 12,000 Horsemen and drink till 3 or 4 a.m. with the soldiers. Then we would pile into cars and drive down Jameson Avenue at 120 miles per hour, ignoring all the roadblocks and leaning over from one car to another to pour beers into the mouth of the guy driving.

Sometimes they would play chicken games like Russian roulette, slapping down pistols on the bar as if in a movie. One by one they would load their revolvers with a single bullet, spin the cylinder, put the barrel of the gun against their head and pull the trigger. Usually when it is spun, the bullet drops down a chamber so it is not in the firing position. But one night in the 12,000 Horsemen, a young soldier did not spin enough and when he placed the barrel against his temple and fired, the bullet smashed into his brain, killing him instantly.

That horrific tragedy did not restrain the boys' daredevil behaviour. *Life was just one big adrenalin rush. We were these farm boys in the Big City. Every time we came out of the tunnel to the other side we'd get up to some adventure and often end up being chased down the sewage tunnels of Salisbury by police.*

Everything revolved round the war, even the music to which they listened. While their contemporaries in Britain in the late 1970s were listening to Abba, Showaddywaddy and Slade, the hits among Nigel and his friends were old Second World War songs reworded to be relevant to Rhodesia. 'It's a Long Way to Tipperary' became 'It's a Long Way to Mukumbura'. All good Rhodies, as white Zimbabweans called themselves, owned the *We Are All Rhodesians* album by Clem Tholet, Ian Smith's son-in-law. The most popular song was 'Rhodesians Never Die' which had the following lyrics:

> *We're Rhodesians and we'll fight through thick and thin*
> *We'll keep our land a free land from the enemy coming in*
> *We will keep them north of the Zambezi till this river's running dry*
> *This mighty land will prosper for Rhodesians never die*

Each morning they would leaf through the *Rhodesia Herald* which would contain a number of reports on the war, all giving the impression that the government was winning easily. *The papers always used to say today we killed 300 gooks and they killed three. Only afterwards I found out a lot of these were women and children and it wasn't glamorous at all, it was usually horrible. A lot of the people I knew who fought in that war either came out stronger and became very good people, perhaps finding God, or a disaster and their lives fell apart. They all saw things they wish they hadn't.*

The freedom fighters were referred to with contempt as 'garden boys' or 'floppies' because of the way they fell when shot. The boys at Prince Edward had all heard their fathers and uncles make derisory comments such as 'Half the time the gooks plant the bloody landmines upside down!' *I thought in wars against blacks the white man always won and definitely thought the black man was a coward and whites better at planning and strategizing.*

They all knew that the first Chimurenga back in 1896 had been easily crushed. Whites did not call it the Chimurenga; to them it was just 'the troubles'. Even though so many settlers were killed, a typical casual white description comes in *The History of Sport in Southern Rhodesia* by J. de L. Thompson, published in 1935. He referred to the Shona Rebellion as 'those wretched skirmishes and wars which interfered with the cricket. It was quite enough to have swollen rivers to contend with.'

The Rhodesian army had two battalions – the all-white Rhodesian Light Infantry, known as 'The Incredibles', and the Rhodesian African Rifles which was all black with white officers and divided into Mashona and Matabele units. Nigel's dream was to be in the SAS or part of the RLI's most feared force, the Selous Scouts, a group set up in 1973 by former SAS officers to carry out so-called 'pseudo ops'. These were clandestine operations to infiltrate the enemy and then persuade them to surrender or kill them.

The Selous Scouts were known by the rebels as *skuz'apo*, meaning 'excuse me for being here', a corruption of the English phrase 'excuse me' and the Shona word *apo* for 'here'. This was an expression used by a pickpocket as he bumped into a victim and sneaked off with his wallet, as the Selous Scouts were seen as those who would steal into the night.

To become a Selous Scout required enduring a selection process that was said to be the most rigorous of any army unit in the world. 'In most armies today I simply wouldn't have been allowed to put these poor bastards through the kind of selection course we gave them,' said Captain Ron Reid Daly, the group's founder, in an interview at the time. 'We take them to the very threshold of tolerance mentality and it's here that most of them crack.'

The 18-day-long course took place near Lake Kariba at Camp Wafa Wafa. The name was carefully chosen and derived from the Shona *wafa wasara* which means 'those who die, die, those who stay behind, stay behind'. The selection process was aimed at virtually dehumanizing the recruits. Their rations were slashed to a sixth of those normally given to a soldier and they were deprived of water, forcing them to live off rats, snakes and baboon meat, and to drink from rainwater found in the carcasses of dead animals.

Even the most battle-hardened soldiers would drop out: on one course only 14 out of 126 made the grade. Tests included being dropped in the middle of the bush amid wild animals with a gun, 20 rounds of ammunition, a match and an egg. The object was to have the egg hard-boiled and ready for inspection the next morning.

To Nigel, this sounded like an incredible adventure and he was longing to get his call-up papers. He felt more part of the war when he returned to the farm for the holidays. Rocket attacks on nearby Umtali had led to T-shirts being printed with the words 'Come to Umtali and Get Bombed' emblazoned over a beer bottle. The road to their farm was not paved so could easily be planted with landmines and there had started being ambushes on vehicles around Headlands, so they were supposed to only travel in convoys with other families. This was not always practical so from the age of 14 whenever they drove anywhere Nigel rode shotgun. *I'd sit in the back with an FN and I always used to think it would be really good to see a black guy and shoot him because then you'd become a hero.*

We didn't have an awareness of who was the real enemy – you assumed it was just a black and white thing. I wasn't old enough to understand the ideology of it – for me it was just the blacks against the whites.

For Rhodesia's white establishment, the war was more than just about race. They believed Rhodesia existed to defend civilized Christian standards from the corruption and anarchy of black Africa, and that they were defending a whole way of life. Max Hastings, then a *Daily Telegraph* reporter who went there in the guise of a game fisherman to report on the war in 1976, found it a 'strange kind of war, the last stand of English suburban values in the midst of the African continent'. He described Salisbury as 'Surbiton, Woking, Tunbridge Wells with the political and social

values of Mr Pooter circa 1890', a place where people still sub-
scribed to the *Telegraph* and *Spectator*, went to the Polo Club and
the races, and *South Pacific* was showing at the theatre. The BBC's
John Simpson had a similar impression in 1977, describing it as
'like coming across a little piece of Croydon which had been
towed out to the African bush and left there'.

The front line was not the towns but the farms. Not only were
they producing the food and earning the foreign exchange that
kept the economy going and Smith's government viable, but also
providing much of the manpower for the war. By the mid-1970s
the farmers had all erected high security fences, not to keep
animals in but the gooks out, barricading themselves in houses
where the windows had been covered with steel anti-grenade
mesh. *Christmas was spent with all curtains blackened and windows
taped and we'd all sleep with weapons by our bed, even the young
guys.* There were no more tennis or squash parties or visits to the
club. Nigel's father, like those of his school friends, was on call,
often going off for 'sticks' – operations in the bush – for eight
weeks at a time. A local radio network was set up linking all the
farms and creating a closer sense of community as well as a feeling
of security. When John Hough was home, every so often the radio
would crackle into action and camouflage Land Rovers would
come and pick up him and his men to take them off to the hills.
*I don't think he played a big part in the downfall of any terrorists
but he loved spending time in the bush.*

*The war had a terrible effect on families because dads would go
off on operations in the bush for eight weeks and experience this
incredible adrenalin rush then come back and be expected to get on
with everyday life.*

Not all came back. Occasionally Nigel would wake in the night
at school to hear the sobs of a boy who had lost his father or
brother. For the wives left behind, the isolation in which they
lived could be frightening. Once Nigel and his sisters were on
their way back to the farm from Rusape with his mother driving

when the car broke down, leaving them to walk through the bush with no idea who might be watching or who they might encounter. *Every little rustle of the leaves made us jump a mile.* Another time they saw a big ball of fire outside and thought they were under attack, only later discovering that it was caused by a man who had lit a cigarette while trying to steal some petrol.

By 1977, Mugabe was running ZANU from Mozambique, issuing daily radio messages in which he referred to the whites as 'blood-sucking exploiters'. Thousands of his Chinese-trained Zanla guerrillas had infiltrated Rhodesia from across the border and, under their field commander Josiah Tongogara, were launching wave after wave of attacks on white farmers. Around Headlands, guerrilla attacks were becoming so frequent that the Houghs decided it was time to move off the farm. They moved into a rented house in the compound of a copper mine, not far away at Nyati. Several other farming families had shifted there and the compound had security guards and electric fences.

Nigel's father continued to go to the farm whenever he was back from operations. When he went in the house he would find that the guerrillas had been sleeping there, eating the family's food and drinking their beer. *After the war Solomon our gardener told us they'd been there all the time, just hiding when we came back, but that the workers had said to them, 'Mr Hough is a good guy, don't kill him,' so they had left him alone.*

Their property might have been protected but it was not easy making a good living from the farm when he was no longer there much of the time to supervise the workers. Major markets had been closed off to Rhodesian tobacco because of sanctions against the Smith regime which meant no one wanted to buy from or sell to the country. Petrol rationing had been introduced and there were constant fuel shortages because Smith had closed off the border with Mozambique where many of the fighters were based, cutting off the vital link to a port.

So Nigel's parents were hardly in the mood for sympathy when they received a call from his school to say their son had been arrested. By the age of 15, Nigel already held the school record for the largest number of sets of cuts – 21 sets of six. Yet rather than deterring him, the beatings seemed almost to serve as a challenge and his nights out on the town continued. The news spread of the butcher's shop from which you could steal biltong and other boys from his house at school started doing the same. Eventually the exasperated butcher went to the police and one evening Nigel and a friend hooked out a piece of the dried meat to find police officers behind them.

Nigel spent an uncomfortable night in Salisbury Central prison, where Mugabe had been locked up until 1974, then returned to school to find that his furious headmaster had called in the Child Welfare department for him to be interviewed by a behavioural psychologist. Were it not for Nigel's prowess on the sports fields, he would have been expelled. *My folks were furious. They beat me and it was very embarrassing. I calmed down a lot after that.*

Although his father never discussed politics with him as a boy, Nigel was well aware that they stood in different places over Ian Smith. *Unlike my mother, my father didn't like Smith: he thought he didn't have vision. Dad was very patriotic, he loved Rhodesia and the Rhodesians, but I think because he was also from Britain and came later he didn't have the same prejudices as those who had grown up here.*

A particular incident always stuck in Nigel's mind. *Once my father came home very distraught from a police anti-terrorist stick he had led where they captured an old man they said was an informer. The old man was shaking with fear and one of the guys in my father's group laughed and tore off this old man's moustache, ripping away the skin. Dad came back very disturbed about it. He thought Smith was responsible for engendering this kind of attitude in the whole country, that he was encouraging these kind of guys, and there would be no justice for people like the old man who'd had his moustache torn off.*

Although both Nigel's mother and father had British parents, so were entitled to British passports, they never considered leaving the country and were contemptuous of the whites who left during the war. The government propaganda unit tried to stanch the exodus by turning out jingles that played on Rhodesian radio warning:

> *Just think for a moment of all you gave up*
> *When you made your mind up to leave*
> *The sunshine, the women, the songs round the campfire*
> *The fishing, the life and the beer*

But then war started coming closer to home. By the time Nigel entered the sixth form in 1978, the war had spread to every rural area of Rhodesia. Main roads and railway lines came under frequent attack and it was clear these were no longer just 'garden boys' they were fighting. *My uncle was part of the Air Wing because he had his own plane and I remember him flying over to visit with all these bullet-holes in the sides.* Some of those killed were people the Houghs knew well. Philip Nicholas, the prefect for whom Nigel had fagged when he joined the school, had been killed just six weeks after leaving school. Yet far from deterring his enthusiasm to join up, memorial services at school for ex-pupils killed in action added to what Nigel saw as the glamour by highlighting the danger. Even though to an outsider it seemed an impossible and unjustifiable war, he and his friends were convinced that Ian Smith was right in standing firm for white supremacy and should not give in to pressure from the British and others to negotiate. *There was no question in my mind that we wouldn't win.*

Besides, he knew that being in uniform would make him more attractive to the opposite sex, in particular to a very pretty blonde girl called Margie, sister of a boy in the year above. School dances held jointly with girls' schools such as Queen Elizabeth College or Salisbury Girls High were the three times a year when the boys got to interact with the female sex apart from relatives. *Girls would be lined up on one side of the hall and boys on the other. We boys would have all this pent-up frustration so would go across and ask the girls to dance and if they accepted then try and kiss them as quickly as we could as those dances only lasted a short amount of time.*

Often such advances would be met by slaps, though that was not as humiliating as crossing the floor only to be refused in front of all their classmates. Nigel might have been rebellious but he was very shy and barely looked at Margie as he asked her to dance. *I thought she was the prettiest girl and was amazed when she accepted.* He was careful to do no more than let his hand slip a little to feel the smooth curve of her bottom. On the second dance together he moved it up enough to brush almost as if accidentally across her pert breasts. Her perfumed smell reminded him of honeysuckle after the rain, very different to that he was used to of boys' dormitory reeking of sweat and damp socks. *At that age attraction was all about physical attributes.*

Margie became his first girlfriend. But Nigel's reputation as a wild boy had preceded him, alarming her parents. After five or six dates, she wrote to him saying, 'I think you should know I'm a Christian.' *I was very offended by this so wrote back saying, 'If you're asking, I'm probably the Devil's Disciple.' That was the end of the relationship. She later told me she had prayed for me every day.*

Although Nigel had been sobered by his brief prison experience, it did not take long for him to return to his wild ways, enjoying the feeling of escaping the authorities, almost like riding the edge of a waterfall. But then something happened that made him think again.

Because I was known as being so naughty, other naughty people used to confide in me, maybe trying to impress. One day this guy from the form below came up to me on the way over to school, all cocky, and said, 'Guess what we've done?' He then told me that they'd driven past a bus stop and dropped a bomb which killed three people. It was him and three other guys led by this 17-year-old guy who everyone called Moonie because of his round face, and they were in a little Mini that belonged to Moonie's gran.

The next day in school assembly it was announced about the bomb at the bus stop and we were asked if anyone had seen anything so I knew it was true.

Nigel did not know what to do. I was shocked. I mean I was naughty but not that kind of naughty. I would never do anything like that. In the end I never said anything and they ended up getting off because the person who'd been a witness at the bus stop had got a digit wrong in the number plate and Moonie's gran provided an alibi. The police and school knew what had happened but covered it up because it would have been such bad publicity.

Suddenly his nightly adventures didn't seem so funny. I was haunted by that because they got off.

Because Nigel had not blabbed the group started seeing him as a trusty confidant, and Moonie boasted to him that those were not the only blacks he killed. He told me he had a friend in the army who he would visit on his base then steal ammunition and break it all down to pack inside an old radio. He would then put the radio on a street knowing some black would steal it and when they got home and switched it on it would blow up in their face.

For the first time Nigel began to understand why his father had been so upset at his men ripping off the moustache of the harmless old man in the bush. War seemed to be an excuse for people doing terrible things and getting away with it and the government seemed to be promoting that kind of patriotism without thought.

7

Marondera, 1980

MIDNIGHT ON 17 APRIL 1980 and there was absolute silence in Salisbury's Rufaro stadium. A blue spotlight quivered birdlike in the air for a moment then focused on the flagpole planted on the pitch. The Rhodesian Signal Corps band struck up 'God Save the Queen' and a young Prince Charles took the royal family's last farewell salute on the continent. Then, slowly but surely, the Union Jack slid down the pole and a new flag vibrant in red, green, black and yellow was raised in its place.

The flag was striped green to represent land, gold for minerals, red for the blood spilled, and black for the people, and bore the Communist star and the soapstone bird of Great Zimbabwe. A few of the whites present muttered sourly that the new flag looked like a deckchair. No national anthem was played because the country's new leader Robert Mugabe did not like any of those written. But as the 21-gun salute boomed out across the hot African night, most of the 35,000-strong crowd erupted into cheers and clapping, a sea of ecstatic black faces, many wearing T-shirts emblazoned with the cockerel of ZANU-PF.

Ninety years after the arrival of the Pioneers at the foot of the small hill called Harare, the land that Cecil Rhodes had tricked from King Lobengula was no more. Rhodesia had become Zimbabwe, the last of Britain's fifteen African colonies to achieve independence. Majority rule meant the end of the days when town councils like that of Fort Victoria could ban blacks from walking in the local parks for being 'too noisy and engaged in unhealthy practices'.

To 17-year-old Aqui, listening to the ceremony on the radio in Marondera, it seemed the best day of her life. *I thought I would burst with happiness. Finally we had our own country.* Never again would she have to suffer the indignity of going into the haberdasher's store to look at the coloured ribbons she had seen in the window and have the white assistant shout 'Kaffirs at the back!' *We would be in charge now.* There was a party at the ZANU-PF office and huge vats of sadza with peanut relish and meat and gravy to celebrate. There was Independence ice cream and cartons of Independence *chibuku* or beer. *We were swaggering around, drunk with freedom.*

Independence Day 1980

In the Rufaro stadium, hardened veterans of independence struggles in their own countries found themselves profoundly moved. Neighbouring Presidents Kenneth Kaunda from Zambia and Seretse Khama from Botswana, as well as Indian Prime Minister Indira Gandhi, were among the many political leaders and dignitaries present to welcome the latest member of the club.

At one point it even looked as if some of those in the VIP enclosure were weeping, but in fact overzealous police, trying to calm the excited crowds, had squirted a dose of tear gas in the wrong direction.

The police struggled to keep control as reggae stars Bob Marley and the Wailers took to the stage. Mugabe had been appalled by the choice of the dreadlocked Jamaican and instead suggested Cliff Richard – a choice that would have appealed more to the old Rhodies. It was perhaps the last time the country's new leader would be overruled. Marley's song 'Zimbabwe' had become one of the hymns of the independence struggle and when Michael Manley, the Jamaican Prime Minister, offered to bring him, the demand for his presence had been overwhelming. As the first few chords rang out into the African night, prompting loud cheers, the crowds outside became frenzied, people climbing on the walls and thronging the streets trying to get in. Those fortunate enough to be inside the stadium ululated, hips swaying like boats on a sea, as they belted out the words:

> *Africans a-liberate Zimbabwe*
> *Every man gotta right*
> *to decide their own destiny.*

The seething crowds outside became desperate, pushing the gates until they shook and began to break apart. Those inside surged towards the stage. The police responded by thwacking people with their batons to knock them back, then spraying tear gas, and a power cut brought proceedings to a halt. 'Madness,' muttered Marley, disillusioned by what he was seeing in Africa's newest independent country and in pain from the cancer eating his body. With tear gas stinging their eyes, the group was shepherded off the stage by police until the lights came back on

Prince Charles carries out the last inspection

and things calmed down, a crisp English accent summoning the group back over the public address system.

Yet the main attraction that night was not the reggae star who would be dead just a year and a month later, but a short, neatly dressed figure with wide-framed heavy glasses. Standing just 5 feet 7 inches, and speaking ponderous but impeccable English, 56-year-old Robert Gabriel Mugabe looked more like a parish priest than a guerrilla leader. He toyed nervously with his spectacles as he took the oath of office to be first Prime Minister of independent Zimbabwe.

'*Pamberi Comrade Mugabe!*' 'Long live Comrade Mugabe!' and '*Viva!*' came the shouts over and over again as 100 soldiers in jungle fatigues, black and white, from three rival armies emerged to present arms. Now marching together under the floodlights, these were men who had been killing each other only a few months before.

*   *   *

After years of vicious fighting in which more than 30,000 people had been killed, in the end the birth of Zimbabwe had all happened very quickly.

It was all the more remarkable because less than a year earlier both sides seemed to have been digging in for a long war of attrition. Mugabe claimed to be confident of military victory while the Rhodesian forces pointed out that the guerrillas had failed to put any of the major roads out of use. What changed was the advent of Margaret Thatcher who had come to power as Britain's first female Prime Minister in May 1979 and was eager to shed awkward millstones from the past. Ever since Ian Smith had declared UDI in 1965, successive British governments had been under both domestic and international pressure to take the rogue state in hand. Thatcher told her Foreign Secretary Lord Carrington that she was determined to be rid of the issue, which meant bringing Rhodesia to some recognized form of independence. The then Commonwealth Secretary-General, Shridath 'Sonny' Ramphal from Guyana, was equally tired of the country's illegal status dominating proceedings at every summit. Although he and Lord Carrington did not get on, the two men worked together through the nights at the Commonwealth Heads of Government Meeting in Lusaka of August 1979 to secure an agreement for Britain to convene all-party talks.

The Independence Day rally was the culmination of the negotiations started at Lancaster House in London that September. Mugabe had travelled to England reluctantly after pressure from the heads of the front-line States, particularly Julius Nyerere, Samora Machel and Kenneth Kaunda, the Presidents of Tanzania, Mozambique and Zambia. The ZANU leader had protested that his forces were winning the war and would soon overthrow Rhodesia's white rulers and capitalist society, so he had no need to compromise with them. When talks with Smith were first suggested, he was adamant: 'The only valid kind of negotiations we are willing to allow with this hard-core criminal is with our

Nkomo and Mugabe

firing squad.' But Machel and Kaunda were so fed up with Rhodesian raids and bombings of guerrilla bases and supply lines in their countries that Machel threatened to shut down the liberation war if Mugabe did not negotiate.

Ian Smith was also there unenthusiastically, having been cut off by the apartheid regime in South Africa which was no longer willing to sustain a war on its doorstep. Under international pressure, he had already made a deal with black moderates to install a supposed representative government. In May 1979 Bishop Abel Muzorewa, a black man with a fondness for Gucci shoes, had become Prime Minister of what was bizarrely called Zimbabwe-Rhodesia. It was a name that, just like its new regime, could not last and most people saw the Muzorewa government for exactly what it was – an attempt to put off the inevitable. But Smith could not see why conceding more was necessary and he was livid. In his last speech as Prime Minister on 28 February 1979, he accused Britain of 'treachery' and dragging his country 'down in the morass of British decadence and decline'.

Only Joshua Nkomo seemed anxious for the negotiations to succeed. He was getting on in years and 'longed for majority rule in Zimbabwe and justice for my people. I wanted these things with as little killing as possible between white people and black people.' But the split between him and Mugabe was increasingly

acrimonious. Mugabe believed that power came from the barrel
of the gun and was furious that Nkomo had engaged in secret
negotiations with Smith the previous year to try to reach his own
deal to come to power. During the Lancaster House talks, which
dragged on from September to December 1979, the two resistance
leaders retained separate headquarters and spokesmen. When they
were summoned one after another to see President Nyerere who
was urging increased cooperation between the two, Mugabe is
said to have refused a seat with the words, 'If you're expecting me
to sit where that fat bastard just sat, you'll have to think again.'

It was a surprise then when after 14 weeks of on-off negotiations
Lord Carrington managed to broker a deal. Under the Lancaster
House Agreement, announced a few days before Christmas 1979, a
ceasefire was declared and a British Governor appointed. The
chosen man, Winston Churchill's son-in-law Christopher Soames,
was sent out to Salisbury to oversee elections to take place at the
end of February 1980.

Both Rhodesia's white minority and Thatcher's Conservative
government had hoped that the winner of the first free elections
would be Bishop Muzorewa, who was prepared to share power
with the whites. In the run-up to the elections there were two
assassination attempts on Mugabe and plans were discussed
for ways to 'ensure' an acceptable outcome. That outcome was
referred to as 'ABM' – anyone but Mugabe.

But African electorates are not so pliable. Although Mugabe
had been prevented by the British from campaigning under the
symbol of a Kalashnikov as he had wished and had to settle for a
cockerel, he secured a historic victory. Voting divided on tribal
lines, which gave an enormous advantage to Mugabe from the
Shona tribe which was almost four-fifths of the black population.
In large swathes of the country, militants from his party had
prevented others campaigning, particularly from ZAPU, despite
repeated warnings from the British authorities for him to call off
the intimidation.

Mugabe's ZANU-PF (Patriotic Front), as it was now called, won 57 of the 80 seats (a further 20 were reserved for whites). Bishop Muzorewa had won only three seats. Nkomo captured the 20 seats of Matabeleland and nothing else. 'I am the Father of Zimbabwe. What have they done to me?' he exclaimed in tears to the Governor. 'You give them one man one vote and look what they do with it!'

Lord Soames's own view of the process was starkly revealed in an interview with the BBC: 'You must remember this is Africa. This isn't Little Puddleton-on-the-Marsh and they behave differently here. They think nothing of sticking tent poles up each other's whatnots and doing filthy beastly things to each other.'

The fierce rivalry between Nkomo and Mugabe was the one cloud over the proceedings that joyful April night in the Rufaro stadium. While Mugabe enjoyed centre stage, the man who had founded the independence movement seemed nowhere to be seen. Nkomo and his wife MaFuyana had been placed far from the VIP stand and well out of the sight of the TV cameras, tucked behind the junior ministers and party officials in the dark beyond the radio commentators' box. 'I was hidden away like something to be scared of,' he would later write bitterly in his autobiography. 'My wife could scarcely restrain her tears at this symbolic humiliation.'

The next afternoon, Independence Day, Mugabe addressed a rally in the stadium at Marandellas, heartland of Mashonaland, which had reverted to its African name of Marondera. It was the first time Aqui had seen in the flesh this man she worshipped. Mugabe, like her, was a product of the missionary system, as were the other African independence leaders Kenneth Kaunda and Julius Nyerere.

It felt as if the whole town had come to celebrate. Farmers had given their workers their lorries to take them to the stadium and also cows to slaughter for meat for their parties. Oh, we celebrated. There were these musicians singing, then Mugabe came to the stadium and we could see him for the first time and say, 'Look, he's our hero because he was the only one brave enough to carry on with the war while others were zigzagging or dropped out.' There was a huge roar. We had our own hero just like those in books I had read at school.

Such was the euphoria that it would be years before questions would be asked about the mysterious deaths of first the party's secretary-general Herbert Chitepo* in Lusaka, then in December 1979 of Zanla's commander-in-chief General Josiah Tongogara, said to have died in a car crash in Mozambique. According to a Rhodesian army officer who examined Tongogara's body, it had 30 bullet wounds. 'There's no question about it, Tongogara was murdered,' he said. 'He was more moderate than Mugabe and he was also a threat.'

Although Aqui felt almost as if she would burst with pride at her new country, she had another reason to be happy. Standing next to her in the stadium was her handsome husband and strapped on her back a beautiful baby girl. The two seemed inextricably linked in her mind with the fight for freedom. Were it not for the war she would never have left the village and by now would be married to some widowed farmer, while if she had not got involved with the freedom struggle she would never have met the man whose hand she now held.

Life in Marondera had been a major adjustment for Aqui. *I had never thought of myself as poor until I moved to the city. In the village, though life was tough, we were better off than others, the only girls to have worn shoes. Marondera seemed very big and cold and all the houses small and neat and clean. The village had been kind of like a family where everyone knew everyone.*

---

* In fact Ken Flower, head of the Central Intelligence Organisation under Smith, later admitted in his memoirs that they had been behind the assassination, believing it would widen the rifts among the terrorists.

Her uncle worked as a woodcutter at the sawmill and she kept house for him, his young second wife and their sons. *In those days we didn't have electricity so I would go and collect firewood in the bush and also cook and wash and iron. The iron was heated by hot coals and very heavy but I was young and strong.* The house was a small place and she worked fast and for the first time in her life found herself left alone for large amounts of time. She would have liked to have gone back to school but there was only one school for blacks and it was full. Besides, she had no means of paying. Eventually Aqui's uncle suggested she go to the Red Cross centre where they offered free courses in hygiene, first aid and childcare. There she made a friend, Hazuinei, who lived nearby.

Some of the people she got to know at the Red Cross were activists for ZANU, taking first aid courses to be able to treat wounded fighters in the bush. One of them had the gruesome task of collecting body parts after bombings. Aqui had never before met women actively involved in the struggle, not simply just feeding the fighters, and she was impressed by their courage and what they had to say.

It was the first time since the stories of Nehanda that I had heard that a woman could do something other than just marry and it was like feeling the rain wash away the dust after years of drought.

As her uncle had warned, in Marondera she encountered segregation for the first time. Her aunt and uncle lived in Dombotombo, one of the so-called 'high-density areas' where shacks were packed together like sardines in a tin and designed to be easily cut off from the main town by a roadblock to forestall any potential uprising. The other side of the railway line and the main road were white suburbs where she was not supposed to go and these had large houses behind high walls with gardens and swimming pools. Sometimes she went to the OK Bazaar to shop for her aunt and there were separate queues for whites and blacks.

Aqui talked about the injustice of all this with her new friends from the Party, some of whom were using the Red Cross as a cover for meeting. *I wanted to be part of the struggle – it was my fight too.* They were equally impressed by her coming from a village, telling her, 'Comrade, that's where the real revolution will come.' Aqui did not like to tell them that no one in the village talked much of these things as they were far too busy trying to coax food from rain-parched lands and that most villagers were as scared of the Comrades as of Smith's soldiers.

She joined a group that was leaving to cross the mountains to Mozambique for training to fight. Aqui began going for daily walks to train herself and fervently hoped her asthma would not let her down on the arduous trip through the Nyanga mountains. But her uncle found out and refused to let her go, saying, 'No, no, no!', she was now his responsibility and her mother would never forgive him.

Aqui was desperately disappointed. But one of the women pointed out that she had a skill with words and convincing people and recommended that she be made a mobilizer. She added that Comrade Mugabe had said that political education was just as important a part of the struggle as fighting. *This meant I would go to youth centres, football matches, anywhere there would be young people who I could recruit to fight. Some people here in town didn't know what it was all about. I was just a young girl but I could try to influence my friends and other young people.*

Smith's regime was very racist and there were many things pulling us apart and I really wanted to help so we could get out of it and have our own very nice government. We used to sing war songs to encourage others to join and tell people to be brave.

It was risky work. If anyone reported her she could be beaten by Smith's soldiers and jailed for what she was doing, but Aqui was determined. *I was quite sure we would win. During training, I had been to a base and seen that our fighters had bazookas, sub-machine guns, land mines, pistols and anti-aircraft guns.*

In the evening she would listen behind closed curtains to

Mugabe's broadcasts from Mozambique, then go and spread the word. *On Saturdays at 5 p.m. we would call people to meet and tell them how we must keep up the fight because how good it would be to be liberated and there were promises, promises, promises of this or that is going to happen, like our children are going to go to school free, and in clinics they would be treated free and no one would pay on the buses. We'd say how good it will be to have our own government, we can do what we like or go where we like, drink anywhere you like, no more whites setting their dogs on you.*

Afterwards she often went to Hazuinei's house and the two girls would weave each other's hair into hundreds of tiny braids and *talk of this and that.* It was there one Saturday evening that Aqui first got a glimpse of her friend's older brother, Tendai Chingarire, who had just come home from playing in a football match.

'He is no good, that one,' warned Hazuinei, following her gaze. Aqui quickly averted her eyes. But she had noticed he was good-looking, how strong he looked in his football kit, the sort of man that could stop a woman falling in the wind. *He was handsome, tall and muscular as I imagined a man should be, but he was also soft in his words.* She told herself she was stupid, he was ten years older than her, why would he be interested in a skinny schoolgirl, one that wasn't even at school?

Even so Aqui managed to find out from Hazuinei that her friend and her brothers were born under the totem of the fish-eagle and not impala like her which would have outlawed any relationship. After that she started taking care in what she wore those Saturdays, secretly borrowing her aunt's mirror and lipstick. She ran her hands down her body and wished she was not so thin, so straight up and down like a ruler. She longed to have plump breasts and a pumpkin bottom like Joy at the Red Cross, something for a man to grab hold of.

But Tendai was noticing her light dusky skin, the colour of the bush in the sunset, her quick dark eyes, soft like those of a duiker, her voice warm as honey and her infectious laugh. Over the following Saturdays, he kept turning up at home when she was visiting his sister. Her fervour for the cause amused him and he laughed out loud when she called him Comrade. He had no time for politics, he said, he was busy in his job as a general hand at a school, and thought weekends should be for sport, beer and lovemaking. He would ask about her village and her meetings, before disappearing off to change, grease back his hair, and preen himself for a night at the shebeen. One day as he was doing up his coat a button fell. As Aqui went to pick it up, he closed his hand over hers and told her to keep it. *In our society this is a traditional token of love to show someone you think they are a desirable woman. I could not believe that this 24-year-old man used to look at me and talk to me and say he'd fallen in love with me. I was 14, just a child, and he was my first love. Life was so difficult, what was in our heads was just war and this was something different.*

When Tendai asked if he could take her to a movie, she readily agreed even though she knew people would talk. It was the first time Aqui had ever been to the cinema. She was not so keen on the film, which was a Western and seemed to involve lots of people charging around on horses and fighting. But while they were seated, Tendai took her hand, lifted it and traced his fingers slowly along her palm. His touch sparked little ripples of electricity running down her body and she could feel her juices inside starting to flow, moistening her pants. She was shocked at herself and pulled away. It was the first time she had let a man touch her since being abused by the headmaster and she had thought she had dried up inside for ever.

There was little entertainment for the women in the township but gossip, and someone must have seen the couple and told her aunt. Aqui realized they knew when she came home from the Red Cross one day to see her aunt and uncle both sitting waiting for her with stern expressions. She was well aware that her aunt did not want to lose having someone to do all her work around the house, while her uncle would appreciate having one less mouth to feed, so it was to him she appealed.

He knew of course who Tendai was and her aunt had filled him in on his reputation as a ladies' man. His father had come from Malawi like many people in Dombotombo in search of work, but his mother was Shona. Aqui emphasized that he had a steady job at the school and had decided it was time to settle down.

I went to my friend's house the next day and when Tendai came home from work I told him my uncle would not allow me to go out with him any more. He said that he wanted to marry me and so I agreed.

Traditionally among Shona, a man has to ask a girl's parents for her hand and then agree the bride price. *The must in my culture is you have to pay lobola of eight cattle to the father and one for the mother, so now you see what women are worth here in Zimbabwe. The mother has to breastfeed the baby, go to the fields with the baby on her back, cook for the husband, iron for him, and all the time he's just talking and drinking, and yet when the child's grown up it's him, the father, who gets the cattle.*

The shortage of cows caused by the war meant that Tendai would have to pay money instead of cattle and would not travel to the village himself. *My father sent a message saying you mustn't send your husband here because the war is hot and if he gets killed it won't be nice so he must give the lobola to a trusted old man who can accompany you.*

It was very dangerous going back. From where the lift dropped us, we had to walk and walk though curfew, climbing mountains to avoid the road because if you saw soldiers they could just kill you straight away. We walked from two o'clock right to ten and spent the night at a place we knew then rose early the next morning to pay the lobola. My father said, 'You mustn't stay here or you will be abducted,' so we left right away.

It seemed much more than a year since she had left the village and Aqui felt very grown up. Her sisters marvelled at her town clothes and her first pair of proper heeled shoes that Tendai had bought for her in the market. She was a married woman and a mobilizer and she lived in a brick house with a tin roof, a real bed and a man who worshipped her.

She liked the fact that she and Tendai had found each other while the whole country was waiting for freedom. 'I want to trace each of your bones,' he said, 'to know your body like this land.' He called her *shamwari*, which meant friend. 'Have you cooked, *shamwari*?' he would ask when he came home from work and kicked off his shoes to tell her about his day.

If she were honest, she would say she missed the mud hut which stayed cool even on the hottest days. In Marondera, she and Tendai lived in his father's house along with her friend, his sister, and their elder brother. Two rooms with a dusty yard in a line of shacks, though they were lucky to have a small toilet rather than having to go to the toilet block. Tendai's parents were separated and his mother lived in Salisbury along with two of the children. His brother was an activist for the other faction of ZANU, that of the party's original leader, Ndabaningi Sithole. *That was a dangerous thing to be – we kept warning him but he didn't listen and was killed. A car crash.*

Within a year of marriage she found herself pregnant and in 1979 returned to the village to give birth. *I had to go back to my family to have the baby. Normally the husband must slaughter a cow, goat and rooster and take them to the family and they cook the meat but this was impossible because of the war. So I took them some money.*

She had known the baby was going to be a girl. It was a tiny thing with a scrunched-up face that came kicking and screaming into the world in the hut where she too had been born 16 years earlier. In Shona custom the husband's family usually chooses the name and Aqui's brother-in-law named the baby Heather. Aqui was pleased they had chosen something which sounded pretty. Heather seemed a watchful, contented kind of baby though she knew Tendai would be disappointed it was not a boy.

Aqui had little time to mull over that disappointment back in Marondera for she was busy with her political work. She had been so successful at recruiting people that she had been made secretary of her local cell despite her young age, and she warned meetings that the new Prime Minister, Bishop Muzorewa, was just a puppet and they should not be deceived.

We told followers of other parties that that is the wrong way, the right way is ZANU-PF. There was Muzorewa and someone had put it in his head that he must become Prime Minister of Zimbabwe then the war would end. He wanted to call the country Zimbabwe-Rhodesia which was very strange. I knew this man was wrong, that he was taking money from the whites and just a traitor behind people's backs. So the freedom fighters stayed in the bush and we kept mobilizing people.

With the war continuing, the Muzorewa experiment did not last long. Aqui was shocked, after all Mugabe had said in his radio messages denouncing whites as 'settler vermin', when he agreed to go to London to participate in the Lancaster House negotiations. *We were winning and I thought it would be better as he had said to defeat the white man altogether and bring down the system.*

The news came back on the radio from London that for the first time there would be elections that all blacks could vote in. Finally there would be a Zimbabwe, the 46th European colony in Africa to win independence. On 27 January 1980, Mugabe returned to Salisbury to a hero's welcome after five years in exile. Aqui campaigned hard for ZANU in the elections, showing people how to put their mark against the symbol of the cockerel, and was overjoyed when the results came in on 4 March and the Party had won so convincingly. *Ah, it was so good to be liberated,* she sighed.

Aqui still found it hard to believe that it had really happened. She and Tendai went to the Independence Day rally together with Heather tied on her back in a cloth, but she returned alone. Tendai had gone drinking with his friends, saying they were going to one of the whites' bars as now they could drink anywhere, in fact from now on the whites would have to serve them. She told them to be careful but she had heard the false note in their bravado and was quite sure they would end up in a local shebeen. Back home, she unwrapped the shawl holding her baby daughter on her back and rocked her in her arms. It was an auspicious time for a child to be born and she was determined to do all she could to make sure that Heather had every opportunity. 'How lucky you are, little one,' she told her. 'You, born free, will have a very different life to me.'

I didn't mind so much that my own dream had gone. I knew I would never be a nurse but I was part of a new country.

Mugabe had already promised secondary education for all and a library in every village; cattle-dipping had started again to protect cows from tick fever; and Aqui knew that Western governments were falling over each other with offers of aid and loans to help Africa's newest country. Already in Marondera she had seen foreigners with Land Rovers taking notes and measuring things. It could only be a matter of time before Nehanda's legacy was fulfilled and they got their land back.

8

Salisbury, 1980

NIGEL PROBABLY wouldn't have seen Robert Mugabe's first speech to the nation had it not been on television just before *Morecambe and Wise*, his favourite comedy show. He and some other sixth-formers were gathered in the prep room of their hostel Rhodes House, a tin-roofed building, where they were supposed to be finishing their homework. *'Morecambe and Wise' and 'The Two Ronnies' were the only things we all watched. We found them incredibly funny and would mimic them.*

The programme was delayed for Mugabe's address and some of the boys booed as the white female presenter stiffly introduced 'Prime Minister-elect Comrade Robert G. Mugabe'. They sniggered as a black man in a sober suit appeared, with glasses wider than his face and thick lenses that he peered through like a rabbit. *To us he was this Marxist ogre who had sworn to exterminate all whites.* But most of them had never actually heard him speak before and they fell silent in surprise at his words.

'There is no intention on our part to use our majority to victimize the minority,' he said in a soft voice. 'We will ensure there is a place for everyone in this country ... I urge you, whether you are black or white, to join me in a new pledge to forget our grim past, forgive others and forget, join hands in a new amity and together as Zimbabweans trample upon racism.'

Nigel was taken aback. *I had been feeling really bleak about the*

Mugabe addressing an election rally, 1980

*future. I remember listening to it and thinking, Jeez, maybe we've
missed everything, maybe he really is a good bloke. He was saying
really conciliatory things, the sort of thing Nelson Mandela would
say ten years later.*

He had had a fluttery feeling in his stomach since that morning
when he had listened to the election results on the radio next to
the school hall. *I remember the results being called out while we
were at school and thinking the worst thing that could possibly
happen was for Mugabe to get a majority . . . somehow we had all
convinced ourselves that the British would never let that happen.
Then the Election Registrar was introduced and I remember so
clearly when he started announcing the results and it was 57 to
Mugabe, 20 to Nkomo, 3 to Muzorewa. Smith won all 20 white
seats. And us all being distraught, saying, 'Well that's it, now we
will all have to leave.'*

To these Prince Edward boys, most privileged sons of a privileged race, Mugabe's sweeping victory signified the collapse of

everything their parents had stood for. Some blinked back tears. A number of Nigel's school friends already had their bags packed and were booked with their families on planes. Within hours of the announcement, resignations started pouring in from the civil service, military and police; husbands called wives from their offices and houses were placed on the market. The one-lane road to Beit Bridge, the border with South Africa, was soon heavily congested with station-wagon loads of families squashed between as many suitcases as they could squeeze in.

Black Marxist government was the greatest fear of Rhodesia's white community. They had all heard about Mugabe's radio diatribes against the white man, vowing to 'blow up his citadel' and 'chase him in every corner'. Such were the scare stories about him that just before his election campaign kicked off, the *Herald* had run a front-page story that if elected he would even ban Christmas, like Oliver Cromwell in the seventeenth century. Even if Mugabe did not physically drive them out, it could only be a matter of time, they thought, before he 'Africanized' their jobs and nationalized farms and industries. They were only too aware of what had happened in neighbouring countries.

The white community stayed home as if in mourning as the results came in. The streets of central Salisbury, which for so long had been a white preserve, filled with cheering, dancing blacks thrusting their fists in the air and shouting, '*Pamberi ne ZANU-PF!*' or 'Long live ZANU-PF!' Many white-owned shops had been boarded up but the jubilant crowds swirled through hotels and department stores they had never before dared enter. There was not a white face to be seen downtown. Those who were not fleeing the country barricaded themselves into their houses or farms, expecting revenge attacks.

The reality had finally struck home of being one of a group of around 200,000 whites, even if they had controlled all the resources, outnumbered by almost 7 million blacks. Many headed south to the Republic, as they called apartheid South Africa, a move that was known as 'Taking the Gap'. That year, 1980, more than 17,000 left, almost 10 per cent of the population.

Nigel's family had most of their money tied up in the farm and could not afford to leave. His father had nothing to go back to in Britain, apart from an ageing sister in Scotland, and his mother had no desire to leave the country where she had been born. Like most whites, they were still in shock at how quickly everything had happened.

We had all really thought that we were winning the war. I couldn't understand why we were giving it over when we were winning so thoroughly. All the communiqués that came through on TV indicated we were winning by miles.

Such was the sense of unreality that at the height of the war in October 1975, after an operation called 'the Big Push', the Rhodesian Security Forces told the press that there were only about 30 terrorists left operating in the country. The following year, columns and columns of newspaper space were devoted to the debate among white residents of Salisbury over whether their rubbish should be collected from inside or outside their gates.

In 1979, on Nigel's seventeenth birthday, his call-up papers had finally arrived and he was furious that shortly afterwards a cease-fire was negotiated. *I had desperately wanted to be part of the war and was bitterly disappointed.*

Many Rhodesians believed that they never lost the war but were simply defeated at the conference table by devious British politicians. They referred to Thatcher's Foreign Secretary Lord Carrington as Lord Carry-on-selling-the-white-man-down-the-river.

The end of the war and transition to majority rule was not the only shock for Nigel and his friends. In his last year at school, Prince Edward, bastion of white supremacy, had finally admitted black students, a major cultural adjustment for both sides. *I was shocked when blacks came to our school and they did just as well as we did. It was hang of a funny in my physics class when the results came out. The top seven students were blacks and the bottom seven were whites. That wasn't at all what we had expected.*

One of them, Max, was immediately nicknamed Comrade Max after the first guerrilla to lay down arms. He was good at cross-country running and would vie with Nigel for who would be fastest. *I remember I used to beat him and my main motivation was that there was no way I was going to be beaten by a black boy.*

Nigel had been sobered by his brush with prison experience and narrow escape from expulsion, and in his last two years at school he had finally decided to settle down and work. As a result he had moved into the A-stream and the one-time naughtiest boy in the school had even become a prefect.

I had a black skivvy called Gabriel and his background was so different to ours. I asked him to polish my shoes and get my case ready to take to school. The next day I found him polishing my case. There was obviously a hang of a communication gap. He just didn't know.

Mugabe's first speech on television just before Morecambe and Wise appeared dancing and singing to 'Bring Me Sunshine' had an enormous effect. Apart from preaching forgiveness, he had assured the business community that there would be no sweeping nationalization, the farmers that property rights would be respected, and white civil servants that their jobs and pensions would be secure. Immediately the panic began to subside. Many resignations were withdrawn and hundreds of houses taken back off the market.

The following six weeks leading up to Zimbabwean independence and Mugabe's inauguration were marked by even more extraordinary gestures. Although the ZANU-PF leader had won an absolute majority, he announced that he was forming a government of national unity. Of his 22-member cabinet, not only did he give his rival Joshua Nkomo the Home Affairs portfolio and appoint three more ZAPU ministers, but he even named two white ministers. The new Minister of Agriculture was Dennis Norman, former president of the Commercial Farmers' Union, the mouthpiece of white farmers, while David Smith, who had been in Ian Smith's cabinet, was named Minister of Industry.

General Peter Walls, the Rhodesian army chief, who had assured Smith 'in the final event we will not allow Mugabe to win', was astonished to be retained as commander of his security forces. This meant he was in charge of his nemesis Solomon Mujuru, aka Rex Nhongo, the guerrilla commander who had led the raid on the Altena Farm and who had been made a major-general. Walls resigned within three months after giving a tele-vision interview in which he disclosed that he had asked Mrs Thatcher to annul the election results. He was replaced by Mujuru, whom Mugabe was said to owe a huge debt for quelling an internal revolt in 1978 aimed at toppling him. Mugabe also kept on Ken Flower, head of the Central Intelligence Organisation (CIO), the secret police, even though Flower had previously spent much time trying to assassinate him. He was also responsible for setting up Renamo, the rebels trying to topple Samora Machel in neighbouring Mozambique.

In his memoirs, Flower recounts how he tried to tell Mugabe about the various assassination attempts against him he had organized. 'Yes, but they all failed, otherwise we would not be here together,' laughed Mugabe. 'And do not expect me to applaud your failures.' So impressed was Flower that he wrote, 'Robert Mugabe was emerging as someone with a greater capacity and determination to shape the country's destiny for the benefit of all its people than any of his four predecessors.'

Word quickly spread that Mugabe had even invited Ian Smith, the symbol of racist tyranny, over to his house in Mount Pleasant for tea, telling him, 'You have given me the jewel of Africa.' When he got home, Smith told his wife Janet he hoped it was not 'a hallucination'. In his autobiography, he wrote that Mugabe 'behaved like a balanced, civilised Westerner, the antithesis of the communist gangster I had expected'. The London *Times* ran a leader dismissing fears that Mugabe was an evil Marxist and describing him as 'clever and well-informed'.

Many were baffled that this man who had so much to hate whites for could apparently be so magnanimous in victory. Not only had he been the target of their assassination attempts but he had spent eleven years in prison, where he had been kept in appalling conditions sharing cells with eight others, at times kept naked, with just a bucket as a toilet. In 1966 Smith had even refused him parole to attend the funeral of his only child. The boy, who was called Nhamodzenyika, which means 'My country is suffering', was only three when he died of cerebral malaria. Mugabe had not seen him since he was three months old and his sister Sabina who brought him the news said it was the only time she ever saw him weep. As for his wife Sally, they had been kept apart for so long that after the independence rally she told a friend, 'In 19 years of marriage we have had only six together.'

But by the time Zimbabwe was born, its leaders had the sobering experience of three nearby independent countries to learn from, all similarly Marxist-influenced. The Mozambican economy was on its knees, besieged by attacks from Renamo rebels, and Machel had strongly advised Mugabe not to do the same as he did and throw out the whites with all their expertise. The exodus of 250,000 Portuguese, destroying things as they went, had left him on Independence Day, 25 July 1975, with just two Mozambican engineers, three agronomists, five vets and 36 doctors for a population of 12 million. In Tanzania, Nyerere, inspired by the Soviet Union and China, had introduced forced collectivization to disastrous effect on the food production. He too advised Mugabe: 'You have inherited a jewel. Keep it that way.' As for Zambia, which had become a one-party state, there was such mismanagement that most of the food produced was being grown by a few whites.

The evening of the independence ceremony Mugabe made

another extraordinary speech, one that for years to come would
be seen as a model of reconciliation. 'If yesterday I fought you as
an enemy, today you have become a friend,' he said, adding that
he would 'draw a line through the past' to achieve reconciliation.

Even so, many whites were uneasy with the new set-up, these
people who called each other Comrade and kept their Chimurenga *noms de guerre*. Joyce Mujuru, the young Minister for Youth
and Sport and wife of Rex Nhongo, had for example single-
handedly shot down a Rhodesian helicopter at the age of 19 and
was known as Comrade Spillblood. The new Security Minister
was Comrade Crocodile, Emerson Mnangagwa. On verandas
across the country, there were sniggers at chickens being kept in
State House, the head gardener being instructed to grow mealies
instead of roses, and the appointment of Canaan Banana as Executive President which provoked the inevitable 'we really are a
banana republic now' jokes. Independence Day itself, with reggae
music and home-made beer, was a stark contrast to Ian Smith's
annual celebration of UDI every November at State House when
he would strike the Independence Bell to polite claps from a
ballroom of men in dinner jackets and women in ball gowns.

Yet though Mugabe and his team still preached socialist transformation, they changed little, and what they did was hardly the
stuff of revolution. They renamed some streets in the capital to
honour their friends Samora Machel and Julius Nyerere as well
as fallen comrades such as Josiah Tongogara, the Zanla field commander who had died in the mysterious car crash many believed
Mugabe to have orchestrated. Statues of Cecil Rhodes were taken
down and Cecil Square, in front of Meikles Hotel in the centre of
Salisbury where the Union Jack was first planted, was renamed
Africa Unity Square and became a flower market. Rhodes' and
Founders' Weekend, the country's main holiday, was renamed
Heroes' and Ancestors' Weekend. The Rhodies promptly christ-
ened it 'Gooks and Spooks'. Only in 1982 was Salisbury renamed
Harare. To this day colonial heroes such as Fife, Abercorn and

Selous still have streets named after them, and David Livingstone continues to point his hand imperiously out over Victoria Falls.

It was remarkable how little was changed. At the Prime Minister's residence into which Mugabe had moved, he even kept the place mats that Ian Smith had used, decorated with pictures of English pubs.

The people with the most to fear were the white farmers like Nigel's father. They were a group of fewer than 6,000 yet they held 39 per cent of the land, and perhaps two-thirds of the productive land, while millions of blacks were squeezed onto reserves in areas of little rain and land degradation. It was a pattern that had changed little since the early part of the century, and it was hard to defend. Throughout the war Mugabe had promised that once the whites were defeated every African would be given land.

During the Lancaster House negotiations, land reform had been the thorniest issue. But the final agreement had meant that for the time being the white farmers such as the Houghs were protected from expropriation. The British government had agreed to help finance land redistribution but stipulated that for the first ten years of independence white farms could only be bought on a 'willing seller – willing buyer' basis.

John Hough was among the farmers who went to Salisbury to meet Mugabe shortly after the elections. *They were expecting this Communist gangster and instead he seemed this very reasonable guy and they were impressed.* Relieved that their farms were not about to be taken from them and that they still had a white Agriculture Minister, they were delighted when Mugabe agreed large increases in the producer price of maize. The first two years of his rule saw good rains and record harvests.

If it was galling to see black Chefs, as the new black elite were known, driving around in flash cars, and to watch state TV turned from a propaganda vehicle for Smith to one for Comrade Bob, they could live with that. How little was changed was reflected by the fact that their biggest grumble at the beginning was that

Mugabe had cut all sporting links with their great rugby and cricketing rival South Africa. 'An entire way of life is at stake,' complained the President of the Rugby Union.

In many ways life had got better for whites. They continued to dominate commerce, banking, mining and industry as well as farming. But there was no more military call-up for sons and husbands, no economic sanctions or petrol rationing, no more driving around in convoys because of ambushes, and farming families could finally sleep through the night without fear of attacks. Instead they could go back to spending weekends at the club, boating and fishing on Lake Kariba or shopping in Johannesburg, and beach holidays to Durban.

The country, which for years had been a pariah, suddenly found itself the darling of the West, and foreign aid poured in. The first year of independence saw pledges of almost £900 million and an influx of aid workers. The resulting economic boom produced economic growth of 24 per cent in two years. Everyone seemed to want to participate in the new Zimbabwe, and some white Rhodesians who had left came back – so-called returnees.

It all happened so quickly that Nigel found himself just months away from leaving school without a clue what he would do. *Throughout senior school I had never had to think about it as it was all mapped out that I would join the army.* His dreams of joining the SAS and becoming a hero now in tatters, there seemed nothing to do but follow his friends heading south. His sporting prowess easily secured him a place at Cape Town University and, leaving behind his newly independent country, he set off to South Africa.

9

Dombotombo township, Marondera, 1986

SLAP. The sound echoes across the small shack so that it seems to Aqui she hears it rather than feels it.

'Tell me, where's the money!'

He's twisting her wrist now, his nails digging grooves into her skin, and she's calling out in pain but she will not tell.

Behind her their two young daughters Heather and Valerie are chewing the collars of their T-shirts and crying silently, their scared monkey faces reminding her of herself as a child.

'Where's the money?' Her husband's fist smashes her face and she feels the salt taste of blood in her mouth. Instinctively she tries to protect her swelling belly. It's a boy this time, she knows it is. She has already chosen the name, Wayne John after the star of the films that Tendai likes. As always the Shona name would be chosen by her in-laws who had given her first child Heather the name Pamhidzai which meant 'Do it again'. Maybe things will be better when he is born.

'Where is it, bitch? I know you have it!' This time the resounding smack knocks her to one side and Tendai begins turning the shack upside down. First he empties the tea tin but there is nothing there. The sugar tin has been empty for a long time. Then he kicks out at the pots and pans, scattering them across the floor. All the time he is cursing, the veins on his forehead bulging. The shelves are almost empty when he spots the sack of maize on the floor. Aqui weeps as he tips what little they have left onto the dusty ground. A column of ants instantly marches out from the bottom of the wall to investigate.

Finally his gaze fixes on the basket full of balls of wool she uses to knit pullovers and bobble hats to sell for chilly winter mornings. It is by the chair where his old father used to sit, the only chair they have.

'No!' she cries and his eyes light up. They both move towards it at the same time.

'Aha!' he laughs.

It was too late. He began tossing out the balls of wool one after another. He pulled out the roll of notes triumphantly from their hiding place then stuffed it in his shirt pocket.

'What about the children, Tendai?' she begged. 'How can I feed them or clothe them for school? And the bills? We'll lose the house.'

But her husband was gone, footsteps fading along the road. Aqui sat sobbing on the floor, the tears mixing with the blood streaking down her chin from the cut lip. She knew he was off to the shebeen. His drinking had got worse after their second daughter was born, and eventually, after too many absent mornings, the school had sacked him. *He would just drink and drink and drink and it was a problem, he was a drunkard.*

Although they had no income apart from odd jobs he picked up, Tendai refused to let Aqui work. *We would have terrible arguments about it. He would just kick me or punch me or chop me and shout, 'Do you think I'm not man enough to look after you?'*

Some of the women in the township made money by taking goods back and forth to neighbouring Botswana where there were products available that could not be found in Zimbabwe because of the country's strict import controls or were much cheaper. When they told her that they were selling the goods back home for more than five times what they paid, she started doing the same. *I would take apples, dried vegetables, embroidered pillowcases, lace shawls and stuffing for cushions to sell and I would bring back tinned sardines, cigarette lighters, mayonnaise, cans of foods and car parts.*

It was an arduous journey. She would get the *Travel with the Lord* bus to Harare then catch the evening train at seven to Bulawayo, crammed in one of the third-class carriages. If she was lucky and there were no delays, she would be there the next morning and in Gaborone, Francistown or the mining town of Selebi Phikwe the following day. She would then sell her goods and use the money to buy as much as she could to take back, mostly from the South Africa-run supermarkets. In Selebi Phikwe she had an uncle with whom she could stay but in the other towns she would have to sleep in the station waiting rooms. These would be packed with men returning from the mines and women like her with mounds of shopping, sitting curled up around their goods to protect them from robbers. Most of the smugglers were female as shopping was seen as a woman's job. When she finally returned to Marondera bus station a week or so after she had set off, she would pay one of the boys with barrows to push the goods to her house.

When people knew I was going to Botswana they would say, 'Bring me this, bring me that,' and sometimes they'd give me half down and then when I brought back the thing they wanted they would just finish up.

The first few times I had come back so proud, saying to my husband, 'Look at all this money,' and he would say, 'Great,' and take it. I'd protest 'But this is for electricity and rent and my children want bread,' but he would snatch it and drink it. So I started hiding it, first in the tea tin, which was too easy, then I got the idea of hiding it in the balls of wool as he would just think this is a woman's thing. He would go mad, scratch and scratch and scratch, looking, but then he found that too. Eesh, I cried, how would I buy more things to sell?

*   *   *

Aqui was not sure which had been the biggest disappointment –
marriage or independence. At the beginning she had been so
proud to be a wife, sweeping and polishing the shack, swabbing
the floor, beating down cobwebs. Once the house was clean she
would go to market, baby Heather tied on her back, weaving
her way through stalls of cabbages, rubber shoes, ngangas with
fetishes, to choose some special food to cook for her *shamari*. *He
loved my food. He said he could eat from no one else.* The hours
could not pass quickly enough for Tendai to come home, put up
his feet, take the mug of *chibuku* which she had ready and tell her
stories about his day. She did not mind that he always went out
after dinner. But three babies in succession had all been girls –
Heather, Valerie, Vivian – and Tendai had turned up late and
breathing fumes of *whawha* for his job at the school one too
many times, and everything had changed.

*We have an expression in Shona: 'The sugar is over,' and that's
how I felt.* She had started carrying a pad and pen to note things.
Thoughts she had; things she remembered.

Tendai hated her noting, tried to grab the pad from her. She
was still secretary of the local ZANU cell but life was no better –
the whites still lived in big houses and just a few black Chefs were
getting rich.

Throughout the Liberation War, Mugabe had promised that
when the whites were defeated every black would have their own
land. Aqui and her friends had imagined some kind of utopia
where everyone would get free electricity and water and no one
would have to pass exams but they would all get jobs. Instead,
life had barely changed. The skies over the township were still
yellow with smoke from all the little fires. It was true that these
were free schools and mobile clinics with free inoculations for the
babies. She, like everyone else, had celebrated when four and a half
of the soapstone birds from Great Zimbabwe had been returned in
military planes from South Africa. But prices had gone up and
there did not seem to be more jobs. Tendai certainly could not

find one. Aqui knew many of the ex-freedom fighters could not get work; she had seen them spending the days roaming around. In a strange twist of fate some of them were now working as security guards for the whites against whom they had fought.

Under the Lancaster House Agreement the government could only acquire land at full market value, which was prohibitively expensive, so hardly any families had been resettled. In 1982 Mugabe had promised that 162,000 families would be resettled within three years of independence. But ten years on less than a third had been given land and these were on socialist-inspired cooperatives which often collapsed because of lack of infrastructure and know-how. Many of the resettled peasants drifted back to towns or commercial farms in search of a steady wage. The whites still controlled more than a third of all land and about 80 per cent of the best.

Aqui's people were still living squashed on the reserve. The name had been changed from Tribal Trust Lands to Communal Areas but nobody brought cattle to replace all those poisoned by the whites or looted by fighters. One of Mugabe's first acts as Prime Minister had been to build Heroes' Acre on a hill west of Harare to commemorate the fallen comrades. There was a 40-metre-high tower protecting the eternal flame, and expensive steel-lined coffins and plaques for those buried there. But in the bush around Zhakata's Kraal, skeletons of fighters were found every year with the rains and no one came with coffins to give them a proper burial.

I would have died for Mugabe but once he was in the Big House he had forgotten all about the people that put him there.

For all Mugabe's conciliatory words at the independence rally, it had not taken long for him to start waging war on his enemies. First of course was the Ndebele leader Joshua Nkomo who had been forced to flee. Less than a year after independence, in January

1981, he had been abruptly demoted from Home Minister to Minister without Portfolio, then in February 1982 he had been sacked from the government. Mugabe had accused him of planning insurrection after a series of bombings and the kidnap and murder of some tourists near Victoria Falls. Aqui did not trust the Ndebele. *I knew them as windy people – like a leaf that if a wind came from the east they would go that way and if a wind came from the west they would go the other way. Like Lobengula they just want nice things, the glitter, they don't care about tomorrow. I used to become angry with the stories from the past when the Ndebeles came and killed our men and took our beautiful women, killed the ugly women and children then went back to Matabeleland.*

Mugabe called Nkomo 'the cobra in the house' and said, 'The only way to deal effectively with a snake is to strike and destroy its head.' So in March 1983, at the age of 66, the head of ZAPU had fled for his life from the country he had helped liberate and was now in exile in London. He spent the third anniversary of independence in a cramped rented flat off the Edgware Road. Aqui was shocked about the things Mugabe said Nkomo had done but she still did not think that was the right way to treat an old man.

Many of Nkomo Zipra fighters had been brought into the new national army at independence, but once he had been sacked and they no longer had any representation in government to protect them, they found themselves increasingly victimized. Some fled back into the bush, taking their weapons with them, surviving by holding up buses, robbing stores and raiding farms. Several white farmers had been killed in the attacks. Such banditry, along with intelligence reports that the apartheid regime in Pretoria was training up ex-Zipra combatants in a so-called 'Super ZAPU' to destabilize the new black government, gave Mugabe an excuse to show what would happen to 'dissidents'. He warned in parliament in 1982 that 'some of the measures we shall take are measures which will be extra-legal . . . an eye for an eye and an ear for an ear may not be adequate. We might very well demand two ears for one ear and two eyes for one eye.'

Nobody could have dreamt how literally this was meant. *When we heard about these dissidents haunting people in the area and the President decided to recruit the Fifth Brigade to fight them I thought he was doing the right thing because I was very suspicious about the Ndebele and Nkomo. He was the one recruiting the dissidents and I thought he was a hypocrite.*

But after a while Aqui began to hear rumours about terrible things going on in Matabeleland, worse they said than what happened in the bush during the war. One of her neighbours with relatives there told stories of entire villages being killed. On a train crossing the barren Matabele plains from Bulawayo to Gaborone train, Aqui first heard whispered the word *Gukura-hundi*, a Shona expression for the storm or wind that blows away the chaff before the spring rains.

It was whispered because these days you did not really know who might be listening. Mugabe said there were a lot of enemies trying to destabilize Zimbabwe and had already arrested some South Africans so it was important to have eyes and ears everywhere.

Aqui knew Mugabe was right that dissidents had to be dealt with and shared his anger that people should be trying to disrupt their new independent country. Large arms caches had been discovered on four farms occupied by ex-Zipra fighters. Because of that he had kept the country in a state of emergency, using exactly the same powers that Ian Smith had implemented. One of the first things he had done was set up a trust to buy out the South African publishing company that controlled most newspapers and sack the white editors. Now the *Herald* and other newspapers sold on street corners were all about his speeches and travels overseas, as was the news on television and radio.

Of course we were proud to have a leader who was met by top people all over the world. Not only was he the newest independence

Mugabe at the White House

leader on the block but in those Cold War days he was seen
as bravely standing against the Soviet Union. In fact he had
no real choice in the matter because of his closeness to China
which had trained and armed his fighters, but that was conveniently overlooked. He had been received by US President
Ronald Reagan at the White House, treated to lavish state ban-
quets in Ireland, and awarded honorary degrees by a number of
universities including Edinburgh and Michigan as well as prizes
by the United Nations.

But what Aqui heard on the train chilled her blood. From the
small fragments she could piece together, Mugabe's armies were
terrorizing Matabeleland and decimating villages. Each time they
left behind a few survivors so they would warn others, making
them watch the rest of their village be burnt alive or dance and
sing songs praising ZANU-PF on the graves of the dead. This,
they were told, was in revenge for 100 years earlier when the
Matabele drove off their cattle, burned huts and took their
women.

One woman in a knitted lime-green cap, whom Aqui had met
on several occasions when going to sell things in Botswana, told
her that after her last trip she used the proceeds to buy maize in

Bulawayo but on the way back to her village it was all taken from her at gunpoint by soldiers. When she pleaded that her family had nothing to eat, they laughed and told her, 'Good, then you will you eat your children and then your dissidents.' Her area had had no rains for three years but their shops had been closed down and aid supplies cut off, forcing them to live on rats, lizards and grasshoppers. In the village where the woman's sister had gone to live, they had herded people into huts, then fired bazookas into them to leave pieces of bodies scattered about as warnings.

The stories the Ndebeles told on the border train were so bad you couldn't believe this could be in our Zimbabwe. I learnt they were even killing the children. I didn't like the way the Ndebeles jumped around like grasshoppers, but hurting children is something that makes me too mad.

None of this was being reported in the state media. These were deaths that would never be registered, and the government denied foreign press reports as propaganda spread by 'Jeremiahs'. When Catholic bishops presented a dossier of atrocities, Mugabe – a Catholic himself – denounced them as 'mischief makers in religious garb'.

Aqui didn't know what to believe. The woman on the train trembled and sprayed flecks of saliva as she talked and spoke of *zambies* with yellow faces and slit eyes and Aqui wondered if she was quite right in the head. But in her experience stories came from somewhere. *There were no flies without dung, we said.*

What would later emerge was that Mugabe had accepted an offer from the secretive Communist dictatorship of North Korea to train a special political regiment to guard him and deal with internal dissidents. A hundred and six North Korean military advisers had slipped into the country in August 1981. The resulting Fifth Brigade was commanded by Colonel Perence Shiri, a former Zanla guerrilla commander, and answered directly to Mugabe rather than the army chief.

The Fifth Brigade was unleashed onto Matabeleland in January 1983. Years later in a brave report called *Breaking the Silence*, published in 1997, the Catholic Commission for Justice and Peace would catalogue in chilling detail how thousands of Ndebele men, women and children were rounded up and taken to interrogation centres where they were held for weeks. Based on testimony from more than 1,000 people, it told of pregnant women beaten with clubs, daily deaths from torture, of people being shot in latrines and told 'filth joining filth', and truckloads of bodies being dumped in mineshafts. At one of the detention centres, Stops police camp in Bulawayo, people were kept in cages smeared with the blood and faeces of previous occupants. Nobody knows how many people died in those four years of madness but estimates are more than 10,000, and twenty years on mass graves are still being uncovered.

The whispers from Matabeleland were not the only troubling matters. Once when Aqui went to Harare to get the train to Botswana, she saw Mugabe's motorcade, his long shiny black Bentley with tinted windows, flanked by a dozen armed motorbike outriders. Everyone froze as they heard the sirens and all the cars on the road had to dart out of the way into side streets or they would be shot.*

She had also seen the new ZANU-PF headquarters, a gleaming black office block with a cockerel on top, paid for by the Chinese Communist Party. Set on Rotten Row, it was the tallest building in Harare and the car park seemed to be full of gleaming cars like Mercedes-Benzes. These belonged to the so-called *Wabenzi*, the Chefs who were getting rich buying hotels and businesses, and demanding bribes for people to do anything. Even the owner of the nearby shebeen in Dombotombo had complained that she was having to grease palms to keep open. Everyone had heard

---

* Later he would bring in a law making it illegal for pedestrians to move their upper body in view of the motorcade.

how the *Wabenzi* all had Swiss bank accounts, sent their children to expensive schools in England and America and held lavish wedding parties for them.

Aqui knew that Mugabe and his wife Sally lived a very decent life, and he had issued a leadership code for senior government and party members to adhere to, restricting their income and forbidding them from owning businesses or more than one farm. But everyone seemed to ignore it. While 30,000 ex-combatants from the war were unemployed, General Mujuru, the army chief, had allegedly made a fortune on kickbacks from defence contracts, and had purchased a hotel, a supermarket chain and three farms. She found it hard to understand why Mugabe could not stop his ministers being so greedy.

For the first few years after he took over she had defended him, telling people that change takes time and pointing out the important work done by Sally's charity, the Child Survival Foundation. *Mugabe was always alone, people doing things behind his back. We saw ministers using the money that should have been for building roads and schools for themselves. Sometimes I felt angry with him because I was the one who was suffering, but then I thought, what could he do?*

But by the late 1980s she thought it was time enough. In 1988 the *Chronicle* newspaper had exposed a car scandal which it called Willowgate. Mugabe had banned the import of cars, resulting in a shortage of vehicles. Only ministers or the well-connected could obtain locally made Toyotas from the state-owned Willowvale factory, so they were buying them, then selling them on at several times the price. A commission of inquiry found five ministers guilty as well as a number of MPs and army officers. One minister, Maurice Nyagumbo, who had actually drawn up the leadership code, committed suicide but the others were granted a presidential pardon. 'Who amongst us has not lied?' asked Mugabe. 'Yesterday you were with your girlfriend and you told your wife you were with the President. Should you get nine months for that?' The only person to lose his job was Geoffrey Nyarota, the editor of the *Chronicle*.

I was disappointed. We knew we were a rich country, you could see in the white man's land, and I thought we'd live comfortably, all of us. But instead they were grabbing everything just for themselves and leaving our children with nothing.

The party was controlled by a Politburo and Aqui's cell did not even seem to have any input into who became their candidate for Marondera in the forthcoming elections. The person chosen was someone who never came to the area. There had been complaints about some of the ZANU-PF youths roaming the streets with bricks and bars, threatening people not to vote against the party. But she never thought of resigning. *It would have been hard to leave the party without raising questions. Besides, Mugabe was the father of Independence.*

Tendai laughed when she talked of such things. 'This is what you wanted, you and your Chimurenga,' he would say. Aqui, the peacemaker, was tired of quarrelling. Was this what marriage was about? she wondered. She found herself staring at other couples wondering if their lives were the same as hers. How could this man who had looked into her eyes with what she had thought was love now kick her like a stray dog? She should have seen the slyness in his eyes. She rarely went out except for party meetings and when she did she felt pitying eyes on her. She could not confide in their neighbours, many of whom were Malawis, like Tendai's late father, who had come to the new Zimbabwe for a better life. But the shacks were so close together and the walls so flimsy that she knew every word and punch was heard.

When she complained to Tendai that the neighbours talked of him as being always out late enough to hear the hippo cough, meaning the early hours, he replied, 'What do you expect? A good Shona bull impregnates many women.'

I knew he was seeing other women. My neighbours stopped me from confronting one at the shebeen but once I managed to get the address of one of his girlfriends and went to see her. I told her my children are going hungry because my husband is spending the bread money buying you beer and trinkets. She just laughed. The woman was sturdily built with thick painted lips pouting as if they had been stung by a bee and tottered on heels sharp as daggers. *I thought she looked like a witch.* Tendai beat Aqui harder than ever when he found out what she had done.

Although Tendai no longer played football, he refereed matches, and would often say he was going refereeing, then come back with lipstick smears on his collar and smelling of perfume. Occasionally when he could not find a lady-friend for the night, he would come home drunk and farting and take Aqui from behind, pumping himself into her as if it were punishment. Even when he hurt her, she stayed quiet, face buried in the mattress so as not to wake the girls. In the morning when she awoke she would look at his handsome features sleeping so gently and hope an arm would reach out like it used to and caress her face. Now he no longer played football he was developing a paunch – he was obviously finding food somewhere even if they were not, a bowl of sadza and peanut relish at the shebeen perhaps. Aqui's stomach growled at the thought.

Aqui's family were surviving on her shopping trips to Botswana but these were becoming riskier. According to the authorities, by 1990 more than 500,000 trips a year across the border were being made by women like her, spending some Z$185m in precious hard currency. It would have been easy to stem the trade by lifting strict import controls to make the goods available in Zimbabwean shops. But instead, the government had started clamping down, opening a new customs post at Plumtree, which meant having to cross the border on bush trails and avoid patrols. The police were so poorly paid that anyone caught could usually bribe their way out, but some women were imprisoned and Aqui decided she would have to stop. *If I was caught, then who would feed my children?*

Not Tendai. As she lay next to him, she wanted to reach out to smooth a curl of his greased-back hair that had strayed onto his forehead. But if he woke, he would shift away angrily and grind his teeth as if she disgusted him.

Her own face was pinched and drawn and her eyes puffy from tears that never seemed to dry. Every day when the girls came home from school she would be crying. *They would say, 'Mama why are you crying?' but I could not stop. In those days, every day I used to cry and cry and cry. It was God who was looking after me or I would have gone mad. The girls were thin and I grew thinner and thinner as if I were fading away.*

10

Victoria Falls, 1990

THE AFRICANS CALLED IT Mosi-oa-Tunya, the smoke that thunders. In his small propeller plane, flying low over the mighty Zambezi, Nigel could see the towering column of spray rising up above the trees from far off, then hear the roar. Then he was lost in a vast cloud of watery smoke, spots of water pinging on his windscreen. Unable to see a thing, for a moment he panicked but managed to hold steady to his course and he was through, seeing dancing rainbows diffracting through the water and glass.

He circled the aircraft around to look over the horseshoe of falls disgorging water with such power that the spray was drenching tourists on the path along the rim. Victoria Falls was an exhilarating sight, even more impressive from the air than land where, seeing it in 1865, the explorer David Livingstone had written of being 'filled with reverential awe' at 'the ceaseless roar of the cataract, with the perpetual flow as if pouring forth from the hand of the Almighty'.

Nigel looked down over the narrow 100-metre-deep Batoka Gorge and the latticed iron bridge which spanned it. It was in a railway carriage on this bridge that in August 1975 one of the most bizarre attempts to end the Rhodesian war had taken place arranged by John Vorster, Prime Minister of South Africa, and Zambian President Kenneth Kaunda. Both men were fed up with the intransigence of the sides they were respectively backing and had begun working together to try and achieve détente to end the war. A sceptical Smith agreed to release the black nationalist leaders from jail for the meeting, under pressure from the South Africans who controlled his lifeline. Kaunda wanted the meeting to take place in Lusaka but Smith insisted it should take place on Rhodesian soil. The compromise was to station a South African Railways carriage on the Victoria Falls Bridge, half on the Zambian side and half on the Rhodesian side.

A white line had been drawn across the centre of the bridge to ensure that the conference car was exactly in the middle. Inside was a long stinkwood table. On one side sat Smith and his delegates and on the other, Nkomo, Sithole and Bishop Muzorewa and their aides, representing three different factions. Only Mugabe was missing, having refused to attend, and he was represented by his friend James Chikerema. At either end were buffet cars, well stocked with everything from Drambuie to whisky.

It was a crush inside the carriage and after Vorster and Kaunda opened proceedings and wished the delegates well, the pair departed to another coach to conduct their own discussions. No Rhodesian really expected a settlement, and the talks broke down by the second day after Sithole and his colleagues demanded one man, one vote, which would mean black rule, and also amnesty for all their fighters, while Smith refused to abandon white supremacy. The Rhodesian Prime Minister left for the nearby Elephant Hills Hotel where he met with his South African counterpart and told him what had happened. When they returned to the train after lunch, they found it deserted, and were told by a steward that the guerrillas had 'drained their saloon dry'.

Nigel circled over Devil's Cataract, the most powerful of the falls, and looked down at the bridge again. 'Angels in flight', Livingstone had written. *It was irresistible.* It was also illegal. A fellow pilot

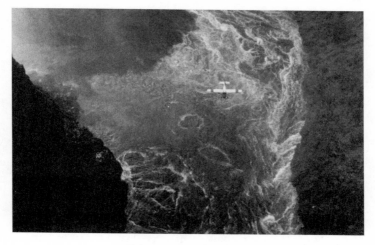

Flying over the Victoria Falls

had asked one of the soldiers if it was permitted for planes to fly over the bridge. 'Yes,' came the reply.

'And under?'

'No, then we shoot,' the soldier had replied. Nigel was undeterred and had arranged for a friend to go on the bridge to divert attention.

He eased the throttle, took a breath and let the plane dive deeply through the spray. The sound was roaring towards him and the gorge was narrower than he realized, churning black waters and rocks below so near. *The turns were very sharp and my stomach was churning around as if I was on a roller-coaster. The sides of the gorge were steep and menacing and this mass of grumbling white water was only a metre or two beneath and flying past us at great speed.*

The wings of the small Cessna seemed terribly fragile and he fought to keep them stable amid the wind currents that came through the gorge from the falls. At the same time he tried to keep an eye out for cables that hang down from the bridge as well as any soldiers. Then he was under the bridge and out the other side, spraying crystals of water like bridal confetti and coming back up through a rainbow.

As I pulled out of the gorge there was a tremendous sense of relief, then almost immediately a need to do it again. Flying was the greatest thing in the world.

Nigel looked fondly at his plane. *I had always wanted to fly. I had grown up with my father's stories of being a Spitfire pilot and my uncle Noel Waller had a Beechcraft Bonanza and during the [Rhodesian] war flew Air Wing. We used to go up with him sometimes and I loved it, it was hang of a treat.*

He was 25 when he bought his first plane, shortly after returning from university in South Africa. He had used all the money he had to buy a four-seater Piper Cherokee PA140 with blue stripes on its wings and its registration painted boldly on the side in black – Zydu Yankee Delta Victor. *It was underpowered and very slow – about 90 knots – but I saw that as an asset because it gave me more time in the air.*

There was, he thought, no better life than as a bush pilot in Africa. *To me the smell inside an aircraft cockpit ignites the senses, a bit like the first swirl of whisky in the mouth. I guess it's the smell of the fuel but I love it. As the props start spinning and the engine takes, a feeling of such freedom follows.*

He loved the thrill of landing on runways hacked out of the bush, makeshift windsocks rigged up on top of a pole, clearing wildebeest and zebra out of the way. *It was great for impressing girls too, taking them up for a whirl with a couple of cold beers to watch the sun setting over the Mazowe hills.*

He also enjoyed the element of danger, often flying to Mozambique where the civil war was still raging on and skimming over the white beaches and the surf of the Indian Ocean. It was there he had his first crash. He was approaching Beira only to find that Russian MiG fighter-jets were doing manoeuvres and would not let him land. As he circled around, he noticed with horror the

Intrigued Mozambicans come to see the crashed plane

warning light on the fuel gauge. Before he knew what was happening, the plane started losing altitude, palm trees racing towards him, and then he was hitting the ground in a cloud of dust. He sat stunned for a moment, then heard excited voices and, testing his limbs to find nothing was broken, managed to climb out. The plane was less fortunate, lying crumpled on the ground with a large crowd of Mozambicans gathered around. Nigel had to pay a large bribe to be allowed to collect the wreckage.

The crash did not put him off flying. His next plane was a Cessna 182, a light four-seater with a propeller and pretty wings that glinted silver in the sun. Its high-wing design was made for bad airstrips and African conditions and it could land almost anywhere.

Nigel loved to set off over the land where for so long white men had fought and scrabbled to secure a foothold. But his Africa was not the dark one of Dr Livingstone. His was the Africa of the steady sun and the long horizon that seemed to stretch to the very edges of the earth. He flew over grasslands, salt lakes, swamps such as the Okavango Delta and Bangweulu Wetlands, the great rivers Limpopo, Zambezi and Congo, and the Kalahari Desert where down below he could follow the small black shadow of his plane on the rolling dunes. *I felt privileged to call this home.*

He took off the doors and sometimes he would notice a splinter of water and head that way to catch sight of a line of elephants going to drink, trunks swaying, trumpeting to the heavens. The only sound then was the drone of the plane. In the distance he might see a spiral of smoke and a few mud huts would come into view, grass-roofed and beehive-shaped just as Livingstone had seen, places not found on maps. Women coming back from the well with jars of water on their heads would look up in alarm. It was not unknown for white pilots to fly low deliberately to scare them, awarding themselves points for making them drop the water. One of Nigel's friends had once flown so low over the Save Valley in southern Zimbabwe that he had knocked the water vessel off a woman's head, sending her sprawling. He had later discovered that she had fractured her skull.

Nigel flew so much that he obtained his commercial pilot's licence and wondered if he could make a living flying. Roads in Africa, where they existed, were often untarred or pockmarked with crater-sized potholes, so the easiest and fastest way to get around was by plane. Many Rhodies had their own plane but it seemed that there was plenty of work for a freelance. Nigel loved the freedom of being responsible only for himself, not like his father dependent on indifferent workers.

His first flying job was for a project to dehorn rhinos in Zimbabwe's national parks. This was a controversial attempt to deter poaching of the endangered creatures by sedating them and cutting off their horns with a chainsaw. He would have to fly low over the bush trying to spot rhinos so that they could be darted. *It was a way of taking exciting flights without having to pay.* But cutting off the horns of these magnificent beasts did not seem right, even if it was to save their lives, and Nigel grew to hate the whine of the saw and insist on blindfolding them before it was done.

Through his old school friend Larry Norton who was making his name as a wildlife artist, he managed to get a contract flying for a *National Geographic* team. They were making a film called *Flight Over Africa* about the life of a bush pilot, following the adventures of a young American called Tom Claytor.

'The film would not have been such a success without Nigel,' said Tom. 'His is the character forged by that land and though we did things he had never done before, he was able to grit his teeth and just do them.'

On that trip Nigel made his first landing on a beach, managing to hold the nose of the plane up so that the nose-wheel did not sink in the sand, as they filmed the Otavi shipwreck in the forbidden diamond area of the Namibian desert. It was an eerie place of abandoned boom towns where miners once paid for whisky and girls with diamonds. Today, the old saloons stand forgotten and half-buried in drifts of sand.

They flew on to Zambia, over the strange sight of Shiwa Ngandu, a towered red-brick mansion built by an English aristocrat in the middle of nowhere. For Nigel, the highlight was flying over the Kafue Plains, vast wetlands inaccessible by road. As they flew low over the watery plains, the game spread out before them as if they were scattering dark seeds. It was a herd of red lechwe, a shy aquatic antelope only found in Kafue. *There must have been more than 2,000 of them and as we came down there was this spray as they all ran off jumping and leaping in the shallow water. In the distance was an African thunderstorm, flashes of lightning illuminating the red sky. It was magical, the most breathtaking thing I had ever seen. I couldn't think of a better way or place to live.*

For all his fears at Independence, Nigel felt that majority rule had made very little difference to his life. While at university in South

Flying over desert sands

Africa in the early 1980s, he had never had any doubt that he would go back home afterwards. *I was very patriotic – I played squash for my country. I used to boast to the South Africans that as you crossed the border into Zimbabwe this weight would come off your shoulders.* But his political views remained those with which he had grown up, based on a belief in white supremacy. At Cape Town University, he and his fellow Rhodesian Pete Moore had been the only members of the student wing of the new ultra-right Conservative Party. Led by Dr Treurnicht, who was popularly known as Dr No, the party had been formed by a right-wing faction of ruling National Party members worried by Prime Minister P.W. Botha's policy of power-sharing which they saw as threatening the apartheid system.

Cape Town University was seen as a sort of spiritual home by many Rhodesians. It was built on land donated by Rhodes and a vast granite memorial stood on the mountainside with a bronze figure of Rhodes looking north over the empire he had dreamed of extending from the Cape to Cairo. Ironically, it was there that Nigel had his first really close contact with blacks, and his view of them began to change. In his first year, 1982, his hall of residence, Smuts Hall, named after General Jan Smuts, became the first hostel at South Africa's oldest university to allow black students. *Smuts Hall was modelled on Oxford, all oak and cut glass, and it was really smart, where the elite guys stayed. You were really proud if you ended up in Smits. So I couldn't believe it that we had to share it with blacks. I ended up in the only flat in the only residence in this white university with black boys. Of the eight of us in the flat, four were black South Africans. They were quite friendly but I would have nothing to do with them because it was just after the war and feelings were high. I was cross too because we used to have inter-house sport and we couldn't compete because these black guys were useless at cricket, rugby and all that. It was very frustrating.*

For the first six months of university, Nigel completely ignored his black flatmates. But then the inter-house soccer tournament began. *Suddenly we were very good because of the blacks and won the whole thing. It was my first time in my life of interacting with black guys on a more or less equal basis and I thought actually these guys aren't too bad and started hearing things from their side.*

They weren't poor blacks from villages, they were from private schools, sons of Homeland Ministers, that kind of thing. Even so my mind was being opened and I was learning that there is another side to everything. At that time I even started listening to what Mugabe was saying and thinking, Well, maybe he is all right. I began to question the attitudes I'd grown up with.

He also began to listen to African radio stations and music. *I really liked this DJ back home called JC Makumba who used to say, 'This is JC James Makumba, your favourite co-pilot.'*

Nigel had done so little work on his business degree that in his final year Pete Moore had to show him where the library was. Even so Nigel was then awarded a place to do his Masters at prestigious Stellenbosch University on a squash scholarship. *I didn't do the MBA; I just played a lot of squash.*

By the time he graduated in 1986, the news from Zimbabwe was not so good. The honeymoon was over, foreign investment was flooding out, and half the whites had left. Most of his friends studying overseas did not return. Nigel's parents had sold the farm and he had returned to find that Mugabe was increasingly blaming the small white community for his problems.

The country had been hit by a shortage of mealie meal and the government accused the milling companies, which were all white-owned, of hoarding to drive up prices. A commission of inquiry was set up which exonerated the millers and instead blamed individuals for taking advantage of Zimbabwe's low fixed price to smuggle the maize across the borders where they could sell it for much more.

'I will never believe the story,' thundered Mugabe. 'That is a lie. I know these millers. Their intention is to suck the wealth of the country and destroy the government ... those whites we defeated are still in control. They own the mines, the factories, the commerce. They are the bosses in our country.'

When he heard the President talk like that, Nigel also began to think about going abroad. He had never been to England where his father was from or to Scotland where his aunt lived, and was keen on extending his sporting horizons. *To be honest, Zimbabwe was a very small pond for squash. I had already beaten everyone.*

His brother-in-law Dave Houghton was a Zimbabwe cricketer and suggested to Nigel that he take up cricket again as he had played for the country's youth team. Nigel thought he had left it too late but then one day in 1989 Houghton asked him for a lift to the airport on his way to play a first-class game between Mashonaland and Matabeleland. *When we got there one of the players had had to drop out because his wife had gone into labour so they asked me to play. In that game I made 180 runs so they then picked me for the B team. We played against Michael Atherton's team and I scored 80 so then they put me in the A team. But I was 29 by then.*

He would fly his plane down to cricket matches around the country. *The cricketers all gave me the name 'ndege' which means plane in Shona. I opened the batting and would often go for a spin in the plane if I was bowled out early, sometimes taking members of the touring team. I remember taking up England players Stephen Rhodes and Paul Parker.*

In between flying and cricket, Nigel found he had little time for the business he had set up – Zimbabwe's first one-hour photo processing shop. But it was a success, developing into a chain, Foto Inn, and he made enough money to buy his first farm and also set up a computer company for data processing. He landed a US$5m contract to carry out the computerization of the Harare Turf Club in a deal that he thought would make him US$2–3 million. *I told my brother, I'll never have to worry about money again.*

Nigel's first farm

But disaster struck. Within ten years of independence, the government had found itself deeply in debt. This was partly inherited from the UDI regime, but also to pay for social reforms to correct the inequities of the past such as funding an enormous expansion in the number of schools, a nationwide vaccination programme, and military spending to support the Mozambique government against Renamo rebels. Many of Zimbabwe's loans in the 1980s had come from commercial banks and as fuel prices rose on the world market by 120 per cent because of the Gulf War, interest rates rocketed. To service burgeoning debts was taking up more than 35 per cent of export earnings, and finally Mugabe, the Marxist, was forced to go to the International Monetary Fund for a loan.

Both the IMF and World Bank stepped in, lending US$700m, but in return they demanded a structural adjustment programme. The government that had professed socialism since independence found itself having to embrace the free market and abolish price controls and exchange controls and reduce import tariffs. In January 1991 an austerity plan was launched to curb the country's

20 per cent inflation. This included cutting the civil service by a quarter with the loss of 32,000 jobs, reducing spending on health and education, and tighter monetary policy. As a result short-term interest rates rose from 27.5 per cent to 44 per cent in a single day, the stock market fell sharply and so did the value of the Zim dollar.

The money Nigel had borrowed (Z$14m) to buy all the equipment had not only become more costly to pay back but was no longer anywhere near enough to finance his imports. *Over the following six weeks the Zim dollar crashed, falling from 5 to the American dollar to 20, while the interest I was due to be paying shot up from 11 per cent to more than 80 per cent. I went from thinking I was going to be rich to losing everything. I lost my farm and my plane. All I ended up left with were 14 ostriches and an overdraft of US$5,000.*

11

Marondera, 1993

Aqui wandered around the double-storey house in
panic, with no idea where to start. *I had never seen such a*
big house, so many bedrooms I couldn't count, five bathrooms, and
I was terrified, wondering how on earth I would clean it all.

It was her first day as a maid at the Loos' farmhouse just
outside Marondera, and her job was to clean the house, wash and
iron the clothes and look after the child. Mrs Loos had one baby
and was pregnant with the second. Aqui did not have to cook;
there was old Julius, the full-time cook boy, to do that, and a
garden boy to tend the garden.

The house seemed a place of many wonders. There were flush
toilets and water that came out hot from the tap without being
heated over a fire. There was a room for eating in and several
rooms just for sitting in and ceilings higher than a person could
reach. The main room had doors opening out onto the veranda
and overlooking a swimming pool that held reflections of trees
and patches of blue sky. On the coffee table in the living room was
a crystal bowl of apples, so perfectly round and shiny that at first
she thought they must be wax, so different were they from the
bruised and battered souls sold in the market in Dombotombo.
Display cases held rows of crystal glasses and china figurines.
There was a grand piano where Mrs Loos would play and sing. A
large wooden cabinet contained a television while another long,

flat and shiny one opened to reveal a Philips radiogram full of
knobs and dials. A fan was blowing cool air. A marble lady
reclined on a plinth and Aqui sprang back in alarm as she realized
she was naked. In one corner was a bar stocked with bottles and
siphons.

Just off the living room was an entire room just of books. *I
could not see how a man could read so many in a lifetime.*

Upstairs, next to the main bedroom, the Madam had a special
room just for her clothes. There were row after row of dresses,
skirts and coats, all hanging on their own separate hangers, some
of them with special dust covers. Aqui thought wryly about her
own few clothes kept in a trunk. She brushed her hand against
the fine materials, then closed the door again quickly. There was
a mirror taller than her and she knew that one day when she felt
braver she might not be able to resist the temptation of holding
one of the dresses up against her. One cupboard was full of shoes
in all the colours of the rainbow and there were shelves just of
hats and another of handbags. *I wondered how the Madam ever
chose what to wear.*

Mrs Loos had shown her around and explained her duties, as
well as warning her not to move the papers on her husband's
desk, then had driven off for a coffee morning at a neighbouring
farm. Aqui put on the crisp red and white checked overall and
plastic sandals that she had been given, collected a mop and
bucket and some cleaning products and went upstairs. The carpet
was plush and thick and the temptation was too much. She took
off her sandals and enjoyed the luxurious feel of the carpet under
her feet. *I had never walked on anything so soft.* She was terrified
she might make it dirty and quickly replaced her shoes in case
someone came.

The baby was asleep in his crib. A procession of coloured
elephants was stencilled around the walls of his room and there
were shelves lined with teddy bears, cuddly animals, and a painted
metal box that played music when you turned the key. Mrs Loos

Aqui as a maid

had opened a drawer to show her row after row of perfect match-
ing vests and baby-grows in pastel whites and blues. Aqui's eyes
had widened, thinking of her own children's few yellowing
T-shirts, not new to start with, then passed from one to the next.

She tiptoed back in the room to check on him, gently lifting
the embroidered cotton sheet. His skin was milky and his arms
and legs were pink and chubby, not at all like the band of scrawny
brown chickens she had given birth to, and he had a dusting of
golden down on his head. *He looked like the angels I had read about
in the Bible.* She stooped to listen to his soft regular breathing and
sweet waves of baby oil and talcum powder wafted over her. Her
own youngest Vanessa was still only eighteen months and she
missed her.

It was so hushed in the house that the sound of all her movements seemed exaggerated to Aqui as if she were an elephant
crashing around. Back in her shack in Dombotombo there was
always noise, a baby crying or the children bickering, sometimes
Tendai shouting and raving. She lived inside tight as a ball, fearing
any moment he might come through the door with beer on his
breath and meanness in his fists. Through the thin walls it was
impossible to shut out the gurgling cough of the neighbour's son,
the radios playing *jit* dance music, and other people's babies and
arguments going on along the street.

In the house of the Loos Aqui felt as if an enormous weight had
been shed from her shoulders. Her mouth was already watering
at the thought of the food she could buy for her children once
she got her first week's salary, a packet of bread perhaps, and
vegetables to mix with the watery porridge they had been living
on.

Still, thinking of all these things was not getting any work done.
She had better stop dreaming and get on with cleaning all the
rooms or she would lose the job she needed so much. Julius
the cook was an old man, older than her father, and she had seen
the sly way he looked at her as if to say he had seen her type

before and she would not be around long. But if nothing else Aqui had been blessed with a golden tongue and she was sure she could win him over. She knew how lucky she was, with unemployment now over a million. *I was scared but also determined – I had been offered a way out.*

Salvation had come to Aqui through the Red Cross. *One day someone came from the Red Cross and said Mrs Musande, this woman who was senior there, says there is a murungu who wants someone to work for her so go and call, Aquinata, because they all knew my situation that I didn't have money to feed my children and my husband was no good and didn't let me work. My husband was out refereeing somewhere so I could go to the Red Cross centre without him knowing and Mrs Musande said there is this white woman who wants to employ someone and she's going to interview many people and you're going to be interviewed and maybe you get lucky.*

So I just said OK but in my heart and mouth I thought I'm not going to be allowed to work. So we got interviewed, there were eight of us, and this lady Mrs Loos asked me, 'How many children do you have?' I said five, four girls and a boy, and she said, 'Oh no, I don't think I'll like one with five kids because the one I am sending away has got pregnant and I don't want people with children but I'll see, give me your number.' I didn't have a telephone but I gave the number of my brother. I was thin and pale, my eyes were puffed up from beatings, and I had five children and I thought, Bother, I'm not going to get this job.

One morning a couple of weeks later, someone came banging on Aqui's door from her brother's house saying she must be there before two o'clock because there was going to be a very important phone call. Quickly, she took off the overall she wore every day and pulled on her best dress, one of her aunt's that she had cut and stitched to fit her much skinnier frame.

Exactly at 2 p.m. that woman Mrs Loos phoned and said, 'Of all the people I interviewed I want you to come and work for me.' I didn't believe it. I said, 'But I still have five children,' and she said, 'The thing is you won't bring them here, you will just leave them.'

Mrs Loos explained that she would come and pick Aqui up the next day and take her to the house every day for the first week, then they would see how the arrangement was working out. If the Looses decided to keep her on, then after that Aqui would have to make her own way there and back.

I was so excited but scared at what I had done. I went home and told my husband and aah, he was too angry, he shouted, 'Work, work. Who said you could go and get interviewed?'

Tendai raised his hand. The slap was so hard that Aqui's head hit the wall and tears sprung to her eyes. She started to slide down like treacle then placed her palm over her cheek and managed to stand firm. *This time I wasn't going to give it up.*

She thought of the salary of 120 Zim dollars a month that Mrs Loos had promised. It seemed a fortune. 'I need food for my children,' she pleaded. 'I go and sell things and you steal my money, you know I'm fed up, I can't carry on with this, I must work.'

She braced herself for another punch. But instead, to her surprise, he lowered his fist. 'OK, you work,' he said. 'But when I get a job, you're going to stop.'

Aqui could not believe that he had agreed. 'Thank you, Lord,' she said to herself.

So when Mrs Loos came to get me I worked so hard, I would not stop, I worked and worked and worked. Later I found that her husband had not wanted to hire me because I was so thin he thought I must have the Sickness.* But Mrs Loos saw something in me, that I was always cheerful.

* 'The Sickness' is a euphemism for AIDS. Zimbabwe has one of the world's highest levels of infection, with more than 25 per cent of the population HIV positive according to the UN.

The only problem was what to do with her own children while she was out working. But Aqui's friends rallied round. *Everyone wanted me to work, so they'd take the children to their houses until my eldest, Heather, came home from school, then she looked after them.*

Eventually Aqui moved to the farm during the week as waiting for buses was taking up too much time and she was spending her wages on fares and the Looses wanted her there in the evenings to look after the baby while they were entertaining. *They loved the fancy life, the smart life, and used to have so many parties where people would sing and dance and braais. But oh, I was too sad to leave my kids behind.*

She would take the children food and blankets at weekends but would later discover that her husband had eaten the food and sold the blankets for beer money. A couple of times she had seen bruises on the face and arms of her eldest daughter and was not at all convinced by Heather's explanation that she had sustained them in knocks during sports at school.

Fortunately Claudia Loos was not a typical madam. Short, dark and beautiful, she was of Italian extraction and loved singing opera. Every afternoon, when she was not giving music lessons at the nearby Peterhouse School, she would take the baby for a walk in his pram along the shady path under the gum trees and when she got back she would ask Aqui about her own children. Sometimes, she would take her with her round the garden to help pick flowers for the house, muttering over her beloved roses which fought a running battle with hungry ants, and would ask Aqui questions about her life.

I had lots of problems. My life was terrible. Mrs Loos was a counsellor as well as a music teacher and she started counselling me over my problems and helped me so much.

Some afternoons she would take Aqui with her to town, stop at OK Bazaar to buy chocolate bars, then drive her to Dombotombo to visit Aqui's children. *I could not believe that a white person could be so kind. The cook boy took advantage of her kindness, always asking, asking for things, more money, clothes, but I did not. We would chat, chat, chat with the children, then she'd say 'Let's go,' and they started crying, the youngest would cry and cry.*

One Thursday afternoon as Aqui was taking a tray of tea and biscuits out to the veranda, Mrs Loos said to her husband, 'Oh Grant, every time we go to see Aquinata's children when we leave they cry very much.'

'So?' he grunted.

'I feel so sad.'

Mr Loos looked up from his newspaper.

'What are you trying to say, Claudia?' he asked.

'I don't know.'

'Why don't the children come and live with us?' he suggested. 'Otherwise next time she will stay with the children and won't come back.'

The couple disappeared inside the house and up into their bedroom to work out a plan, leaving Aqui almost rigid with astonishment. She had never really felt before that her presence mattered to anyone. They came back and told her that when she finished work the following day, Mrs Loos would take her home, then return to pick her and the children up at 4 p.m. on Sunday when they should all be ready to move into the servants' quarters where she was staying. *It was such a happy day for me, I clapped my hands.*

It was a good place, two rooms just for us and I had a bathroom with a geyser and hot shower and everything. They even gave me a plot where I grew my mealies, big pumpkins, carrots and tomatoes. When they saw how nicely I was growing them, they put a fence around and a tap just for me.

Away from the township and with better food, her children finally started to put some flesh on their bones. But leaving Dombotombo meant the end of her marriage. *My husband used to come to visit every week, then every two weeks, then once a month,*

then not at all. He got a job in Harare with the municipality and
everyone knows there are beautiful women in the city.

Sometimes in the evenings, Aqui took out the black-and-white
wedding photograph she kept in her mother's Bible. She ran her
fingers over the gawky 14-year-old in a puff-sleeved dress and
borrowed hat, her arm hanging on to that of this handsome man,
and would feel sad. But she knew she had done the right thing.
Once I started working I started changing, even my body got nice
and plump, simply because I was staying on my own.

Aqui never quite got used to the size of the Looses' house. *They*
were always changing things, new paintings, new furniture. To her
it was like a palace and she wondered if this was the sort of place
that people were talking about which Mugabe's new wife Grace
Marufu was building. It had been a shock, learning about Grace
in the newspapers. She had been Mugabe's secretary and was
40 years younger than him. It turned out that they had been
having an affair for years, long before the death of his much-loved
wife Sally in 1992 from kidney failure. Everyone had thought he
was childless but the newspaper revealed that he and Grace already
had two children.

The start of a new decade had seen sweeping changes in much
of the rest of Africa with the demise of nine presidents between
1990 and 1991, the highest turnover since the Organization of
African Unity was founded in 1963. But Mugabe was still very
much in power. His face stared out from photographs everywhere
Aqui went, even the office in town from which Mr Loos ran his
construction company.

Most of those nine presidents had been removed at gunpoint
or fleeing from rebels, as was the case of Ethiopia's President
Mengistu, the Marxist overlord, who had been given sanctuary in
Harare by his friend Mugabe. But in March 1991 President
Mathieu Kerekou of Benin had become the first dictator in post-

colonial Africa to be beaten at the ballot box in a display of people power, followed by Zambia's Kenneth Kaunda a few months later.

Mugabe had no intention of leaving open such a possibility. There had been a series of elections since independence, but by abolishing seats reserved for whites, intimidating voters, and making a Unity Accord with his old rival Joshua Nkomo, he had turned Zimbabwe into the one-party state he had always wanted. Aqui had just given birth to her son Wayne when on 30 December 1987 a special ceremony was held in which Mugabe had himself declared Executive President by Parliament amid loud applause. Joyce Mujuru, the Minister for Women, had led women dancing and singing a chorus of 'You Are the Only One'. This meant Mugabe was both President and Prime Minister, and had sweeping powers to dissolve Parliament or to declare martial law as well as the right to run for unlimited terms of office. The 1990 elections had left ZANU-PF with 117 out of 120 seats. He could be President for the rest of his life.

Aqui was not at all sure this was the best thing for the country. It was hard for her to criticize Mugabe as a fellow Zezuru. But she did feel that he was almost 70, older than her father, and should be thinking about retiring and making his peace so new blood could come forth. *There is something about our African men when they get power. They want it to put things right but then they enjoy it too much. They like too much being the Big Man. They forget what is real and what not. So when people started being bussed in to clap at his rallies instead of flocking by choice, didn't he know they were bussed in?*

For some time she had been leading the weekly motivational singing with the ideological choir at her local ZANU-PF branch with less enthusiasm. *But it was not a light thing to leave the party.* The 1990 elections had been heavy with threats of violence and many who spoke out against Mugabe seemed to meet untimely ends in road crashes. Edgar Tekere, Mugabe's former close ally in the liberation war, had been expelled from the ZANU-PF

after criticizing the corruption in the government following the
Willowgate car scandal. He had set up a new party called Zimbabwe
Unity Movement (ZUM) that had a lot of support from students
and said he was going to stand against Mugabe for President.
Mugabe was so furious that when police clashed with protesting
students he closed the university for the first time in its history.
He even seemed to give his supporters licence to kill, boasting, 'I
have a degree in violence.' A television advertisement for the
ruling party in the election campaign showed a gruesome car
accident. 'This is one way to die,' said the narrator. 'Another is to
vote ZUM. Don't commit suicide, vote ZANU-PF and live.'

Aqui's full-time job and the fact that she had moved out of
town meant it was difficult for her to keep running the local party
cell. She handed over responsibility with some relief, though she
remained a party member.

*Mugabe was still our hero, he liberated us, but we were not happy
with what he was doing.* Apart from the lack of political freedom,
the economic situation was deteriorating. Between 1991 and 1995,
after imposing the World Bank's structural adjustment programme and following two terrible droughts, Zimbabwe's economy averaged only 1.2 per cent annual growth, far below the
yearly population growth of 3.1 per cent. The country was still
self-sufficient in food because of the commercial farms, but per
capita income was less than US$400 per annum, lower than at
independence. Thousands of people had been laid off

Aqui knew how lucky she was to be protected by the Looses
but was aware of the growing disillusion with Mugabe. *It's like if
you are a mother, your children are looking forward to you giving
them food and carrying out other duties for them, then you stop, the
children might rethink their opinion of you. So for example I am
asthmatic and I know if I don't get my medicine I will die. When I
started going to the hospital and they didn't have medicine yet in
the streets I saw the Chefs with those big black cars, I began to think.*

But there was one hope. The Lancaster House Agreement,

which had protected white farmers, had expired in May 1990. A few months later, in January 1991, Mugabe signed a constitutional amendment that gave his government the right to order compulsory purchase of white-owned land. 'What we are doing is bringing about justice for our people,' he said. 'We will ask the owners of the land to sell it but if we need it we will not take no for an answer.' Although he would still need to pass a Land Requisition Act to be able to expropriate the farms, the announcement was greeted by much singing and dancing.

Internationally, Mugabe's image remained the great liberation hero, the horrors of *Gukurahundi* conveniently ignored, the evidence buried deep in the earth of Matabeleland. In 1994, during a state visit to Britain, Mugabe was awarded an honorary knighthood by the Queen on the recommendation of John Major's government.* *We still felt proud to have such a leader.*

---

* Mugabe was made Honorary Knight Commander of the Order of the Bath, a title he still retains despite calls for it to be withdrawn.

12

Guanghzou, China, 1991

THE OSTRICHES LAY DEAD AND DYING on the dusty street. A chattering crowd of Chinese watched on in astonishment as Nigel and an assistant ran from one to another trying to resuscitate those still hanging on. The ostriches struggled and panicked, flapping and kicking out with their long ungainly legs as the two men desperately tried to hold up their heads and prise open their beaks. All but one of the Chinese helpers had fled, scratched and frightened by the birds' flailing legs. Nigel managed to squirt glucose solution into some of the ostriches' beaks, while others he injected with massive steroid doses that brought some of them round temporarily. But it was too late and many more died.

It was like the killing fields. I was shaken to the core. I hated the sight of the dead ostriches, and all the Chinese kept doing was taking photos.

Nigel felt sunken. Importing ostriches into China was supposed to have been his path to fortune. Instead, 67 of the 93 ostriches now lay dead, leaving him with a large debt. The sinister Chinese businessman to whom he had sold the birds, stood staring grimly at the feathered mass.

The idea of selling ostriches had come to Nigel after his losses during Zimbabwe's Black Friday left him with nothing but 14 ostriches. He managed to sell them to a farmer in Scotland and,

as part of the deal, travelled out on the cargo plane with them. Afterwards he had stayed in Glasgow for a year playing cricket for a small club called Hyndland. He was their first overseas professional and the local paper had run a front-page story about the team signing on a 'hard-hitting international test batsman'. After that in the first five games he had only scored four runs. *It was humiliating as the kind of teams we were playing were not even as good as an under-13 B team back home.* Nigel was so embarrassed that he told the club that until he started scoring he would go without the fee of £100 a match they had promised him.

Apart from his frustration at failing to notch up runs, Nigel found himself yearning for the sun-drenched colours of home. One particularly drab day, he escaped from driving rain down some steps into what he thought was a coffee bar but which turned out to be a church-run shelter for down-and-outs. Not wanting to go back out into the rain and feeling slightly awkward, he randomly picked up two books from the rack and sat down to read. One was the Bible and the other a book about finding

Christianity called *Beyond Ourselves: A Woman's Pilgrimage in Faith* by Catherine Marshall. *It was the strangest sensation. Perhaps because I was alone and far from home, I felt as if God was speaking to me.* Although Christianity was seen by many Rhodesians as a fundamental part of their identity, Nigel's family were not church-goers and he had always rather derided such faith. *The first person I thought about was my first girlfriend Margie who all those years before had thought of me as the devil's disciple and said she would pray for me. Suddenly I understood.*

Shortly after that, Nigel started notching up plenty of runs. But the club fell into disarray as Hyndland's captain, who was also the treasurer, ran off with the kitty. Nigel might have found God but he would need to find another source of income. One evening, he was having dinner in a Chinese restaurant, staring absently at a scene of willow trees and pagodas painted on a mirror, when his mind turned to ostriches.

The good thing about ostriches is that you get multiple offspring, maybe 35–40 chicks a year, and very good feed-conversion ratios. For the amount of food you're putting in you get much more meat than cows, say, because part of an ostrich's digestive system is like that of a chicken so they convert food very quickly and part is like a horse so you can give them very cheap feed. Also ostriches only take nine and a half months to be ready for sale compared to 18 months for cattle.

Nigel thought that China, with its huge population needing food, would make an ideal market. *I thought even if I did not sell ostriches I would get to see China.*

Once the cricket season was over, he flew to Hong Kong and went to see a Chinese tycoon in Kowloon who produced ostrich-skin handbags and shoes. Nigel's plan was to convince him that it would be far more lucrative to source the material himself and raise ostriches in China.

The man was a tough character who had fled Mao's China by swimming across the Sham Chun river to Hong Kong. From there

Ostriches produce as many as 40 chicks a year

he had gone to the United States where he had set up a chain of restaurants and made his fortune, then returned home. When Nigel turned up to see him in jeans and scruffy T-shirt, he was not impressed. *He was very disparaging about my clothes but I managed to turn that to my advantage by saying I was not there to sell him clothes but to teach him how to make a fortune out of ostriches, which he seemed to like.*

Some days before the meeting, Nigel had gone to a church service in Kowloon where he had met the sales manager of a multinational food and drink company. This man had advised him that the key to selling products successfully in China was to imply that they might boost male virility. So, apart from offering his prospective buyer some cooked ostrich meat to taste, Nigel went armed with photographs showing some rather well-endowed male ostriches.

I took in cooked ostrich, which he tried, and it was tender with no fat so it was easy to sell that aspect. I then showed him a picture of the male ostrich's winkie, which is huge, and said, 'Eating it will help all you guys with that part as well.' I got him going really big-time. He started asking if he could eat that bit.

The South Africans had long dominated the ostrich market through the Klein Karoo Co-operative which had been set up in the Eastern Cape back in 1945, but Nigel pointed out that the South African ostrich was much smaller than its Zimbabwean cousin. *It was easy for me to say, 'Look, ours is so big, massive compared to theirs.' But if I'm really honest, theirs is a better ostrich because it is domesticated whereas ours are wild and hard to control.*

The businessman was convinced and ordered 93 ostriches. The deal was written on a piece of paper. The birds were to cost US$3,000 each plus transport, half up front and half on arrival at the airport. *My profit would have been US$27,000, which was a fortune to me then. I could taste the money.*

He paid the half up front but after he took delivery he never paid the other half. Worse was to follow. For some reason he had only wanted Nigel to transport the ostriches to the airport, then sign them over. *I had warned him that transporting ostriches was quite a tricky business but he would have none of it. About seven hours later, I was summoned urgently. They had transported the ostriches in closed trucks that became ovens and 67 ostriches died of heat exhaustion and suffocation. It was one of the most terrible days I have ever had.*

On the train back from Guangzhou, the Chinaman refused to speak to Nigel and forbade his staff from having anything to do with him for the whole 110-mile journey. Everyone sat silent, shocked at what they had seen.

Afterwards Nigel sat in a café near the station, head in hands, counting his remaining yuan. The place was packed with Chinese workers and he tried to block out the sound of them crunching ducks' feet or slurping from bowls of what to him looked like frogspawn. What on earth was he doing there, he wondered, a White African farm-boy in China? The loss on the ostrich deal was enough to bankrupt him and he had no idea how he was going to pay the farmers back in Zimbabwe for the birds. Not only had he lost all his money but he could not get the picture of dead ostriches out of his head.

For the next few days he went and sat outside the businessman's office, refusing to move until eventually he was granted an audience. But the Chinese man would not keep to the contract. *The cause of death was quite clear but he tried to insinuate that it was disease. Fortunately we had a vet who was present at the autopsy and the official finding was suffocation.*

Although Nigel found a lawyer who thought he had a good case, the man asked for a substantial sum as down payment, and he had nothing to pay him. Desperate, he went back to the businessman and asked, 'Why are you doing this? We could go into business together and sell ostriches to the whole of China.' A slow, unpleasant smile spread across the Chinese man's face. 'You're just much too stupid to be my partner,' he replied. 'Look how easily I tricked you.'

For Nigel it was the start of a love–hate relationship with ostriches. With no money to go back home, he was forced to stay in China. For the next six months he slept on a mat on the floor of the apartment of his friend from the food and drinks company and lived on noodles from roadside stalls. *It was the darkest period of my life.* All that kept him going was his new-found faith and his interpreter Shen Yingran, the only one of the businessman's staff who had really tried to save the dying ostriches and whom he subsequently employed.

To try and find buyers for ostriches, he and Shen travelled round China by train. The country had not yet opened up to tourists and Nigel was stared at in astonishment by peasants who had never seen a *laowei* or foreigner before. He had endless meetings with businessmen followed by interminable dinners of strange-looking food like soups made from baby owls or from bull-penis, and goats' testicles on sticks. The Cantonese have a saying: 'Anything that walks, swims, crawls or flies with its back to heaven is edible,' and at times Nigel felt he was being served the whole gamut.

Toasting was always a central part of the meal, people constantly raising their glasses to the visitor and shouting, '*Kan pei*,' which means 'Bottoms up!' This was usually rice wine, sometimes flavoured with mice or lizard, but Nigel stayed sober by saying he did not drink and mainly sticking to Coca-Cola. *Afterwards they usually expected to go to the whorehouse where women would come up and feel my thin arms and say, 'How strong you are!' while I tried to escape.*

Finally he started getting deals and making money. Over the next four years he sold 3,000 ostriches – about US$10m worth – all over the Far East from Inner Mongolia to East Timor where he set up the island's first ostrich farm. *What had happened with Tai Mak had been a hard blow but was valuable training in dealing with that part of the world.*

In Indonesia he linked up with a businessman called Charlie Kumalo, who was an associate of President Suharto, and survived the corrupt environment by doubling his price per ostrich to US$3,000 up front and US$3,000 on arrival. That way, if they failed to pay the second tranche, he had still covered his costs, while if they did pay he would have a very healthy profit.

His ostrich business was soon thriving though he almost lost some beasts at Shanghai airport when a crate of six male ostriches was lifted by crane and the bottom fell out. They ran out onto the runway, forcing the airport to be shut. Ostriches are second only to cheetahs as the world's fastest animals on land, and chasing them was no easy business. They are also easily stressed, and when they had finally been rounded up, the hysteria of the Chinese ground staff caused one of the male ostriches to have a heart attack and die.

The first ostrich farm in East Timor

But Nigel could not get Zimbabwe out of his blood. He had rented a cramped flat in Hong Kong's Kennedy Town on the 37th floor above a pig abattoir. Sometimes he would lie on his bed in the room where he could reach out and touch all four walls, and dream of home, wondering if the jacarandas were out, dusting the streets with their fine violet blossom, or remembering dusk on the farm when the flying ants stream from their dry dusty holes in the ground and birds arrive in all directions.

Then one day in 1995, he fell sick in Indonesia. First the shakes and high temperatures of malaria and tick-bite fever, then he contracted hepatitis on top and was rushed into a Jakarta hospital, weak with vomiting. In just one day he lost 22 pounds and was so dehydrated that the hospital could not get an intravenous drip

Exporting ostriches

into his arm. *I lost about seven days of my life drifting in and out of consciousness.* So ill was he that an Indonesian priest was brought in to administer the Last Rites. *I heard him ask God to forgive all my many and obvious sins and say that all my suffering was a direct result of my trespasses. I was so annoyed that somehow I managed to find the strength to object and it seemed to revive me.*

It was, he decided, time to go home.

*   *   *

It was the light that hits you first, he thought, that ultra-blue sky, the feel of space, the sun that shone almost every day of the year. And the smell, that familiar sweet primeval smell of wood-smoke and dust from his childhood. His spirits were already rising as the taxi drove out of Harare airport, through Independence Arch, trees either side of the avenue. The green msasas were coming into pod and the flamboyantes dressed with spectacular red flowers. Soon it would be November, the rain month.

In all his travels, he had never come across anywhere to touch Rhodesia, as he still thought of it, for its climate. Despite its location within the tropics, Zimbabwe rarely experienced the unpleasant combination of high temperatures and humidity that in Indonesia had left him feeling like a wrung-out rag. The seasons ranged from mild winters of cool nights and sunny days between May and August through the hot days of September and October to the wet and warm months November to March.

Nigel wound down the window and breathed in the air. It was more than five years since he had left. The world had changed a lot in that time with the fall of the Berlin Wall, the end of apartheid in neighbouring South Africa and the release of Nelson Mandela, and the collapse of the Soviet Union. But Zimbabwe had not changed, still governed by a Communist-inspired Politburo who called each other Comrade and berated the World Bank and IMF while reluctantly implementing their liberalization programme.

In Nigel's brief phone calls back home or dealings with the Zimbabwean farmers from whom he had bought ostriches, he had heard ominous mutterings about the deteriorating situation, so he was relieved to see that Harare still appeared prosperous. The supermarkets sold everything and now had far more imported goods, and unlike almost anywhere else in Africa the traffic lights worked. The cinemas were showing recent films. The only change as far as he could see was that the window of Edgars department store had its first black mannequins.

But on closer sight, the place which once boasted of being the cleanest city in Africa was now littered with piles of rubbish and many of the roads had potholes. Nigel had heard the stories of Harare's Mayor Solomon Twengwa who had taken office promising to eradicate corruption and wipe out the housing waiting list of 100,000, and instead spent £1m building himself a new mayoral mansion. By the time he was suspended in 1999 for gross mismanagement, the city's finances would be in a far worse mess and the housing backlog would have doubled, leaving half the population in shacks and squatter settlements.

Even so there was no doubt that, for those with money, Zimbabwe was still a good place to live. Fifteen years on from independence, the whites numbered only about 80,000, far less than 1 per cent of the population. Yet they still controlled business, mining and farming, and cheap black labour remained plentiful. *Blacks didn't understand that you needed to start off small and build up, they wanted to be big right away, and also when they did make money they spent it on flash cars and things rather than reinvesting, so very few were getting anywhere.* The long-threatened land reform had not really materialized despite the recent Land Acquisition Act, and the country still had a white Minister of Agriculture, Dennis Norman. It was a peaceful place too, beset with none of the civil wars of its neighbours such as Mozambique or Congo, nor ethnic carnage like that which had shocked the world the previous year in Rwanda where Interhamwe militias of the Hutus had slaughtered more than half a million Tutsis in just 100 days.

Nigel had made enough money from the ostrich business to buy a good farm, and at 33 he was ready to settle down. He wanted his children to grow up as he had with plenty of sunlight and space to roam. Farming, after all, was in his blood. His grandfather had farmed there since 1919. There was just one thing missing. *I knew a farmer needs a wife.*

The previous year, in 1994, his sister Shirley had told him she

Nigel back in Africa

wanted him to meet her friend Claire with whom she played hockey and who also taught at the convent. She had fixed up a date for a time when Nigel was visiting from China. But by then Claire had met someone else so the date had been cancelled.

When Nigel moved back to Zimbabwe, his sister told him that Claire and her boyfriend had broken up so he half-heartedly suggested another blind date. Shirley arranged the place but forgot to tell her brother, leaving Claire to be stood up. That same night, while Claire was waiting alone in the bar, Nigel was out drinking with his old school friend Larry Norton. *I was bemoaning my single status and complaining that it looked as if I would be a bachelor for ever.*

When Nigel learnt of Shirley's blunder, he felt sorry for Claire and telephoned the next day to ask her out. She agreed to meet for dinner that night. Nigel drove to her house feeling apprehensive about the dull evening he expected lay ahead of him. *Try as I might, I could not conjure up my idea of a princess out of any of the hockey-playing teachers I knew. Then I saw Claire at the gate and she was stunning and from that moment everything I said seemed clumsy and stupid and everything she said mesmerized me. I knew straight away that she was the one.*

We went to The Cellar, which was the best restaurant in Harare. I knew it would put me back in overdraft but I didn't care. At that stage I would willingly have gone bankrupt.

Nigel was mortified because he knew he reeked of ostrich dust. *When you went on the ostrich farms you got ostrich dust on you and you stunk. Even if you bathed for four days you couldn't get rid of the smell.*

But he kept his distance and she didn't seem to care. To Nigel the dinner passed in an instant. When he dropped her back at her house, she invited him in for a coffee. He was pleased but thought she might just be being polite. They talked and talked and only when he saw Claire yawn did he look at his watch and realize it was 3 a.m.

That night, back at his sister's house, he did not sleep a wink. *My mind was racing. Claire was beautiful, smart, and also shared my faith in God. I felt something I had never felt before but I had seen no indication of how she felt about me. I vowed that I did not care if I made a fool of myself. I would do everything possible to be with her.*

That one evening had changed his life completely. He felt as if he had never before really lived, had never really noticed the sun rising and setting, or the perfume of the blossom on the breeze. All that mattered was seeing the light in one woman's eyes.

Two days later they went out on another date. By the ninth day, Nigel was desperate. *I still had not kissed her – the stakes were*

too high – I really wanted her and didn't want to ruin it. On the
ninth day she had been to watch me play cricket, then we met up
later at the Italian Bakery. I was desperate but instead of saying
how I felt, I very clumsily asked, 'Where is this going?'

Claire pushed back her honey-blonde hair and looked at him
quizzically.

'It's just that I'm too old for this if you think it isn't going any
further,' added Nigel.

'I think it could,' replied Claire.

'How much further?' he asked nervously.

'A lot further.'

Somehow Nigel told her that he wanted to spend the rest of
his life making her happy, and they finally kissed. By the time he
drove her home, they were engaged.

That night he slept properly for the first time since they had
met. Within three months they were married.

13

Marondera, 1999

IT WAS A DREAM and it wasn't a dream. Aqui had woken in the middle of the night remembering a scene from her childhood. *My grandmother had built a goat shelter near the yard and we were sitting round the fire in her hut talking. My uncle was playing the mbira and it was so nice, my grandmother was humming, rhyming to the mbira in a kind of trance as she did when the spirits possessed her, when suddenly we heard a terrible roar outside. My grandmother was so happy, clapping and cheering, and I asked, 'Why are you so happy? I am scared of that terrible noise.'*

She replied, 'I am happy because there was a leopard outside wanting to eat my goats but a lion has killed it.'

She would not let us go outside to look because it was too late, but the next morning we woke early, early to see, and, yes, there was a leopard lying there dead. My grandmother called her brothers to collect the leopardskin, then she went about making the clay pots that she sold to buy cattle.

I could see then there were many things that would always be mysteries.

Aqui hummed to herself as she vacuumed and scrubbed and polished the house. These days she moved around without hesitation, no longer fearful of its large rooms. She was so happy, and for the first time even managing to save a little money. Almost more than having the money, she enjoyed thinking of what she might do with it, perhaps buying her eldest, Heather, a dress, or football boots for Wayne. She would like to build another room onto the house in Dombotombo but that would have to wait.

Sometimes, when Mrs Loos was out, Aqui would make herself some tea and sit in one of the fine chairs that sank feather-soft as you sat in them. Then she would imagine what it would be like to be the mistress of such a grand house looking out over her land.

She never sat for long – although she would hear Mrs Loos's car driving in with plenty of time, there was far too much at stake. Aqui did not often talk to other servants but from the little she picked up she knew that she was lucky and the Looses were good employers. She was very proud of her vegetable patch with its own tap where she could grow her relish and occasionally stop to look up at a sky that was once more filling with dreams.

The memory of her grandmother and the leopard distracted Aqui a little and that afternoon she inadvertently walked in on a heated discussion between the Looses. Mrs Loos seemed tense and her dark eyes were red-rimmed from crying and the couple fell silent on seeing the maid. Aqui began to fear that they were going to fire her and wondered what it was that she might have done. She started working harder than ever, rubbing and rubbing surfaces of tables and cabinets so that they gleamed like mirrors. In those dry September days, it was a constant battle against dust, particularly when Mr Loos kept leaving windows open, but she was determined that not a speck be allowed to settle.

One day Mrs Loos called her in to the drawing room and gestured her to sit.

'Aquinata, I have to tell you something,' she said.

'Yes, Madam.' Aqui knew it was something bad by the way Mrs Loos was not looking straight at her.

'There's no easy way to tell you this,' she began. 'Grant, that is Mr Loos, and I are moving to South Africa. I'm terribly sorry Aqui, but Mr Loos doesn't like the way the economy is going down here and thinks we should move for the sake of the children.'

They gave her an extra two months' salary and promised they would send for her once they were settled. Everything in the house was packed up in boxes and crates and the dates on the calendar crossed off faster and faster until it was the day to depart. The children were crying and Aqui sniffed noisily as Mrs Loos suddenly reached out her arms. Aqui had never been hugged by a white person before. Her nostrils flared like an animal's at the fragrance enclouding her and which she recognized from the pastel-coloured soaps shaped like shells that had filled a glass dish in the bathroom. *I was crying, everyone was crying.* Mr Loos shook her hand and pressed a wad of notes into it, then placed his arm round his wife and led her to the car. In a flurry of waves and spiralling dust they were gone.

Without Mrs Loos's flower-patterned curtains, the windows of the house looked blank and unwelcoming and Aqui had no wish to hang around. Her own belongings had already been strapped onto the farm truck and she clambered in to be taken back to the shack in Dombotombo.

The driver was slow but she felt as if she were hurtling downwards, mocked by every bump in the road. The iron bedstead crowning the pile of furniture was a sign of success, something everyone in her village had aspired to, and she remembered how as a child she and her sisters had crowded admiringly when one was lifted down from the bus in the township. But in every other sense it was to Aqui a journey from white to black. Over the railway track, past the big grey rock from which Dombotombo got its name, *the place where long, long back when there were wars between the tribes, the men would take their wives and children into the rock to hide.*

Then it was past the bus station on the left with the sail-skirted women selling packs of Lobells biscuits and bright-coloured juices in plastic bags, and on the right came the bottle store where the Saturday drinkers were already gathering, and the butchers *For the Cheapest Meat Special.* A right turn-off led into the grid of mud lanes past the line of shacks, each with a small wire fence and doors painted with black numbers, B401, B402 . . . until they got to B438 though the eight had dropped off.

Aqui's shack in Domobotombo

Back in the township things had deteriorated, or perhaps, thought Aqui, she had never really noticed before. A pipe had burst, oozing green-frothed sewage all along one side of the road, and someone's goat was nosing in a pile of rubble. In her yard, a dragonfly was drinking at the puddle where some water had leaked. Above, the pregnant sky that would not bring forth rain seemed filled with foreboding.

As Aqui started trying to squeeze the furniture from the truck into the three-roomed shack, a loud wailing started up. She looked outside to see a crowd of people passing along, some carrying umbrellas against the unforgiving sun. It was a funeral party. *I thought it was the Sickness but later I heard that it was someone*

Aqui's kitchen-cum-bedroom

shot by police in food riots in Harare. People had gone into the
streets to protest against the price of rice and cooking oil, which
had doubled in a month, and of maize meal, which had made
three serious leaps in price in three months. There had been
several bread riots since the unpopular IMF programme was
imposed back in 1991 but the protests of December 1998 were the
most violent since independence and the police lost control.
Troops were brought into the streets for the first time and opened
fire on the protesters. At least ten people had been killed and
hundreds injured. One of them was a woman from Dombotombo
who had gone to the city to look for her son who had been trying
to find work there. She was just a bystander.

Aqui had forgotten how noisy the township was. Angry noises,
like a kind of constant buzzing of bees. Radios played, people
argued, someone was trying to coax a coughing motor into life.
Everyone seemed to be complaining – about the price of bread;
the lack of medicines; the doubling of the size of the cabinet to

42 ministers and their 133 per cent pay increases while the health budget was almost halved; the way you needed so many more Zimbabwe dollars to buy anything. The very same week as the food riots, the government had spent US$2m buying 50 new Mercedes-Benz saloons for ministers. Aqui was unwilling to enter into the general outrage. *I did not really believe that Mugabe would do such things.* She told everyone that she would soon be moving overseas.

Each night she lay awake in the cramped kitchen, her small bunk wedged in under a shelf shared by face-lightening cream and cooking oil and almost touching the two-ring stove balanced on some concrete bricks. She stared at it, remembering how once she had dreamt of owning a store-bought stove with four rings and a refrigerator. The five children – Heather, Valerie, Vivian, Wayne and Vanessa – slept in the bedroom, sharing the iron bed crammed between the wardrobe and a sack of mealie meal.

While Aqui was living at the Looses', they had given her a television and an old brown sofa, and somehow, pushing and wheezing, she managed to squash these into the tiny second room of the shack. The sofa was one of those plump ones, which at the Looses' had been lost in the corner of some spare room and had fitted nicely in her living quarters. Here it was so wedged between the walls that if you tried to take it out, Aqui thought the whole shack would collapse like a house of cards, while if you stretched out your legs they would hit the TV. But it would double as a bed for a couple of the children and maybe her mother or visiting sister and her child. The television was mostly an ornament. Even if she could afford the electricity, there were constant power cuts. That February, the electricity company had been declared bankrupt, largely because of theft and fraud by its own managers. Anyway, she knew she was not missing much. ZBC had turned into 'what the President did today' in between scenes of scantily clad village people dancing and drumming. She had heard Mr Loos refer to it as 'the drums and bums channel'.

*   *   *

With no job to fill her days and the children all at school, Aqui moved listlessly, like one of the mombes she used to tend all those years before. She had even begun to miss Tendai. He soon heard she was back and turned up one Saturday. There was no way of stopping him getting in if he wanted to; the door was far too flimsy. She could smell the alcohol on his breath but she let him in and for a while believed him when he said he had missed her and traced out her new fuller figure with his hands. That night she enjoyed the familiar comfort of his strong chest to lie on and his warm beery breath on her neck. He even played with the children the next day, kicking a ball down the street with Wayne and buying them sugary Fantas in the store. While they were out she counted out fifty of the precious dollars from the Looses to buy some meat so there would be a decent meal and dressed in the polka-dot skirt Mrs Loos had given her in a bag of cast-offs. The Looses had eaten meat every day, sometimes twice. As she spooned out the stew and piled the sadza into a thick white cone, she carefully gave her husband the least gristly pieces of meat.

The next morning Tendai was leaving early to get the bus to Harare. Aqui woke at dawn to heat water for him to wash and to make tea, enjoying the bustling sense of being a real family.

'Ugh, what's this?' he asked, spitting the brown liquid onto the floor.

'It's tea.'

'Where's the sugar, bitch? You know I take sugar.'

There had not been sugar for a long time. Nobody had sugar. Surely he knew that. He seized her wrist and began to twist. Aqui's wrist bones felt as fragile as chicken bones and she shrank inside as she watched the web of tiny red blood vessels spreading across the whites of his eyes.

'You've been spending all that money from those *murungus* on fancy clothes instead of food for your family!' he shouted.

'Mrs Loos gave me the clothes,' she whimpered.

'What are we now, beggars from the whites?'

'It wasn't like that, they were good people,' she said.

'Aah, they'll forget all about you now they've gone,' he snorted. 'The whites will all be gone soon, you mark my words. I've heard them talking in those government offices where I clean.' He flung her to the ground and stormed out of the door.

'Momma!' In the doorway she could see little Vanessa, the six-year-old's, eyes wide with terror.

Later, when the children had gone to school, Aqui opened the sugar tin to get some money for buying an onion and found that the thick wad of notes had disappeared. She lay on the room-sized sofa, staring at the paintings that had been her farewell present from the Looses. They were very different. One was of waves crashing on dark rocks and the other of a line of elephants walking trunk to tail across flat yellow savannah. She wondered how they felt, finding themselves here in this ramshackle shack, rain pinging on the tin roof, instead of that big white house lulled by Mrs Loos's tinkling of the piano.

The weeks went by and she waited and waited but no letter came from South Africa. Each night she prayed and prayed for it to come but her God was not listening. Instead she woke up with a sour taste in her mouth one morning and felt the telltale swelling of the breasts. She could not believe that she had fallen pregnant again. The bottom of the sack of maize was already visible. They were barely surviving on the watery sadza and soon there would not be any left and the talk was that the government was planning to bring back school fees which would mean taking the girls out of school. She was sure Tendai would not help them – she knew from his sister that he had taken another wife in town. Finally one day she went to the post office and there was an airmail letter for her in Mrs Loos's writing. Her whole body sagged with relief – this would be the summons to move south. She would not open it in the post office where everyone watched each other's business but placed it carefully in her bag and walked away with a spring in her step. Back home she first made tea then took out the precious envelope. In her eagerness to open it she did not notice that instead of South Africa it was postmarked New Zealand.

Dear Aquinata, she read in neat black ink that she could picture Mrs Loos writing, her pretty face scrunched up with concentration. She smiled at the thought then read on.

So terribly sorry but our plans have changed.

The rest of the letter swam into a blur in front of Aqui as a life selling potatoes or firewood by the side of the road stretched ahead of her. She had always thought she was more than that. 'You think you're better than the Malawis in the township,' Tendai had jeered. Maybe he was right. As a black woman it was not enough to have a school certificate, and hers was anyway only a primary school one.

That evening she snapped at her children to do their homework. 'You Born Frees don't know how lucky you are,' she scolded. The children raised their eyebrows at each other, waiting for the familiar refrain. 'You must work hard so you can get a good job, not end up like me, scrubbing other people's dirt if I'm lucky.'

But her words lacked conviction. Those starry-eyed days when they would dream of their independent Zimbabwe as a paradise seemed like a figment of her imagination now, part of the time when Tendai cast her body in golden light. Every year the colleges turned out thousands of graduates who would not find jobs. There were more than 260,000 school leavers each year, compared to just 30,000 in the early 1980s, but only about 8 per cent would find jobs. Some of them were working as queue boys, waiting in lines for whites at petrol stations where most days boards outside read 'No Fuel'. The clinic where she used to get her asthma medicine now only had aspirin. Even the main public hospital in Harare, the Parirenyatwa, which had once been the finest in southern Africa and where Aqui dreamed of nursing, was now regarded as a death trap. Before independence it was called Andrew Fleming Hospital and offered treatment as good as anything you could find in England, but was only for whites. Now anyone could go there but it was running short of bed linen and unable to replace broken equipment, and many of its nurses and doctors had moved abroad. The Looses had paid for Aqui's healthcare, but that was all gone now, and since the World Bank reforms the children's schools were no longer free.

One morning in December 1999, Aqui had seen the children off to school and was leaving to join a queue for a cleaning job when she noticed her neighbours pointing at something. During the night a series of stickers had appeared along the fence, proclaiming *Chinja Maitiro*, 'Change, Now is the Time', under an open black hand – the opposite to the clenched fist that had replaced the cockerel as the symbol of ZANU-PF. *We didn't really know what it was but one of the neighbours said it was a new political party. When he said that we were a bit scared and all went back indoors or on our way.*

The new party was called the MDC, which stood for Movement for Democratic Change. Its leader was a stocky ex-miner named Morgan Tsvangirai, who like Aqui had been one of those in the dancing, cheering crowds in 1980 when Mugabe's election victory was announced. He was then a 28 year old working in a nickel mine and had gone on to become a trade union leader. His arrest and detention in 1989 during student protests against corruption had turned him into a national figure.

Aqui thought Tsvangirai poorly dressed and like a bulldog with no neck, but as head of the 400,000-strong Zimbabwe Congress of Trade Unions (ZCTU) he had become popular for his crusade against the government's extravagance and the high living of its ministers. Even some of Mugabe's staunchest supporters were shocked by the lavish ceremony on 17 August 1996 to wed his long-time mistress Grace. The *Herald* described it as 'the wedding of the century', costing £2 million, and some 10,000 guests turned up for the celebrations. The best man was Joaquim Chissano, President of Mozambique, and many other African heads of state were present, including Nelson Mandela. Mugabe resented Mandela's status eclipsing him as Africa's leading star of liberation since his release in 1990 and was said to be enraged by the loud cheers that greeted the South African President's appearance.

As a Catholic herself, Aqui was astonished that the Catholic archbishop had agreed to perform the ceremony when the couple had already had two children out of wedlock. While Sally Mugabe had been extremely popular and regarded as a sensible woman who did lots of good works, nobody in ZANU-PF respected Grace. Her well-known fondness for expensive clothes and shoes had made her one of Harrods' best customers and she was inevitably dubbed the Imelda Marcos of Zimbabwe. Party members were outraged at the lavish house Mugabe had built for her, which they named Graceland.

People had really liked Sally, she was a very good lady that one, but Grace was different. People mocked her. All she was interested in was clothes and jewellery and we all knew about her building herself a fine mansion and commandeering the national airline to go shopping in London or Paris.

By contrast, Tsvangirai's badly cut suits that always looked creased reflected his very modest lifestyle. He had been born in a poor rural family in Buhera, Manicaland, in 1952. His father was a bricklayer, and as the eldest son Morgan had left school early to work in a textile mill to support his eight brothers and sisters. From there he moved to a nickel mine, becoming a foreman at just 23 and eventually leader of the whole trade union movement. But he still lived with his wife and six children in a very ordinary bungalow.

Aqui had first heard his name in December 1997 when he organized a mass stay-away to protest proposed tax increases. It had brought the country to a standstill and she remembered Mr Loos grumbling because he needed to finish a building project.

Mugabe and Grace

A few days later, a group of thugs burst into Tsvangirai's tenth-floor office opposite Meikles Hotel, beat him almost senseless, and tried to throw him out of the window. The union leader was a burly man and managed to hold them off just long enough for his security guards to rescue him.

Aqui thought he must be a very brave man but ill-advised. *Everyone knew that no one stood up to the Big Man and survived. If my mhondoro grandmother had still been alive, I am sure she would have been predicting trouble.* Yet she was aware from her neighbours in Dombotombo that there was a growing appetite for change. ZANU-PF continued to win all the elections with sweeping majorities largely because of lack of choice and a persisting belief that it was unpatriotic to vote otherwise. In the last elections in 1995, the party had won 147 out of 150 seats. But the electorate had shown their feelings by the falling turnout. Back in 1985 more than 90 per cent of the electorate had turned out; ten years later the turnout was only 32 per cent.

But the first group to really shake the Mugabe regime would not be outsiders. Instead the threat would come from those at the very heart of the struggle for independence.

Afterwards people would say it was a funeral, an army officer and a young clerk called Shepherd that started everything. In December 1996, a well-known veteran from the liberation war called Mukoma Musa died so destitute that his friend Brigadier Gibson Mashingaidze had to pay for his burial. The army officer was so angry that he used the funeral to denounce the government. 'Some people now have ten farms to their names and luxury yachts and have developed fat stomachs when ex-combatants like Comrade Musa lived in abject poverty,' he said. 'Is this the ZANU-PF I trusted with my life? . . . To the majority of Zimbabweans I say our party, which I believe is still a great party, has abandoned us.'

The war vets had long felt aggrieved that they had given up so much of their lives for the struggle, suffering injuries and losing friends, yet instead of being rewarded with the long-promised land and freedom, most had been left destitute. To them it seemed that the system they had fought to dismantle was still in place, just that the faces at the top had changed colour. Zimbabwe now ranked alongside Brazil as the countries with the world's biggest gap between rich and poor. So there was fury in 1997 when the news emerged that the War Victims' Compensation Fund had been suspended because all the money had disappeared. The fund was supposed to provide disability allowances to ex-combatants but documents leaked to the press by a young clerk called Shepherd Mongu in the Social Welfare ministry revealed that a massive Z$1.5bn had been handed out between 1992 and 1997, mostly on fraudulent claims to government cronies.

The war vets were livid and began to campaign for their money. Their leader was a man called Chenjerai Hunzvi, who had emerged from nowhere to become chairman of the War Vets' Association, even though his own war record was highly dubious. He claimed to have been a member of the Zipra high command (Joshua Nkomo's forces) during the liberation war, but in fact had never seen action. After joining Zipra in 1977, he was sent to Romania then Poland for training and enrolled at medical school. It was uncertain whether he had ever graduated but he set up in practice and married a Polish woman. She later left him and wrote a book about her life of domestic violence with him entitled *White Slave*. Back in Harare, he had set himself up as a doctor and become an assessor for the War Vets' Association, producing medical reports on disabled ex-combatants that would decide their payouts.

Despite his questionable background and strange combination of high-pitched voice with thuggish appearance, Hunzvi was a determined leader. In July 1997, when Mugabe refused to grant an audience to the war vets to hear their grievances, Hunzvi and his supporters took to the streets of Harare, banging drums and chanting Chimurenga songs outside the President's office for three days running. A commission of inquiry into the benefit scam was set up but this did not appease them. At the annual Heroes' Day commemoration in August at which Mugabe usually spoke for an hour, they drowned him out, forcing him to desist after just ten minutes.

Aqui followed events avidly. *It was easy to see why the war vets were angry. We all felt we'd fought and got nothing whereas the*

Veterans sing revolutionary songs in protest

white guys still have the big cars, so we became bitter, saying, 'We were in the bush but you forgot about us.' But I thought they were wrong to blame Mugabe. He was the one who got the country for us. The problem was Mugabe was always alone with people doing bad things behind his back.

The President was clearly rattled and finally met with Hunzvi. Despite the parlous state of the economy after the failure of the structural adjustment plan, he agreed to give a lump sum of Z$50,000 (then worth £3,000) to each of the 50,000 war vets claiming compensation as well as monthly pensions of Z$2,000 (£125). They also demanded land which he promised would be forthcoming.

The total cost of the deal was Z$4.2bn (then around £280m) which he promised to pay by Christmas. The government had no money to pay this and the horrified World Bank suspended its lending. Investors pulled out their money from Zimbabwe. On the morning of 14 November 1997, a date that became known as Black Friday, the Zim dollar lost 74 per cent of its value in just four hours. The Zim dollar that had been stronger than the pound at Independence was now worth less than three pence.

Many Zimbabweans were angry and more so when the tax increases were announced that would fund these payments. It was unclear why there were now 50,000 war vets when only 30,000 had been demobilized at the end of the war. Aqui felt that they were being asked to pay for the fact that the top guys had stolen the money. *I was a war vet if it came to that, most of us were.* When price increases of basic goods followed, so did the food riots.

When the commission issued its report on the benefits scam the following year, it confirmed Shepherd Mongu's revelations that the main recipients of the missing funds were Mugabe's own family and top lieutenants. The President's brother-in-law, Reward Marufu, had been awarded Z$822,668 (about US$70,000) on the basis of ulcers and a scar on his left knee. This '90 per cent disability' had not stopped him being posted to Zimbabwe's diplomatic mission in Canada where he was known for 'playing a mean game of squash'. The Police Commissioner, Augustine Chihuri, had received Z$138,645 for 'toe dermatitis of the right and left foot'. The Commander of the Defence Forces, Vitalis Zvinavashe, got Z$224,395 for 'a skin allergy and chest injuries'; while former Minister of Women's Affairs Joyce Mujuru pocketed Z$389,472 for 'poor vision' and 'mental stress disorder'. Many reports for politicians who had been given big payouts were simply described as 'missing'.

The man who had been leading the war vets' campaign, Chenjerai Hunzvi, was himself implicated. Not only had he provided many of the assessments, but he had been awarded Z$517,536 for 'impaired hearing' and 'sciatic pains of the thigh' even though he had never seen action.

A High Court judge ordered the return of the money, but as usual this was ignored. Shortly afterwards, Shepherd Mongu, the young whistleblower, was found dead. The police report put his death down to suicide, but the way Aqui heard it, a petrol siphon had been forced down his throat and rat poison poured into it.

It was amid the mounting public anger over the benefits scandal that Tsvangirai and his ZCTU joined a wide alliance of civic organizations, churches, human rights groups and lawyers to demand constitutional and electoral reform. Together they formed the National Constitutional Assembly (NCA) and one of its main aims was to prevent Mugabe running for election again. In February 1999, some of those involved decided to form a new political party to challenge ZANU-PF in the June 2000 elections.

Mugabe was furious, dismissing Tsvangirai as 'a tea-boy' for his lack of education and involvement in the liberation struggle. 'People must weigh themselves and see what they are good at,' he sneered. 'Some drive trains, some are foremen . . .'

Tsvangirai retorted: 'This government has lots of people with degrees and doctorates but they are not doing such a good job of running the country.'

Never one to be outmanoeuvred, Mugabe responded by setting up his own commission to draw up a new constitution that would provide him with vast powers. It also allowed the compulsory acquisition of white-owned farms and declared Britain, as the former colonial master, responsible for paying compensation. Britain had given £44m towards land reform since independence but suspended payments in 1996 because of the lack of progress on a transparent programme.

A referendum on this new constitution was to be held on the weekend of 12–13 February 2000. Not surprisingly, white farmers put their weight behind the No camp. Mugabe had appointed a slick new spin doctor called Professor Jonathan Moyo who had once been a staunch critic. Moyo responded with a propaganda blitz declaring that whites and the British government were behind the new opposition. Blacks voting No were branded 'sell-outs' in an echo of the liberation war while a Yes vote was equated with patriotism and loyalty.

One day Aqui switched on the television and saw an advertisement showing a small black boy standing at a gate with a big 'No Entry' sign. The boy was staring wistfully into the fields beyond. Then the gate opened and as the boy ran in, a voice said, 'Vote Yes.' *They tried to convince us that if we voted Yes, white farmers would lose their land and we Zimbabweans could reclaim our rightful inheritance.*

The weekend of the referendum, Aqui stayed at home, fully expecting the government to win. She had lost the baby and did not feel like going out and, besides, Mugabe had never lost an election. So she was stunned when two days later the results began leaking out. The turnout had been very low, only a quarter of the electorate, but the No camp had swept the country. *Everyone was whispering to each other, 'Mugabe has been beaten.' Some people were even saying 'This is the end.'* Even in places like Chimanimani and Mutasa that had returned ZANU-PF MPs with overwhelming majorities in every election since 1980, more than 60 per cent had voted No.

That night Aqui watched as Mugabe appeared on television in a smart blue suit to concede defeat. He looked old and tired and his hands shook as he read from a paper. 'Government accepts the results and respects the will of the people,' he said. 'The world now knows Zimbabwe as a country where opposing views and opinions can be found alongside each other peacefully. Let us all, winners and losers, accept the referendum verdict and start planning our way for the future.'

The national anthem played as the large bespectacled face faded from the screen.

Behind his conciliatory words, Mugabe was furious. It was the first time he had been confronted with proof of his own unpopularity and there was no way he would take this lying down.

Three days later an emergency meeting of the ZANU-PF central committee was held inside the gleaming glass party headquarters in Harare. The atmosphere was acrimonious and there
was a gasp around the room as Dzikamai Mavhaire, MP for
Masvingo, told Mugabe he should step down. The President stared
at him impassively without replying. Then he accused party
members of failing to fight an effective campaign and warned
them never again to be caught 'flat-footed in the future'.

Amid the part-fearful, part-excited atmosphere of a nation that
had finally stood up to its leader, Aqui had another reason to be
hopeful. She had received a message that a white family in Marondera called the Houghs were looking for a maid and nanny for
their young children and she had been recommended.

Early one morning she set off to catch the bus for an interview
at their farm in Wenimbi Valley, which was about ten miles
outside Marondera, just off the highway to Mutare. By the side
of the main road, she passed a gathering of people in white robes
in a small dip known as The Hole. *They were Apostolics and a
man they believed was a prophet lived there who had told them that
Mugabe would be President for life.* Aqui had disliked the Apostolics since childhood and she shivered as she walked past. The
shortage of fuel meant there was no traffic on the once busy road
and she could hear the sound of their robes flapping like crows.
*I was worried. People in Dombotombo were partying believing there
would be change and things would get better. But Mugabe was too
much stubborn, I knew he would not step down and there would be
retaliation for the vote.*

It would not be long before the country saw what Mugabe
could do.

14

New Life Centre Church, Marondera,
16 April 2000

THE HOUGH FAMILY had gone to church as usual on Sunday morning. It was a glorious late summer day, a few small puffs of cloud chasing each other across the sky, and sun streaming through the church windows trapping long fingers of dust. As always, with getting the three children ready, they arrived late, creeping in the back expecting to find the service in full swing. *Instead the congregation was very, very solemn and praying and we didn't know what was going on so we stayed at the back trying to find out.*

Marondera was one of the richest tobacco-growing areas in the country, and some of Zimbabwe's biggest farmers were at church. The New Life Centre was non-denominational and its Sunday morning service very much a social occasion – a chance for farmers and their families, often living on isolated homesteads, to get together. Afterwards they would head to the club for a braai or a roast beef lunch and a game of tennis or golf. It was their one chance in the week to take a break from worrying about absent rains or indolent workers.

But that Sunday was different. All around the Houghs familiar white faces were stained with tears or drawn tight with terror and there was the occasional stifled sob. *It was clear something terrible had happened.* Eventually someone whispered something

The Hough family

so shocking that at first they thought they must have misheard.

A local farmer, David Stevens, had been murdered by war vets. Just round the corner in Borradaile Hospital, three other farmers who had tried to save him lay seriously injured. John Osborne, Gary Luke and Steve Krynauw had all been bludgeoned to unconsciousness and dumped in the bush. Two others, Stuart Gemmill and Ian Hardy, were still missing and a search party was under way.

Nigel and Claire were horrified. The results of the referendum in February had been followed by invasions of hundreds of white-owned farms by people demanding land. They called themselves war vets but most of them were youths who could not possibly have fought in a war that had been over for 20 years and were probably just drawn from the million-plus unemployed. Each invasion followed a similar pattern. Gangs armed with axes and pangas would move onto a farm, round up the workers, beat them and force them to attend all-night *pungwes* and chant party slogans as they had during the bush war. But until then nobody had been killed.

The Stevenses were not just anonymous figures to the Houghs. They had been friends of Dave Stevens and his vivacious Swedish wife Maria with her mass of curly black hair, and their children had even played together. The Stevenses' farm was only about 13 miles away and Maria had just recently visited them to look at their ostriches. Now she was widowed at 39, left alone with four children, Marc, 15, Brenda, 13, and two-year-old twins Warren and Sebastian. Claire had taught with Gary Luke's wife Jenny, and both the Lukes and the Osbornes were members of their church. *It was a real shock. These were people just down the road, not in Bulawayo or the lowveld; it was someone here, part of our community, people from our church.*

Most of the congregation were farming families and the service ended with more prayers offered for the injured and missing men. *I think every one of us was thinking. That could have been me.*

Afterwards, they huddled together in a state of shock to discuss what had happened and piece together what they knew.

As on many farms, war vets had been squatting on Arizona Farm in Macheke for about a month, constantly demanding food from Dave Stevens and harassing his workers. On the previous Friday evening, the squatters had beaten up some of the workers and allegedly raped the daughter of one. The following morning the farm-workers had retaliated and chased some of the war vets away. Police arrived and detained some of the workers. A large group of war vets then returned, this time armed, and demanded to see Stevens. He radioed the local network for help and telephoned his friend John Osborne. But before Osborne could arrive, Stevens had been overpowered, his hands bound up with wire, and pushed into the passenger seat of his own Land Rover. He was then driven off, in between a car containing two armed men and a minibus packed with around 30 war vets. The group that remained set fire to the tobacco barns, then looted the house.

Osborne had rounded up two other farmers to help, Gary Luke

and Steve Krynauw. They arrived at the dust-track turn-off to Arizona Farm just as the convoy was roaring off along the road spraying dust. They saw Stevens's vehicle and he lifted up his wrists to show that he was handcuffed so they raced after it to Murehwa, about 25 miles away. As they entered the township, one of the war vets opened fire on them out of the window of a vehicle, so they drove into the courtyard of the police station to seek refuge. But the police simply stood by as the war vets marched in, one of them waving a rifle, and seized the farmers one by one.

Osborne was the first taken, driven along the road to the local ZANU-PF office where he was beaten with fanbelts and sticks until his glasses were smashed and his head was pouring with blood. Then he was thrown into a room at the back where Stevens was lying on the floor with his hands tied. Both were beaten once more, then put into a car with a blanket over their heads and driven into the bush. There they were dragged out, harangued for not supporting ZANU-PF and struck with clubs and iron bars over and over again. Suddenly a shot rang out and Stevens's body slumped to the ground. Osborne waited in horror for the same to happen to him when the voice of a woman he had once helped suddenly called out, 'He's all right, he's Mr Bluegums!'

'Yes, he's all right, he's Mr Bluegums,' shouted someone else. Osborne had no idea what they meant, but his life was spared. Bruised and bleeding, he was left at a house in the township from where he was evacuated to Borradaile hospital at about 10 p.m. on the Saturday night.

Meanwhile Steve Krynauw and Gary Luke had their hands and feet bound with wire, then were blindfolded and bundled into Stevens's Land Rover. They were bumped around for a while until the vehicle lurched to a halt and a heavy object was thrown on top of them. It was ice-cold and with dread they realized it must be the dead body of Dave Stevens.

The two farmers were taken to a hill north of Murehwa where another mob had gathered waiting to beat them senseless. 'You're

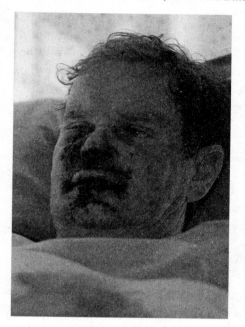

Steve Krynauw

MDC supporters and you're going to die!' shouted the crowd as they pounded them with iron bars, axe handles and large rocks. Convinced they were going to be killed, the men were tossed into a Toyota pick-up and driven around as they drifted in and out of consciousness. The vehicle eventually broke down and they were whacked a few more times and left for dead on a bridge.

Both men came to in the early hours and managed to untie each other's hands. It was raining heavily and the waters of the river below were rising. The two men began to fear that the pick-up would be swept off the bridge and they would be drowned, thinking that perhaps that was why they had been left there. They managed to break out of the back and started walking, barefoot and bleeding, through the bush. After about ten miles

they came to a farm, only to find the owner had fled. But he had
left his Land Cruiser so they broke in and drove to safety. They
too were taken to the hospital in Marondera. There it was discovered that, aside from massive bruising, Luke had a fractured
skull and Krynauw a fractured cheekbone.

Two other farmers, Ian Hardy and Stuart Gemmill, who had
driven into Murehwa to try to find out what had happened to the
others, had been taken to the ZANU-PF headquarters. There
they were savagely beaten, then driven to some hills where they
were forced to walk up to a cave. They were beaten long into the
night and eventually abandoned, gagged and bound with nylon
rope, bleeding from their wounds. At the time of the church
service they still had not been located.

As the Houghs listened to the initial garbled accounts of what
had happened, Claire felt her insides twist with terror. They had
bought their farm, Kendor, for US$350,000 just after getting
married in 1995 and put everything they had into it. Apart from
growing tobacco, they kept ostriches and had borrowed a further
US$200,000 to set up a factory producing shoes and bags from
the leather as well as safari clothes. Until that Sunday morning,
they had thought the farm invasions were just a ploy to intimidate
people before the forthcoming elections in June. Now it was
something much more sinister. As they left church, other farmers
from the area around Arizona Farm were arriving in Marondera
in pick-ups piled high with cases, all fleeing Macheke.

She could not imagine what Dave Stevens's widow must be
feeling. Maria Stevens was not even from Zimbabwe but had met
Dave while working for an aid agency, so she had not grown up
through the experience of war like the rest of them. *The only
blessing was that she and the children had been away on a trip to
Harare when the attack happened.*

Maria's good looks had made her a talking point among the

male farmers. *She was a very energetic lady with lots of hair,* said Nigel. *This guy Sir Nicholas Parr used to sit next to me at the ostrich meetings and he'd say very loudly in his posh British accent, 'I only come to these meetings to look at Maria Stevens's lovely legs.' He was deaf and didn't realize that everyone could hear and I used to be very embarrassed.*

Stevens seemed an unlikely victim for a racist attack. While some white farmers still whipped their workers and one even had a portrait of Mussolini over the fireplace, he had been regarded as a good and fair boss. With interest rates that had hit 55 per cent, and inflation more than 60 per cent, it was increasingly difficult to make a living from farming. But even though his 400-hectare farm was heavily in debt like those of most farmers, he maintained a school and beer hall for his workers and gave them 10 per cent of his earnings as an annual bonus.

It was clear that Stevens had been carefully targeted to send out a warning for another reason, and it was this that really alarmed Claire. Mugabe's proposed new constitution, which would have enabled him to seize all white land, had galvanized many white farmers into getting involved in politics for the first time since independence. They had helped the newly formed opposition Movement for Democratic Change (MDC) with funds, offices, organizational skills and transport to take workers to vote No in the referendum. This enabled Mugabe to blame a 'conspiracy of whites' for blocking his new constitution, and his spin doctor Moyo even claimed that they had brought fellow whites from South Africa for the weekend to vote.

Stevens was an active MDC supporter and had paid for his backing with his life. The reason that Claire was so worried was that Nigel too had been helping the MDC. So involved was he that an official letter from its leader Morgan Tsvangirai was on the desk in his study, authorizing him to solicit funds in South Africa.

When they got home from church, the couple sent their children outside with their maid Aqui to play on the trampoline and in the Wendy house. Their wide-screen satellite TV was usually tuned to sport but that Sunday they switched it over to news. On every channel – Sky, BBC, CNN, SABC – Zimbabwe was suddenly the headline story. The Commercial Farmers' Union had hired planes to search for the missing farmers Gemmill and Hardy, and they had finally been found and also taken to hospital in Marondera. The BBC had already interviewed some of the survivors, lying in their hospital beds, bloodied, bruised and deeply traumatized. John Osborne had an ugly black eye, and had suffered concussion, five broken ribs and a collapsed lung. 'It was unreal,' he said, breathing with difficulty. 'These guys are not playing, they are deadly serious and out of control.'

Television footage showed the blackened remains of the Stevenses' farm. It had been razed to the ground along with the couple's entire tobacco crop and many of the workers' houses. All 300 workers were now left homeless and jobless. Other farmers were filmed fleeing the area – around 50 families had left Marondera that day.

As Claire watched the reports, with the bright sun outside and the sounds of the children playing happily with Aqui, laughing and clambering over her, she felt a cold dread creep over. *I had young children and I suddenly felt very vulnerable. If it came to it, how would we know who to trust? I wanted to leave.*

That morning Mugabe had flown back from Cuba where he had been visiting his friend and ally Fidel Castro and attending a summit of developing countries. The BBC report showed him arriving at Harare airport to be greeted by large crowds of toyi-toying supporters in T-shirts bearing his bespectacled face or wrapped in bright cottons printed with cockerels.

Nigel turned up the television. *We expected him to condemn the murder and rein in the war vets.* Instead, they watched the President be warmly welcomed by the war vet leader Chenjerai Hunzvi, who had recently adopted the name Hitler. Mugabe was on fist-waving form. 'There is an expectation that I will say

Mugabe and Hitler Hunzvi

to the war veterans "Get off the land,"' he said coldly. 'I will not do that . . . we warned the white farmers not to be provocative, not to take up weapons. If you do that you will suffer the consequences.'

As he watched Mugabe speak, Nigel's usual cheerful bluster deserted him. *I realized that we were alone.* The government was not going to do anything to stop the invasions; in fact it was beginning to dawn on him that it might even be behind them. Many of the farmers whose land had been invaded had reported that the squatters had been brought in on government and army trucks.

Although the identities of the Macheke war vet leaders behind the killing of Dave Stevens were well known to the police, no action was taken for the killing of Stevens. Later, government authorities even blamed Stevens for his own murder, and claimed it was he who had provoked the violence. Mugabe told journalists: 'He was the one who started the war. He was the one who started the firing.'

What had happened to Stevens meant there was always this fear, that threat, there was now an uncertainty all the time, you never knew how far they'd go. They'd learnt the procedure where they'd go and get the guys drunk and high on mbanje. Then they'd come and jambanja you and once in that state anything could happen and you knew the authorities would do nothing.

Two days after Stevens's murder, Nigel played his weekly tennis match with some farmer friends. He was astonished when one of them asserted that Stevens had brought his death on himself by getting involved with politics, and soon found himself in a bitter argument.

I said, 'So that's his crime, that he did the right thing?' recalled Nigel. *There were a lot of mixed feelings among our community about the situation: Do you do the right thing and openly support the MDC, or should we help them and do it quietly, or should we stay away altogether like the whites had done in Kenya and say, 'It's their problem, the blacks, nothing to do with the whites, let them sort it out.' A lot of people argued that we should work with the government of the day, they're the people in power and we have to work within their system.*

Tuesday 18 April 2000, three days after Stevens's murder, was the twentieth anniversary of independence. It was a national holiday, but, far from celebrating, the white farming community watched the proceedings with trepidation, radios and mobile phones at the ready for any emergency.

Soon the radios and telephone lines were buzzing. Early that morning a second white farmer had been murdered. Forty-two-year-old Martin Olds had been surrounded at Compensation Farm in Nymandlovu near Bulawayo by around 100 war vets, some armed with AK-47s firing into the house. One of the bullets hit his leg, smashing the bone. He radioed for help but local farmers could not reach him because police roadblocks had been set up to stop them getting through. Olds managed to splint his shattered calf with a chair leg and for three hours held off his attackers by crawling from room to room firing out with a pistol.

Martin Old's burnt-out car and farm after his murder

Eventually they set his house on fire by throwing in petrol bombs fashioned from beer bottles to smoke him out. He started running a bath to escape the smoke but he was gunned down in the bathroom and forced outside. As Olds lay spread-eagled on the ground, he was shot, then hacked to death.

There was no doubt that the brutal attack was a deliberate targeted killing with the collusion of the authorities. After killing him, the attackers returned through the police roadblock waving their guns and singing liberation songs. Like Stevens, Martin Olds had been an active supporter of the MDC. He left behind a disabled wife, Kathy, and two teenage children who were away in Bulawayo during the attack.

It was not the only incident that day. Later it would emerge that the same morning the car of the MDC leader had been ambushed in Buhera and set on fire. Tsvangirai was not travelling in it but his driver and colleague were both killed.

Once again, instead of denouncing Olds's killing, Mugabe's Independence Day address to the nation was laden with anti-white rhetoric. 'What we reject is the persistence of vestigial attitudes from the Rhodesian yesteryears – attitudes of master race, master colour, master owner and master employer,' he said.

Afterwards he gave an interview to Reuben Barwe of the ZBC that left no room for doubt over what he thought of the whites. 'Our present state of mind is that you are now our enemies because you have really behaved as enemies of Zimbabwe,' he complained. 'We are full of anger. Our entire community is angry and that is why we have the war veterans seizing land.'

But far from a spontaneous uprising as Mugabe claimed, it was increasingly clear that this was an organized campaign. The war vets' trucks were brazenly left in the car park of the ZANU-PF headquarters and Hunzvi said the party had paid him 20 million Zim dollars (then about £330,000) to carry out the invasions. This was the 'Unfinished War', with prominent ZANU-PF figures and army officials from the liberation struggle directing events. One of the key organizers was Perence Shiri, head of the air force and former leader of the notorious Fifth Brigade.

He could hardly have chosen a more unpleasant figure to implement his operations than Hitler Hunzvi with his black leather trench coat and 'Ride of the Valkyries' ringtone on his mobile. Apart from his dubious war record and his ex-wife's allegations of domestic violence, his surgery in Harare was becoming notorious as a torture centre. The red-bricked building in the township of Budiriro with 'Dr CH Hunzvi' written in black over the entrance looked innocuous. But it was well known that anyone suspected of links with the opposition might be kidnapped from the streets and dragged inside to be beaten senseless with iron bars or clubs wrapped in barbed wire. Only when one man was tortured so severely that he died, sparking off riots in the township, did police intervene. No action was taken against Hunzvi.

Hunzvi himself did nothing to dispel his violent reputation. 'If the white farmers do not give us what we want they will bury themselves down six feet!' he told cheering supporters at a rally.

Despite such provocation, the white farmers' union urged their

members to show restraint and avoid confrontation, recommend-
ing in a special leaflet that 'farmers endeavour to be constructive'.
Instead the CFU leadership took the legal route to court to contest
the invasions. But the High Court order they obtained declaring
them illegal was simply ignored by the police.

By the end of April 2000, nearly 1,000 farms had been invaded
and the numbers were increasing every day. Those under occupa-
tion faced daily harassment. Throughout the country, mobs were
holding white farmers hostage inside their farms, smashing their
windows with iron bars if they tried to resist. Makeshift roadblocks were springing up – logs balanced on oil drums manned
by thugs who gave themselves names like Saddam or Napoleon
and whose telltale red eyes usually meant they were high on
mbanje. Rural Zimbabwe once more felt as if it was in a state of
war, dark columns of smoke rising from burning fields.

With the President having declared farmers as enemies of state,
ZANU-PF offices being used as headquarters for invasions, and
the police refusal to uphold the court order, more and more
farmers started to flee. Rumours abounded. According to one of
the most widely believed, all the whites were going to be killed
en masse on Easter Sunday. Trucks packed up with household
contents started to be a regular sight, and auction houses were
doing a flourishing trade in velour sofas, tasselled lampshades
and Andy Williams LPs.

First thing every morning, long queues formed outside the
British High Commission in Harare to apply for passports. Many
had relinquished theirs because Mugabe had made it illegal to
retain two nationalities. But the British government had revealed
it had plans for the evacuation of its 20,000 citizens in Zimbabwe
and everyone wanted to book their place on the plane out if it
came to that. White farmers who had never queued for themselves
in their lives stood meekly in line for hours.

Farm invaders

The British evacuation plan was a sign of just how powerless
Tony Blair's government had found itself in trying to contain the
Zimbabwean President. Mugabe had always been an Anglophile,
a professed admirer of the Queen, and a lover of cricket which
he described as 'a game that civilizes people and creates gentlemen'. Once he was even rumoured to be trying to purchase a
castle in Scotland. But when he met Blair at the Commonwealth
Summit in Edinburgh in 1997 just after the Labour leader had
become Prime Minister, the two men had not got on at all. The
relationship soured further when Clare Short, the International
Development Secretary, wrote a tactless letter to Mugabe's Agriculture Minister, stating that the Blair government did not accept
it had any responsibility to meet the cost of land reform in Zimbabwe, despite what had been agreed at Lancaster House in 1979.
'We are a new government from diverse backgrounds without
links to former colonial interests,' she wrote. 'My own origins are
Irish and as you know we were colonized not colonizers.'

Mugabe had, however, struck a chord with Peter Hain, the

ambitious junior Foreign Office minister. The perma-tanned Hain saw himself as a son of Africa, having been born in Kenya and active in the fight against apartheid as well as leading demonstrations against Ian Smith's Rhodesia. The two men had a long meeting on 31 October 1999 during a visit to London, with Mugabe affectionately slapping Hain's knee by the end. But the following morning, as Mugabe emerged from St James Court Hotel in Buckingham Palace Gate to enter his limousine with Grace for a shopping trip in Harrods, his right arm was grabbed. His assailant was the Labour activist Peter Tatchell, who had been inspired by the arrest of the former Chilean dictator General Pinochet in a London hospital the previous year while recuperating from minor surgery. 'President Mugabe, you are under arrest for torture!' yelled Tatchell. 'Torture is a crime under international law!'

Zimbabwe's President visibly shook with rage. He was not used to coming in contact with the public; by then his motorcade had grown to 22 vehicles, including truckloads of crack bodyguards bearing AK-47s, and it had so many motorcycle outriders that locals referred to it as Comrade Bob and the Wailers. Worse still, Tatchell was a militant gay rights campaigner and Mugabe abhorred homosexuals, referring to them as 'worse than pigs and dogs'.

As a dictator himself, to Mugabe it was unthinkable that such a thing could happen without Blair's approval, particularly as a Sky TV crew had been on hand to film the incident. He immediately denounced the Blair government as 'little men' and accused the British Prime Minister of 'using gay gangster tactics'. Hain he described as 'the wife of Tatchell'.

From then on, the Zimbabwean leader would lose no opportunity to irritate Whitehall. A few months later, he ordered customs officials at Harare airport to break open a British diplomatic bag in breach of international law. This prompted Hain to appear before television cameras on the steps of the Foreign Office and thunder, 'This is not the act of a civilized country.'

To call Mugabe 'uncivilized' was one of the most provocative things he could have said to an African leader, and played right into his hands. Hain's unfortunate words enabled the Zimbabwe President to portray himself as the upstart leader whom the old imperial power could not stomach. They would make it extremely difficult for any African leader to be seen to be supporting the British against him and indeed only Mandela would dare criticise him.

In the increasingly paranoid mind of Mugabe, Blair was lumped with white farmers as part of the great conspiracy against Zimbabwe along with trade unions, non-governmental organizations, the World Council of Churches, the IMF and the BBC. It was a remarkably similar 'axis of evil' to that which was once the bane of his white predecessor Ian Smith. Barely a Mugabe speech went by without a tirade against the British Prime Minister, and the fact that the mobile latrines used in much of the country were called Blair Toilets would be endlessly milked.

Britain seemed to be at a loss on how to react. Development aid was frozen and a shipment of donated Land Rovers withheld. But Blair would soon be far too involved in the aftermath of 9/11 and the war on terror to focus on a small bankrupt African state with a pesky leader.

Some farmers were calling for foreign intervention, but Nigel was quite sure this would never happen. *We had no oil or resources that really mattered to anyone. To the Blair government we white farmers were a hangover from colonial times, almost an embarrassment. Just like during the war we were on our own.*

Networks of support were set in place as they had been during the bush war, with so-called Godfathers responsible for each area. No one went anywhere without a radio or mobile phone. Farmers and their families took to sleeping in tracksuits and shoes and had backpacks ready packed with torches, Swiss army knives, compass, matches, ammunition, bandages and their most important personal papers.

As in the war, the CFU began issuing sit-reps, at first weekly, then daily, with lists of violent incidents in each province. Stress seminars were organized and the Marondera Club held a two-day Medical Air Rescue Service course in which the unit on snakebites was replaced with one on treating gunshot wounds and setting up a makeshift drip.

The Houghs started keeping their gates locked during the day as well as at night. Every morning there was a roll call over the radio of the 24 farms in Wenimbi Valley. One by one their neighbours started radioing the chilling words, 'They have arrived,' and Nigel and the other men would rush to help. Although Kendor Farm had remained untouched, the mood was tense. Nigel's involvement with the MDC hovered over them like a warning sign. *There was a feeling we were overtly political. People backed off from us.*

I was nervous, very nervous, said Claire. *Every time there was an attack on a white farm in their area we heard everything on the radio so we were aware all the time what was going on, we heard everything, guys screaming, 'They're at the door, they're at the door, we're going to shoot!' I knew that what Nigel was doing was the right thing to do but I worried about the consequences.*

As the centre for growing tobacco, still Zimbabwe's most lucrative export, Marondera was becoming the front line in the battle for land. The fact that it was only an hour's drive outside Harare made its farms particularly in demand. Gangs rampaged along the North Road only a mile or so from the centre of town, and there were stories of horrific beatings in workers' compounds, of men being abducted and women raped. Deserted farms were turned into re-education centres. Workers would be rounded up en masse in stolen trucks and trailers and forced to chant ZANU-PF slogans and songs through the night. During these *pungwes*, lists of people said to be MDC supporters would be read out and those individuals beaten and whipped.

Claire was particularly shaken when one day on the radio she heard the cries of her friend Joanna Faber who had been surrounded by war vets as she drove into the yard of workshops and barns in her farm. They surrounded her and she was trapped inside for two or three hours while the guys were rocking the car back and forth, all broadcast over the airwaves.

I sat glued to the radio following everything. Men from the area went there but couldn't get to her because of the war vets. Then the army had come and formed a cordon around the farmers. It seemed like a set-up so that the farmers would shoot and then the army could move in on them. It always seemed like a set-up but amazingly it never ignited.

In May 2000, a month after David Stevens's murder, Sidney Sekeremayi, the much-feared Security Minister, held a rally in his constituency of Marondera. That morning the entire town was closed down by ZANU-PF youths. Buses were prevented from leaving and youth militia went from door to door ordering people to attend. Some of Nigel's workers were among the 10,000-strong crowd. Once there, they were not allowed to leave.

Those present were left in little doubt about what might happen to anyone daring to vote against the ruling party in the June elections. With a flourish, Comrade Sekeremayi produced fifty MDC T-shirts, some heavily stained with blood. 'If we eventually find that you are lying to us, we shall meet each other,' he thundered. 'Like we say in the Shona proverb, you can't hide from the truth for ever. After the votes we will see who has been fooling who and we shall deal with each other.'

A few days later, on 24 May 2000, Mugabe signed a decree empowering the government to seize farms without paying compensation. These, he said, would be distributed after the elections.

A list of 805 farms to be seized was published in the *Herald* on Friday 2 June:

> 'NOTICE is hereby given in terms of subsection (1) of section 5 of the Land Acquisition Act [Chapter 20:10] that the President intends to acquire compul-

sorily the land described in the Schedule for resettlement purposes . . .'

The announcement was followed by seven pages of farms – 'The List', as it became known. Like farmers all over the country, Nigel flicked through, hands shaking as he scanned the names. There seemed no pattern. Among those included were tobacco farms, cattle ranches, dairy farms, flower exporters, safari parks and producers of mini-vegetables for British supermarkets. Some were more than 30,000 hectares, others fewer than 50. Many of them were in Marondera and belonged to people they knew. As Claire waited anxiously, Nigel scanned back and forth over the pages, then breathed a sigh of relief. Kendor Farm was not on the list.

15

Zhakata's Kraal, 2001

THE RED DRALON THREE-PIECE SUITE by the side of the highway was an incongruous sight. It had clearly been looted from one of the farms that had been seized. From the bus leaving Marondera to go to her village, Aqui saw a white farmer in the briefest of shorts overseeing the loading of cows onto a truck, his face red-blotched with anger, watched by a war vet in a ZANU-PF T-shirt and Marlboro cowboy hat looked on. Alongside, the farmer's terrified wife and children stood in a huddle trying to guard a pile of belongings.

It was hard to feel sorry for those white farmers. They had air-conditioners and cars and refrigerators, ate food from packets, and went shopping in South Africa and on holiday in Mozambique. We had grown up living on leaves and locusts and walking an hour each way to fetch water and firewood. And some of them had treated our people very bad.

It seemed as if more than a hundred years after that season of drought and locust when Nehanda led the first Chimurenga against the whites, the bones of the Shona resistance leader were finally rising again as she had predicted. *When the farm invasions started we were very happy. People were saying, 'It's over against the whites, we're going to get our land back,' and planning what they would do with their land. But others would say, 'Look at this country. It's going to get destroyed.'*

Mugabe had even taken to describing the land invasions as the Third Chimurenga. 'Perhaps we made a mistake by not finishing the war in the trenches,' he told members of his party. 'We were modest and rushed to Lancaster House. If the settlers had been defeated by the barrel of the gun, perhaps we would not be having the same problems . . . Our revolution has not ended. We want it to end and the starting point is land.'

Barely a day went by without Mugabe complaining that the whites still owned 70 or 80 per cent of land. In vain the Commercial Farmers' Union kept pointing out that its 4,000 members owned 8.6m hectares, which was only 21 per cent of the land, while seven million blacks lived in communal areas covering 16.3m hectares or 41 per cent of the land, though there was no doubt that the whites had the better land.

But nobody questioned Mugabe as to why he had made so little effort to redistribute the land for the first twenty years after Independence. His government had acquired 3.5 million hectares on a willing-seller willing-buyer basis paid for by donors and created a number of Chinese-style collective farms to resettle people, but almost all had ended up wrecked and abandoned and some had never been occupied.

As Aqui's bus turned off toward Hwedza, the sky blackened with smoke. By the roadside trudged a line of people with bundles on their heads or pushing barrows full of pots, pans and bedding. The driver slowed down and spoke to them. They were farm-workers who had been rendered homeless when the white farmers they worked for were evicted by war vets. The war vets had accused them of supporting the farmers and the MDC and burnt their huts down. Now they were trying to get back to the rural areas that their families had come from originally. The bus passed an entrance to a farm, the name Greenfields scrawled out with a black pen, and posters of Mugabe plastered over the gate.

The tar road ended just past the wire fence of the last farm, then they were over the dry bed of the Sabie river and into the rocky landscape of the communal lands. The bus was crammed with people, some of whom had been waiting days as the fuel shortage had left transport very sporadic. There had been no rains that year and the bus windows were all jammed closed. The white heat of an unforgiving sun turned the airless bus into an oven, cooking the smells of sour armpit, carbolic soap and stale meat pies, until temples pounded and eyes bulged. At Aqui's feet her own bags bumped around – a precious loaf of bread, a pack of sugar and a live chicken tied in a plastic bag – all gifts from the Houghs.

She was relieved when the dark bulk of the Daramombe Moun-tains finally loomed into view on the right-hand side which meant they were nearly there. Aqui was going back home for her brother's funeral. The Houghs had let her have the weekend off, even given her money for the bus fare as well as food for the funeral party. *Boss Hough and Madam Claire weren't like other whites. They treated me almost like part of the family.*

Aqui did not know what she would have done if it had not been for getting the job with the Houghs. *They were good people, paying for my asthma medicine and for my children to go to school.* They were paying for her to do a cookery course. They even ran an orphanage for the growing number of AIDS orphans left by farm-workers and gave them milk from their own cows. Aqui had heard that one person was dying of the disease every 15 minutes* and most of her neighbouring families in Dombotombo had lost a mother, father or brother or had someone lying ragdoll-like on a bed as life seeped away from them. People were even forming burial clubs, macabre saving schemes modelled on Christmas clubs so their children could afford to bury them in ever more crowded cemeteries. In many families both parents had died, and aunts and uncles too, leaving children as young as seven to become heads of households. Yet she knew that many men like her late brother

The way to the village

* By 2005, according to Unicef, the country had 1.3 million AIDS orphans and 318,000 child-headed households.

refused to use condoms, believing that AIDS was a myth propagated by whites to keep down the black birth rate. Some even believed the way to get rid of it was to sleep with young virgins.

The bus cranked to a halt at the Sadza growth point from where Aqui walked for the three hours across the land of the dead and the thorn bushes to the village. She was exhausted by the time the old sacred muchakata tree came into view and the line of huts, and she felt something was different but was not sure what it was. Then she realized. She could not hear the thump of the hard *mukonono* wood pestle against the softer *mukuyu* block, the sound of grinding millet that she used to listen out for as a child coming back from school to know she was almost home.

Some children appeared and ran ahead to tell her mother she was coming.

'*Mangwanani*,' Aqui called in greeting and they dropped their heads shyly, mumbling back, '*Mangwanani*.'

Aqui's mother outside her hut

Her mother was waiting at the door of her hut, wrapped in a luminous pink shawl that Aqui had given her. As Aqui handed over her gifts, she clapped one hand over the other then took the bags in both arms to indicate how generous it was. Inside, Aqui crouched on the ground by the fire in the middle, not on the bench around the side where the men sit, and let her eyes accustom to the smoke. She noticed the poles that framed the doorway were worn and exposed like bone. But there was a new shiny black floor and shelves. Her mother explained that one of the villagers had found a stone in the river, which if you ground it with the mud from the anthills, gave this pewter-like sheen, and now they were all using it.

She had been looking forward to her mother's sadza and perhaps some pumpkin leaves but could see there was nothing in the pot over the fire. Her mother noticed her looking and smiled wryly.

Inside the hut

'No food,' she said. 'Even the store has no mealie meal and I have killed my last goat for the funeral.'

Life seemed much harder than when I was growing up. The store was empty. There were no more mobile clinics to vaccinate children and men who were away working on the farms were coming back with empty hands.

Soon her mother's hut was filled with aunts and others come to see Aqui back and express their condolences. Many of them had white rashes from vitamin deficiency. It took time for each person to have his or her say, and everyone seemed to think that her brother had died of TB. Then they asked after her children and her 'top-flight administrative job' and she smiled, knowing her mother had been exaggerating. In turn she asked about the situation in the village and they told her that the previous year during the campaign for the elections the candidate had held a meeting at the growth point and they had all been told to go and they would get food. The store was now run by a ZANU councillor and you needed to show a party card to get maize, but the villagers were all ZANU members anyway.

The biggest problem was that the rains had not come. Just that day the elders had sent young virgin girls to get the water from the well and grind the rapoko to make beer for the an-cestors. *This would be brewed by the oldest women who were no longer sleeping with their husbands, offloaders we call them. This beer should have no men inside.* Once the beer had been made, the women would leave it under the tree about four or five in the afternoon. The elders would then come back the next morning to check the pots to see if the beer had been drunk by the spirits. *Usually the pot would be only half full and every-one would start clapping their hands, beating drums, whistling and shouting, saying the ancestors have accepted the beer so we are going to have some rains. I was too suspicious about where the beer had gone. Then if the rains didn't come they would say something had been done wrong in the brewing of the beer.*

Aqui walked down to the fields where the dried maize stood in sharp brown stalks like spears waiting for battle, and snapped a piece off to chew. The abundant silence seemed to hold too many memories, both good and bad. In these fields belonged the dreams she had had as a girl and the injustice that had burned inside over her brother being allowed to stay at school and being granted his own plot of land by the chief while she got nothing. None of it seemed to matter now.

The sun fell behind the Daramombe Mountains and Aqui was startled out of her thoughts by a strange flapping sound. At the other end of the field she could see a tall man from the village who had recently returned penniless after the farm he had worked on for twenty years was taken over. He was waving a long stick at the birds flying round and round in the fast-falling dark. She wasn't sure why. Nothing was growing and there were no longer any cows. She could not help thinking of Boss Nigel's farm with its green fields of tobacco and maize, water so plentiful that it filled a swimming pool and thousands of silly lolloping ostriches.

Back in the village, people were retelling the old stories of Nehanda and talking excitedly about how they would soon be getting plots of good land where they could grow wheat, tobacco and cotton like the white man. After the previous year's elections, Mugabe had announced a so-called Fast Track scheme where groups of poor blacks would be taken to a white farm and the land shared out among them. A ZANU official had come through the village and told them to put their names down, and that once land had been designated a truck would come and take them there. But they had heard no more. Villagers knew that Aqui had been a party official and thought she would know when the truck was coming.

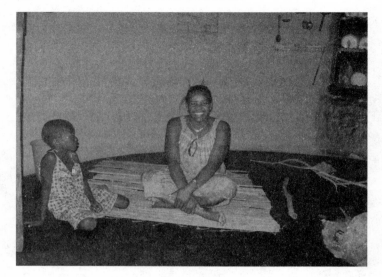

Aqui in her mother's hut

Aqui had also put her name down on such a list. *I agreed with the fact that the land should be shared, particularly as there were those whites who were greedy and had vast farms or three or four farms they weren't even using. But because I worked on a farm I knew that to be an owner you had to be very experienced and have lots of capital. I didn't agree with the idea that people with nothing could come in and just take over.*

She could not help remembering the words of her late *mhondoro* grandmother who warned: 'It is the envying eye that will destroy us.' For what she had seen back in Marondera was that it was not the poor landless blacks who were being given the land. Crowds of dispossessed people who had worked on farms had flooded into Dombotombo. Many of them originated in Malawi so they had no home to go to and were sleeping in people's yards. *Twenty people in a shack again, just like in wartime.* Nor were the land invasions spontaneous, as Mugabe claimed when he told the

Herald, 'They are just demonstrating their greatest disappointment that there was this No vote [in the referendum].' Sinister
men had appeared in leather coats and bush hats, party bigwigs
and Hitler Hunzvi, the war vets' leader who had become an MP.
These were the people driving the invasions and getting the farms,
not landless poor. They were even charging locals, real war vets
like her, a hundred dollars to go and peg out plots of land which
she thought they would probably snatch back again.

If they did, nobody would complain, for fear stalked the air.
Torture, beatings and people disappearing in the night had once
again become part of life just as they had been during the liberation war. The Zimbabwe Human Rights Forum had catalogued
more than 3,100 murders, rapes and abductions during the campaign for the June 2000 elections and a further 10,000 huts burnt.
The true figures may have been ten times more. In many constituencies, opposition candidates had been completely unable to campaign. In some places such as the lakeside resort of Kariba, they
were hounded out of town and coffins erected with their names
on. Posters put up by their supporters in the dead of night were
torn down next morning by ZANU-PF militia. Mugabe had not
unleashed so much violence against his own people since the
Gukurahundi in Matabeleland, and this time the Shona too were
targeted. Even before the votes were tallied, European Union
observers (amongst whom no British had been allowed) denounced the elections as 'marred by violence and intimidation'.

Despite this carrot-and-stick combination of repression, rigging
and promises of land, the ruling party only scraped a narrow
victory. ZANU-PF won 62 seats with 48 per cent of the votes,
while the new MDC, which was just nine months old, secured 57
seats on 47 per cent of the vote. But under the constitution
Mugabe had the right to appoint a further 30 seats, giving him a
clear majority.

For Mugabe and his cohorts, this was a drastic fall compared
to almost 82 per cent of the vote in previous elections in 1995,

and there was no doubt that the people in the urban areas wanted change. The MDC had won all the seats in Harare and Bulawayo and ten of the twelve constituencies in Matabeleland. ZANU-PF had been reduced to a party dependent on rural Shona votes, retaining only one urban constituency in the whole country. Seven cabinet ministers lost their seats, including the Justice Minister Emerson Mnangagwa, who was expected to eventually succeed Mugabe. Four whites standing for MDC won their seats, despite Mugabe's vicious anti-white campaign. In Marondera, the Security Minister Sidney Sekeramayi hung on but with his majority slashed to just 61 votes even though the whole town knew that the ballot boxes had been stuffed.

The vote reflected the mood. People were not happy. By 2000 the population was 10 per cent poorer than it had been ten years earlier and the country had begun to default on its debt repayments. Zimbabwe had boasted the highest literacy rate in Africa but the number of children completing primary school had fallen from an impressive 83 per cent in 1990 to less than 63 per cent. Government spending on education had been slashed, while, without consulting parliament or cabinet, Mugabe had taken the country to a costly war 1,000 miles away in the Congo. Some 11,000 Zimbabwean troops – then still receiving British training – had been there since 1999 to prop up the tottering regime of President Laurent Kabila against Congolese rebels. Only a year later did Britain halt arm sales to Zimbabwe.

Intervening in a foreign war in which Zimbabwe had no interest, at a time when the country's finances were collapsing and the government heavily overborrowed, seemed like the sort of thing only a megalomaniac would do. Keeping the troops there was costing the country £20 million a month, and for the first time since independence Zimbabwe was in recession. But some important people were benefiting. Kabila had handed out diamond, cobalt and timber concessions to Zimbabwe's generals. The country's army chief, General Vitalis Zvinavashe, owned the haulage business that won the lucrative contract to transport supplies into Congo, and was building himself a palatial glasshouse with its own elevator on a hill in Borrowdale Brook, Harare's most prestigious private estate. Mugabe's new blue-tiled pagoda-style palace was also being built there and the local Spar supermarket stocked Johnnie Walker Blue Label, Cuban cigars and Mozambican lobsters. As if to emphasize the origins of the money, General Zvinavashe's driveway had been tiled in a diamond pattern.

Mugabe was still said to lead an ascetic life, up at 5 a.m. as he had been since prison days to use his exercise bicycle and practise his own form of yoga, and despising smoking and drinking or any form of excess. But like a spider sucking in flies, as his public support waned, Mugabe seemed to encourage those around him to indulge in corruption and looting to retain their support. ZANU-PF had acquired numerous businesses and increasingly the country was being run by a mafia, many of whom had joined in the farm snatching with great enthusiasm. Through his ever-expanding secret police, Mugabe kept files on them all and would pull them out the moment anyone showed signs of disloyalty.

Aqui's favourite singer, Thomas Mapfumo, had been forced to flee the country after criticizing this corruption in his new album *Chimurenga Explosion*. With lyrics like 'the beautiful country that Mugabe has turned to hell', he also questioned why the government was spending so much on someone else's war when its own people were perishing in hospital through lack of drugs. One of the country's top musicians, Mapfumo had been a great supporter of Mugabe during the liberation struggle and was even jailed by Smith in 1979. Yet now his songs were banned on the radio using the very same Censorship and Entertainment Control Act that Smith had introduced in 1967, and he had fled to America.

Most ordinary people kept their words to themselves. But no one could hush the news of what happened in Yugoslavia in

October 2000 where people had come out into the streets of Belgrade to occupy parliament and overthrow Slobodan Milosevic, and it gradually percolated though the cities. Mugabe was said to have kicked his television in anger when he saw the news and ordered a steel ring of roadblocks round the main cities of Harare and Bulawayo, which were well designed by the colonial regime to be easily sealed off. But unlike Yugoslavia, most Zimbabweans had no access to independent media. The opposition was scared of which way the army and police would go, and anyone who spoke out soon regretted it. The government had its eyes and ears everywhere and people had even been arrested for criticizing Mugabe on a bus. The *Daily News*, the only daily independent newspaper, which had been launched in 1999, had been bombed in January 2001, destroying its printing press.

In the increasingly ludicrous state *Herald*, Mugabe blamed the economic crisis on Britain, from the fuel shortage, which he said was caused by Royal Navy submarines intercepting oil tankers bound for Zimbabwe, to poisoning fish in Lake Kariba. The revelation that Whitehall had a contingency plan to evacuate all 20,000 British citizens was interpreted by ZBC as a massive military operation to be launched from Botswana for the 'reconquest' of Zimbabwe.

Aqui did not really believe this. The radio was pumping out so much Rwanda-style hate-speak against the whites, yet those she had come into contact with had treated her well. *You could no longer be sure of getting facts from the radio. If something was green the radio reported it as yellow. If it was brown they called it white.*

She thought about the Houghs, the way Boss Nigel asked her about her life and what she thought about things, even discussing her doubts about the Old Testament. She knew he was involved in the MDC, that he went out at night with some of the farmworkers putting up *Chinja* stickers. She knew Madam Claire was scared about this and saw the way she hugged her children close each time more news came that another farm nearby had been

Mugabe and Grace in his open-top Rolls Royce

invaded by men with pangas and names like Comrade Slit-eyes or Comrade Double-trouble. She felt bad for them that they might lose their farm.

But then she thought about her people in Zhakata's Kraal with their bare shelves and standing under the sacred tree calling to the spirits for rains. She thought about the ageing President, his skin like a turtle's, haunted they said by the ghost of General Tongogara, the murdered commander of the bush war. She imagined Mugabe alone in his big palace with his shopaholic wife, rumoured to be kept under house arrest after being caught in the embrace of another, poring over the latest catalogues from Harrods, while he sent troops off to far-away lands. She thought about her born-free children, growing up now with no signs of the jobs as accountants, nurses or top-flight secretaries that she had imagined. It was clear that nothing was going to change unless you did it for yourself. *Of course I wished I had a house like the Houghs instead of this small shack, all squashed up like a nest.* Then she checked herself. *Jealousy doesn't work. It makes you destroy people.*

16

Kendor Farm, May 2002

OUT OF THE CORNER OF HIS EYE, Nigel could see them building their huts at the bottom of the garden. Their leader was a short, pugnacious man who called himself General Tongogara after the commander of the liberation fighters in the bush war who had died in Mozambique. He was strutting around directing things, though clearly unsteady on his feet after a night's carousing. Yet again that morning, Nigel had found the carcass of one of his cattle, all the meat pulled off. They had cut down several of his beautiful trees for poles for their huts and firewood.

The reign of fear of the war vets had been going on across Zimbabwe for more than two years. It had not stopped with the elections in June 2000, or even the death from AIDS of Hitler Hunzvi* in June 2001. Nor had it stopped after the presidential elections of March 2002 that had seen the 78-year-old Mugabe elected for another six years in a vote so rigged that Britain, the US, the EU and even the Commonwealth had refused to recognize the result. Before the elections the head of the European observer mission had been expelled. The EU had reacted by imposing sanctions on Mugabe and 19 others including the army chief,

---

* Hunzvi, master of torture, was declared a national hero and given a state funeral, then buried in Heroes' Acre.

Wilfred Marimo, leading war vet

preventing them from travelling in Europe and freezing their assets. But Nigel knew that would not stop him.

Nigel no longer thought that the farm invasions were just an electoral ploy; that no government would deliberately destroy the farms that fed and employed its people; and that things would soon go back to normal. This was war, as the President had said – 'a real war, a total war' – and his main enemy was clear. 'The white man is not indigenous to Africa,' he told rallies. 'Africa is for Africans.'

It was only the Houghs left now in Wenimbi Valley. The area had turned into a battlefield with roadblocks everywhere manned by youths in red bandannas and Mugabe T-shirts, all high on *mbanje*. A war vet called Wilfred Marimo was directing the invasions in between giving interviews to foreign journalists and asking them to post their articles to his family in Norway. There was no more morning roll call on the radio as all the other 23 farms in the valley had been taken over so there was no one to call out for help.

Every evening before they went to bed Nigel checked all the doors and windows in the house, but he knew that if the war vets wanted to get in with their axes, *pangas* and guns, no amount of locks or burglar bars would stop them. The eight-bedroomed house that he and Claire had loved so much, and planned to fill with children, was starting to feel like a prison. Claire had stopped going for walks round the farm or using the swimming pool because she felt threatened. But Nigel refused to let his wife pack and had even encouraged her to put up the new curtains she had wanted.

We were always hopeful we would survive. Lots of people had packed up their stuff and moved it to Harare or lived out of boxes, but we never did. We hadn't packed a thing. It felt like that would be giving in to them.

At night they lay in bed listening to the drumming and chanting outside, wondering if it was getting nearer or if that was just the way the wind was blowing. Nigel knew the war vets were rounding up his workers to sing liberation songs. He found himself having

The Hough family behind their locked gate

to shout at them to do things because they were coming to work so tired and sluggish after being kept up all night. Henry, his farm manager, told him they had no choice. Nigel supposed he and Claire were lucky. In some places white farmers and their wives had been marched out of their houses and made to dance and chant ZANU slogans. His friend Roy Bennett's wife Heather had miscarried her baby after war vets abducted her at knifepoint and forced her to dance for hours in the rain.

The arrival of the war vets at the bottom of the garden had made the Houghs suddenly very aware of being the few surrounded by the many. It was a sensation similar to what the first settlers must have experienced when the Shonas, whose land they had taken, began hacking down the people they called 'strangers'.

It was the same madness that I had felt years before, landing in my plane in Burundi when the genocide had just taken place next door in Rwanda. There was that smell of fear and everyone edgy and the feeling of being on your guard but not knowing what against. In Burundi a few days later the killings had begun.

So far the war vets on the Houghs' farm were no more than a nuisance, chopping down trees and stealing pumps and equipment. Occasionally General Tongogara lurched over to the door and asked for 'donations' of meat or maize, saying, 'Aah, we are too hungry,' in a very proper British accent. When Nigel asked to see his war veteran's card, he became very angry and shouted, 'We are the really war veterans.'

I knew it was a bit pointless refusing, they would only kill another one of the cattle, but it was just to feel I still had some power over the situation.

It was not easy living in fear. One evening the family were having supper when the house was suddenly plunged in darkness. *We thought this is it, but it turned out that the war vets had stolen the electrical cable.* Sometimes at night the roof would creak or a twig snap and they would wake, hearts thumping. Claire kept imagining she was seeing a figure at the window that melted away

again. *The endless stream of anti-white propaganda whenever you turned on the radio was really getting to us.* Everyone was snapping at each other and the children had grown clingy, biting at their sleeves and reluctant to go to school or nursery in case their parents were not there when they came back. Even the ostriches seemed to sense that something was wrong.

Ostriches are highly strung beasts and very stupid, with a brain the size of a chicken's. The security fence had three horizontal wires along the top and they kept poking their heads out between two of the wires then twisting round and trying to get them back through the other and suffocating.

The Houghs had 3,000 ostriches on the farm and Nigel worried that the stress would start killing them off. *Ostriches have no more ability to defend themselves than a chicken and, because of their size and the fact that they are roaming around outside, they are much more exposed to the environment, so vulnerable to lots of diseases. I was watching them all the time. What was going into the system and what was coming out and also their mood, if they seemed a bit listless. Any signs of a problem, I would isolate that ostrich. We once*

Trying to herd an ostrich

had Newcastle's disease go through the flock and it wiped out 400 or 500.

Apart from keeping ostriches, cattle, sheep and chickens, they also grew tobacco. Nigel should have been preparing the winter seedbeds but did not know if they would still be on the farm by harvest time. He had already loaded ten of their twenty remaining

Megan's Christening on the farm

cows onto a truck for slaughter. *We were losing them at the rate of one a week so there seemed no point in keeping them.* Much of the milk went for the orphans at the orphanage so he was reluctant to send away more.

When he was really depressed, he would go to the msasa trees overlooking the rocks where they had christened their four children, including the most recent, little blonde Meggie, only the previous year.

It was this that had made them fall in love with the farm from the start. *There was this drive down the valley through the msasa trees and stunning granite rocks, then you came to the highest point in the area and could see thirty miles in all directions over this canopy of msasas. We both just loved it.*

There was something spiritual about the place amid the trees and the strange slabs of stone. There he would feel close to God. He sat on a rock and thought about all he had gone through, the good and the bad, the bankruptcies, the ostriches in China, and the happiness of meeting Claire, to have this. They had sunk everything they had into the farm; gone without holidays or the jewels he would like to have bought for his wife, to buy feed for the ostriches and to make a legacy for their children in the country that was their home. He was determined not to let General Tongogara and his bunch of thugs take it over and destroy it.

Once it had become clear that the farm invasions were not going to stop, Nigel had been to England where Claire's brother and sister were living to think about moving there, but could not face living *so squashed up under such small skies.* Like many white farmers, his brother had moved to Australia, and under pressure from Claire he had started the process of applying for visas. But he could not imagine leaving the land that felt so much a part of him.

This was the best farming land in Africa. Zimbabwean farmers held world records for yields in cotton, wheat, soya and tobacco production. Everyone called it the breadbasket of southern Africa. But since the farm invasions had started in 1999, the annual production of its staple crop, maize, had fallen from 1.5 million tonnes (most of its yearly need of 1.8m) to less than 200,000, little more than enough for a month. The number of cows had fallen by more than half, causing a shortage of milk. Apart from feeding the nation, the commercial farms had produced 40 per cent of export earnings, and provided jobs and homes for 350,000 workers (supporting more than a million people) as well as another 250,000 seasonal labourers. As he walked back across his farm, Nigel just could not believe that any nation's ruler, however despotic, would let all that go to waste. Yet, as each day passed, more farms were being taken over.

The land was bone-dry, crunching underfoot, for the rains had failed that season and he wondered why the blacks, with all their beliefs in spirits, did not see why the gods might be angry. Everyone knew that the drought was not the main reason for the shortage of food or the 200 per cent inflation or the fact that the Zim dollar, which at independence had been stronger than the British pound, was now worth less than 1p. Very little farming was going on at the farms that had been seized. The invaders had been dumped there with no inputs such as seeds or fertilizer and absolutely no idea about running a large farm. He had seen some of them trying to plough these enormous farms of thousands of hectares with just a donkey and plough. High-tech irrigation systems had been pulled up and sold for scrap metal and thick black smoke billowed across the land from their fires as they reduced state-of-the-art commercial farms to large slash-and-burn subsistence plots. Even the farmhouses had been destroyed. The new inhabitants were tearing out baths and toilets, removing window frames and even stripping electrical fittings, all to sell.

Nigel knew the situation had been unfair, with whites still owning most of the best land. *But I had done all I could to be a model farmer.* He had given land at nominal rent to a local black mechanic, Mr Chirashi, who had repaired his tractor and told him he had nowhere to graze his cows. Their factory employed 150 workers and they were training local people and exporting their products to earn valuable foreign currency. With one in three of his workers dying of AIDS, he had founded an orphanage for the children of deceased farm labourers. He had helped set up a school in Marondera and was the chairman of a local employment creation committee that had enabled hundreds of students to start up projects.

I had done everything I could for the local community. On every single criterion the government said it had for keeping your farm, I passed, except for one thing. I'm white.

But he could not ignore the fact that the situation was getting worse and worse. Over the previous two years, more and more lists had been published in the *Herald* of farms designated for expropriation. Each time he would search with dread for the name Kendor Farm. More than 3,000 farmers had been issued eviction notices giving them 30 days to leave. Nigel's brother and his sisters had all had their farms taken over, as had Claire's sister and brother-in-law. But even those not on the list were being tormented by war vets, stopped from planting, their fences removed and sold, their trees cut down. Like Nigel, each morning farmers would find carcasses of dead cattle or discover that their children's ponies had had their legs broken, forcing them to be put down.

The relentless harassment was causing marriages to break down, families to turn on each other, and producing many new chain-smokers. Many whites were leaving, not only those who had been turfed off their land. Others just fled, unable to bear the tension of wondering when it would be their turn for the door to be broken down, leaving them running for their lives. No one wanted to be added to the statistic of 13 white farmers already killed.* One cattle farmer down in Mazowe valley drowned himself by walking into the dam after his farm was seized. Nigel had heard of one case where a farmer had just walked into his bank manager's office, flung the keys of his farm on the desk and said, 'I've had enough.'

It was not just whites fleeing; there was also an exodus of black professionals, doctors, accountants, teachers and nurses.† *Sometimes I wondered if Mugabe wanted to reduce the country to a nation of peasants.* One of the President's closest allies had said as much. Didymus Mutasa, secretary for administration in the Politburo, told journalists: 'We would be better off with only six million people, with our own people who support the liberation struggle. We don't want these extra people.'

*   *   *

* The murder of 68-year-old Don Stewart at the end of November 2005 brought the number of white farmers killed to 18.
† According to a study by the South African church group Solidarity Peace Trust, 3.4m Zimbabweans had left the country by 2004, a number it described as 'a staggering 60 to 70 per cent of productive adults'.

Aqui playing with Oliver

As Nigel reached the house, he saw Aqui playing with the children on the lawn and smiled. *She kept us sane. Within a few months of employing her she had already become the heart of the family and within a couple of years we couldn't imagine life without her. I liked the fact she shared my faith and always had big a smile on her face. The kids adored her.*

She seemed to have endless patience. When the children had chicken pox, she would sit for hours wiping their fevered brows, and when Christian put his foot through some rotten wood, she spent hours picking all the chagga worms out of his feet. She was always good-humoured even though Nigel knew she had had many problems in her life. *I guess what surprised me most was how bright she was. You never had to explain things twice to her.*

He liked to talk to Aqui about the differences between blacks and whites and was fascinated when she replied, 'Jealousy.' *She insisted to me that whites don't get jealous in the same way as blacks. That was one of the reasons when the black guys seized the farms they always stripped the houses, otherwise someone would get jealous and come and take it from them. Similarly if we ever gave her anything, she didn't want me to drop it off at Dombotombo because others might see and want a share.*

She told Nigel about her experiences during the war and being surrounded in a pit and spat at by the Rhodesian soldiers. *I felt guilty. It could have been me doing that.* He remembered stories told by some of his friends in the army of the terrible things they had done to the village girls, such as sticking hot pokers up their vaginas, and wondered if more had happened to her than she was saying.

He worried about what would happen to Aqui and the 300 staff and all their family members living on the farm if it were taken over. Every time he drove into Marondera, he saw farm-workers camped along the roadside, destitute after having been kicked out when the farms where they worked were taken over. Just as in the bush war, it was the rural poor who were suffering most.

Nigel was so intrigued by his conversations with Aqui that he set up a local mixed-race discussion group looking at what each race thought about the other to try and promote understanding. *It was quite funny. All the white guys said there is no industry among the blacks, they are lazy. Then all the blacks said the whites are not industrious. I was incredulous. I said, 'How can you say that? We create all the business in this country, run the mines, grow the food.' They said, 'Yes, that's what you do, you create things, but you don't actually work, you just sit and watch and we do all the work.'*

All the time he waited for his name to appear on a list. In theory, Kendor Farm did not fit the government's criteria for being taken over. Unlike some farmers who owned two or three, it was Nigel's only farm. Nor had it come from the largesse of Rhodes handing out plots to the Pioneers for just the price of a stamp and the sealing wax. He had bought it fair and square for US$350,000 and obtained a government certificate that they had no interest in acquiring it. The title deeds lay in a safe at his bank.

But Nigel knew in his heart of hearts that such legal niceties did not matter any more. The land grab had become chaotic. with people simply turning up at the gate clutching a piece of paper, often just torn from an exercise book, saying this was now their farm, whether or not it was on any list. In the beginning many of the invaders had let people take their equipment and cattle, but now farmers were lucky if they escaped with their lives.

The invasions had taken a more sinister turn with the deployment of youth militia. This was an initiative of one of Mugabe's protégés, Border Gezi, who had risen from government clerk to be Governor of Mashonaland Central. The so-called Green-bombers were unemployed young men who were drilled in ZANU-PF ideology and trained to terrify the population. Their name derived from the khaki fatigues they wore but also because a green-bomber was a species of fly that ate off faeces. Nigel had seen the Border Gezi training camps that had appeared in large white tents in rural areas and heard from his workers about their brigades roaming the townships, using broken bottles to carve the initials MDC in the backs of suspected opposition supporters or raping their women.

Farmers had long before learnt that it was no use appealing to the police. The Police Commissioner, Augustine Chihuri, was a war vet too and openly ZANU-PF and had himself seized a farm. The police had become an instrument of the party, used during the elections to torture opposition supporters. Not only were they turning a blind eye to the plight of farmers held hostage in their homes, they were actively helping the invasions.

Any chance of the courts intervening to help farmers like Nigel vanished with a government campaign to hound the Chief Justice out of office. 68-year-old Anthony Gubbay was a British-born judge whom Mugabe had appointed as Chief Justice in 1990. But at the end of 2000 the Supreme Court on which he sat along with

one other white judge, an Asian and two blacks had issued two
rulings declaring the seizure of farms illegal. They described the
resettlement programme as 'entirely haphazard and unlawful',
and went on to say that the farm occupations amounted to unfair
discrimination because the selection process was controlled by
ZANU-PF committees. Several ministers had announced that
only ZANU-PF supporters would be resettled.

It was a courageous move and it was clear that the white
judges' days were numbered when the Justice Minister, Patrick
Chinamasa, started talking about exorcising 'the racist ghost of
Ian Smith' from the judiciary. He added, 'The present compo-
sition of the judiciary reflects that the country is in a semi-colonial
state, half free, half enslaved.' Shortly afterwards around 200 war
vets invaded the Supreme Court building, shouting 'Kill the
judges!'

Eventually in July 2001, Gubbay was forced to resign after a
campaign of threats denouncing him as a 'British imperialist
agent' and a letter of dismissal appearing on the front page of the
Herald. He was replaced by a ZANU-PF loyalist, and the bench
was expanded to include three new judges. All were known supporters of the ruling party and two had been given farms. One of
the first things they did was to overturn the ruling that the land
invasions were illegal.

Senior army and police officers and the heads of intelligence
and prisons were all given farms, as was the Anglican Bishop of
Harare. For the most part the list of new owners of farms read
like a Who's Who of ZANU-PF. Joseph Msika the Vice-President,
Patrick Chinamasa the Justice Minister, Ignatius Chombo the
Local Government Minister, and Jonathan Moyo, Mugabe's chief
spin doctor, were all among the beneficiaries. Ray Kaukonde, the
Governor of Mashonaland East province, which included Marondera, turned out to have seized eight farms. Mugabe's family also
got in on the act. His sister Sabina, herself an MP, drove her
Mercedes to take over one of the country's largest dairy farms in

Norton, while his brother-in-law Reward Marufu grabbed two farms.

Nigel knew that his own political activism was making him more of a target, particularly with Mugabe describing the MDC as the 'manifestation of the resurgence of white power'. It was through his involvement in the church that Nigel had started working for the party. He had got to know fellow Christian David Coltart, an extremely brave white lawyer in Bulawayo who had helped document the *Gurukahundi* atrocities. Coltart was the party's spokesman for legal affairs and one of four whites elected as MPs in 2000.

Like Nigel, Coltart had a wife to whom he was devoted, a lovely home and four beautiful children, yet there he was, risking his life for his country. Nigel felt inspired by this mild-mannered, dedicated man whose study door bore a poster proclaiming Hope. After talking to him, Nigel decided he would like to meet Morgan Tsvangirai and was initially impressed by the MDC leader. *He seemed to represent a new kind of Zimbabwean, urban and modern. I was impressed by his wife, she's a schoolteacher, a very normal sensible person, and I felt at least he has someone behind him giving him sensible advice.*

Nigel began fundraising for the party among businessmen in South Africa. Although their President, Thabo Mbeki, continued to stand by Mugabe, South African companies were the biggest investors in Zimbabwe and increasingly worried about their neighbour's deteriorating economy. He also organized a series of talks for Tsvangirai in Cape Town and Durban, arranging through his contacts for him to stay free in hotels. *I got to know him well. For me, Morgan was a good trade unionist and a nice guy, but that was it. I didn't feel he was a real leader, definitely not the calibre of a Mandela, but at the time I thought he was the best alternative.*

Apart from raising money, Nigel became involved in cam-

Christian fishing on the farm

paigning for Tsvangirai during the presidential elections. He and some of his workers would go out in the dark on clandestine missions, putting up Tsvangirai posters and MDC stickers around Marondera, switching cars and number plates to avoid being tracked.

We would go out at night between 10 p.m. and 3 a.m. We plastered these MDC stickers showing an open hand all over Mugabe posters. Every night we would put our hand stickers over Mugabe's clenched fist, then the next day the ZANU people would go and rip them off. When they pulled off the sticker it left a white hand rather than black and they'd have to put new posters up and then we'd go out again. It was going on like this all the time.

The cat-and-mouse nature of the electioneering gave Nigel the same kind of adrenalin rush that he had felt during his school days. *I thought it was important work and I had to admit I enjoyed it. It was good fun, exciting like in the war, and there was this camaraderie because you felt you were on the right side, even though most of us had been on different sides in the past.*

Nigel had obtained some bright neon spray paint and one evening they crept into the field of a farm that had been taken over by a ZANU-PF official and sprayed all his cattle with MDC slogans.

Another evening they were driving towards Marondera when they saw a white Mercedes broken down on the road. *My guys stopped me, shouting, 'That's Wilfred Marima's car, that's Wilfred Marima's car!' Wilfred Marima was the guy in charge of farm invasions locally and everyone hated him but the black guys hated him the most. We'd made these stickers you couldn't pull off so we went and plastered his car with the MDC hands, then watched for him to come back. He was apoplectic.*

But he knew Claire worried about his MDC work and wanted him to stop, and he wondered if he was being selfish. The last thing in the world he wanted to do was hurt the woman he adored. Nigel had hoped he would be safe because of his good works in the community, helping the school, and his orphanage, but in his heart of hearts he knew it made no difference. Ian Kay's wife Kerry had worked tirelessly to try and secure awareness of and treatment for AIDS among farm labourers but that had not stopped her husband from being the target of a vicious attack that almost left him dead, or their son from narrowly escaping being blown up by a booby-trap mine.

Although Ian Kay went on to stand as MDC candidate for

Marondera, many white farmers had decided it was too risky to continue supporting the party. Allan Dunn, another white farmer who had helped the MDC, had recently joined Dave Stevens and Martin Olds on the list of those killed.

As the campaign for the presidential elections continued, Nigel had grown disillusioned with the MDC leadership. Through his church connections, he had made contact with the Republicans in the US and leading members of the Moral Majority, the fundamentalist Christian coalition that formed one of America's largest conservative lobby groups. They had put him in touch with two top election gurus, Argentinian Felipe Noguera and American Wayne Johnson, who had run campaigns all over Central and South America as well as in the US and Europe. *I went to see them in Washington and they agreed to run Morgan's campaign and I got the big tobacco guys here to agree to finance it. Then I came back here and had meetings with Morgan and David Coltart and it was agreed they'd have these guys and the tobacco companies would pay. It was going to cost US$3m and I had put a lot of pressure on the tobacco guys to come up with the money. Then with no explanation, Morgan suddenly decided to go with this other guy, a disreputable former Israeli spy based in Canada called Ari Ben-Menashe.* He never even phoned Felipe to apologize. When I spoke to Morgan's right-hand man Gandi to ask what was going on, he said, 'We thought if we hired your people, you white guys would have too much influence.' I was really disillusioned. They'd made pledges and never followed up.*

It was a decision that came back to haunt them. In February 2002, three weeks before the elections, Australian television broadcast a grainy video apparently showing Tsvangirai plotting the assassination of Mugabe in meetings in London and Montreal.

---

* Born in Iraq and educated in Israel, Ben-Menashe worked for Israel's intelligence service until 1987. He claims to have then worked as a secret adviser to Yitzhak Shamir, then Israel's Prime Minister, and sold Israeli warplanes to Iran, though this has always been denied by Israeli officials.

Two weeks later, he was charged with treason,* a crime punishable by execution.

The video had clearly been edited, but even so it seemed clear that there had been discussion with Tsvangirai about the 'elimination' of the head of state. The tape turned out to have been made by Ben-Menashe's consultancy, Dickens & Madson which, it transpired, was actually also working for Mugabe.

Despite Nigel's fury over what had happened, he carried on helping the party. But as the election day of 9 March approached, the climate of fear intensified. Thousands of people were bussed into Mugabe rallies to see their leader, in an incongruous white baseball cap, rant about Blair and Britain† and accuse Tsvangirai of planning to give the land back to the whites. By contrast, those attending MDC rallies knew they risked beatings and haveing their homes burnt down.‡ Mugabe appointed retired military officers as chief election officer and head of the electoral supervisory commission. The locations of polling stations were kept secret till two days before voting so that the MDC did not know where to deploy their agents, and the party was not allowed access to the voters' roll. The number of polling stations in urban areas was reduced so that voters would have to queue for many hours while those in rural ZANU strongholds increased. When people turned up to vote, thousands found their names missing while many dead people's names appeared, the so-called zombie votes.

Nigel and his friend Barry Percival, headmaster of the Christian

---

* He was eventually acquitted in October 2004 after a long court case clearly designed to drain him of energy and the MDC of resources and in which Ben-Menashe appeared as State witness. Ben-Menashe later told Canada's *National Post* on 25 June 2005, 'We didn't break the law but we weren't innocent bystanders either. We do break eggs to make an omelette.'

† The *Daily Telegraph* correspondent in Harare, David Blair, counted the mentions of Britain in Mugabe's speeches and estimated he averaged 43, around one every two minutes.

‡ I met many people who bore the scars of such beatings, including a terribly injured 14-year-old girl near Mutare who went to a rally to be able to report on it to her disabled father.

community school which Nigel had helped build, monitored four polling stations in Marondera. It was no easy task as the stations were far apart and the MDC election agents kept being chased out. People in the queues were subjected to harassment from ZANU-PF workers with cameras, saying, 'We know who you are.' *Yet large numbers turned out to vote. There was a real mood of bravado. You really felt there was a groundswell, a sense of it's now or never.*

So when the election results came in on 13 March declaring Mugabe the winner with 56 per cent compared to 42 per cent for Tsvangirai, the MDC leader was stunned. He declared the result 'daylight robbery' and Zimbabwe was suspended from the Commonwealth. But Mugabe stood defiant. Far from heeding international calls for a rerun of elections or talks to form a government of national unity, he unleashed a campaign of retribution against opposition supporters, more terrifying than anything that had yet been seen. As the World Food Programme declared 7 million people – more than half the population – at risk of starvation, he issued yet more lists of farms to be seized driving to Parliament in his open-top Rolls Royce. In Harare, where 75 per cent of voters had voted for Tsvangirai despite all the attempts to deter them, people waved red cards indicating Mugabe's time was up and waited for a signal from their leader. But there was nothing.

The MDC's lack of strategy came as no surprise to Nigel. *I thought they were visionless and lazy. If we white guys didn't do things for them it didn't get done. All the money was raised by us and we organized all the logistics. They said they were afraid of provoking a bloodbath but I kept saying to David, 'It's not enough to be gentle like a hawk. The scriptures say you also need to be wise like the serpent.' I had never seen Morgan as the answer for Zimbabwe; the problem was there just wasn't anyone else.*

17

Kendor Farm, 5 August 2002

IT WAS THE PHONE CALL Nigel had been dreading. He had been worried about leaving the farm to go to Harare but he had an important meeting arranged.

A week earlier a woman called Netsai had arrived at the farm gate with a group of eight war vets including her boyfriend Shasha and the one who called himself General Tongogara. 'I want to move into my house today,' she demanded, gesturing at the farmhouse. 'This farm has not been sectioned,' replied Nigel. Under the law when farms had been listed to be taken over, farmers first received a Section 5 notice declaring that the government wished to compulsorily acquire the property. They would then be issued with a Section 8, which meant the owner must leave within 90 days. Nigel had received neither.

Netsai laughed unpleasantly and pulled out a typed piece of paper stating that Kendor Farm was now hers. 'This is my farm,' she said. 'These are my ostriches. And this is my house.'

After some argument, Nigel had managed to get rid of them but they had clearly just gone off to marshal more forces. His meeting in Harare was finishing when Henry, his farm manager, telephoned to tell him that Netsai had now come back with a much larger group and they were refusing to leave. Aqui had apparently let them in the gate so they could shelter because it had started to rain. Nigel's first concern was for his family and he was relieved to hear that the two elder children, Jess and Emma, were at school and Claire had left the house to take their son Christian to nursery. Only the youngest, baby Megan, was at home with Aqui. To the Houghs' relief, Aqui had shown the presence of mind to take Megan to their friend Roseanne Percival who was on the farm running the factory and tell her to leave quickly out the back gate. Thank God for Aqui, thought Nigel, not for the first time.

By a stroke of luck, his old university friend Pete Moore was visiting. Back in the war days, he had been a member of the Rhodesian SAS. *He was cool and calculating, a great guy to have in a crisis. We drove like mad back to Marondera, and when I got home there was a fire in my driveway and these guys had all settled around the house and taken chairs and tables from the veranda and plonked themselves down as if they owned the place.*

Nigel was furious and barged his way through, shouting at them, 'You can't take my house!'

'This is not Rhodesia,' roared General Tongogara as he swayed around, clearly drunk. 'There is no space for you in this country!'

'Whites out! Whites out!' chorused the others.

Somehow Nigel and Pete managed to get through and inside the house and bolt the door. Pete ran round locking all the windows. Nigel was shaking as he called the police. He knew the local inspector who answered, but the man told him it was 'a political matter' so they could not help. He then tried the local Lands Committee, which was in charge of redistributing the farms, only to be told, 'You're not on the list so we can't do anything.'

Outside Netsai was snarling at him and to his alarm he saw that General Tongogara was waving a pistol. Then it went quiet. *They went off and got all these guys, plied them with beer and mbanje so they were rabid, then came back and started doing all their song and dance, banging a large drum, waving sticks and shouting 'Hondo' [war].* By that time there were more than 50 of them.

That's when he saw Aqui. *To my horror I realized that Aqui had joined the group and seemed to be its leader. I couldn't believe it. Not Aqui. I don't think I had ever felt so betrayed.*

The war vets began rattling the windows. There was a sound like a shot and Nigel and Pete looked at each other in horror. *It was hard not to think of Dave Stevens and Martin Olds and all those other guys who had been killed in their houses.* Then he realized it was the sound of breaking glass. *They were trying to get in.* Desperately, he called his friend Barry Percival, headmaster of nearby Langley Park School, begging him to get the police. Claire, who was staying with the Percivals, came on the line. *While I was on the phone they started breaking down the door. We had a grille so they couldn't get through. Claire could hear the noise in the background and was really worried so I tried to be cool and joke, 'I don't think we need TV any more, we've got enough entertainment.' But I could tell she was terrified.*

As darkness fell, the group surrounding the house swelled to more than a hundred and the drumming became more persistent. 'Whites out! Blacks in! Whites out! Blacks in!' came the chant.

There were still no signs of police. Nigel took out candles and torches in case they managed to cut off the power.

'Let's see what weapons you have because we might need to start shooting and we need a strategy,' said Pete.

'Pete, I don't think that's the right way to go,' replied Nigel.

'Listen, I don't care what happens, if those characters break down this door, I'll start shooting,' replied his friend.

Reluctantly Nigel unlocked his gun cabinet.

'How many guns do you have?' asked Pete.

'Two.'

'How many bullets do you have?'

'About 150.'

Nigel remembered his school lessons about Allan Wilson and

the Shangani patrol killed by the Ndebele as they sang the national anthem.

I didn't want to die like a hero. I didn't want to die.

A few miles away at the Percivals' house, Claire and the Percivals had been repeatedly calling the police with no success. There was no way they were going to intervene in a farm seizure. In the end Barry drove to Marondera to plead with the police and tricked them into accompanying him by telling them it was a domestic situation with a man about to kill his wife. A policeman and four reservists went with him to the farm.

The police went to the back door and Barry telephoned Nigel to let them in. Outside the crowd surged forth, yelling 'Hondo! Hondo! [War! War!]' and trying to push their way through. *It was awful to see my own workers among the war vets. I went to talk to two guys among the group whom I'd helped a lot, my own farm-worker Wonedzi and another guy Norman, who worked for my neighbour.*

'Wonedzi, how could you do this after all we've done for you?' he asked. 'And Norman, I got you that job, how could you do this?'

The men said nothing.

The police managed to calm the crowd down, but were clearly not pleased to have been tricked into coming out.

'This farm has not been sectioned,' said Nigel. 'Can't you get rid of these guys?'

The policeman smiled. 'We have not had a directive,' he said.

After the police had left, the war vets began singing and dancing again, rattling the windows all around. As Nigel peered out, he could see Aqui there in the thick of it, shouting, 'Blacks in! Whites Out!' and 'Down with whites!'

To me it looked like she was leading the lot. I said, 'I don't want to ever talk to her again. I've trusted her as a member of the family and can't believe she is doing this.'

He thought about all they had done for her, the medical insurance, the school fees for her children, the uniforms, even sending her second daughter Valerie on a secretarial course. Aqui herself they had just sent for some cookery lessons.

It was not just the money but the utter sense of betrayal. *You have these people as part of your life, they are exposed to all your private stuff, you trust your children to them, then that day you suddenly see her transformed into this rabid character leading the pack of war vets shouting 'Get out, whites!' and 'Death to whites!' I wanted to kill her.*

The two men stayed awake all night, terrified of what might happen. Nigel opened a bottle of whisky but they drank little, wanting to keep their wits about them. The war vets had lit several fires all around. At times the sound seemed to swell and they were sure the group were going to burst in. Then there would be a brief lull and he could hear the strange cries of the ostriches in the distance. He hoped the birds were all right. At about 5.30 a.m. the first streaks of pink lightened the sky and the group started singing again. But this time they seemed a little subdued. *They were clearly tired and hung-over and you could sense a lot of tension building up.* One of Nigel's must trusted workers, Bennett, phoned to tell him that both the workers he had spoken to had died in the night. Wonedzi had had a heart attack about two hours later and Norman had gone home and hanged himself in his room.

I knew these guys have a hang of a lot of superstition about these things. I could see they were all full of fear and subdued.

There had been a lot of talk that ZANU-PF was haunted after three of the main driving forces behind the land invasions had died over the last year. First Hitler Hunzvi, then Border Gezi, the man behind the Green-bombers, and Moven Mahachi, the Defence Minister, both apparently in car crashes.

To wind them up, Nigel opened the kitchen window and deliberately asked Shasha about the two missing men.

'No, they are dead,' replied the war vet, clearly irritated.

'What, and you guys are still carrying on with this thing, despite that?' asked Nigel. Aqui had disappeared and he could see some of the crowd looked distinctly uncomfortable though they still waved their sticks at him, menacingly.

But the intimidation continued. Someone started up a new chant, clearly remembered from the presidential elections.

'Down with whites!'

'Down with colonialism!'

'Down with Britain!'

'Down with Blair!'

'Down with the cup he drinks his tea from!'

For two days we were locked in that house, being moved further and further in. We were really scared, not sleeping, and thought in the end we'd have to turn our weapons on them. It was quite clear that Aqui was on the other side and I couldn't bear to think about that.

'It was like a game where everyone knew that the final outcome would be Nigel losing his farm,' said Pete Moore. 'The question was just how long it would take. Although it was terrifying I never really thought we would die.'

Finally, more policemen came, led by Inspector Julius Chikunda whom Nigel knew as a ZANU-PF henchman. The two white men were told they were under arrest and should follow in Nigel's pick-up to the office of the Member in charge of lands in Marondera. Netsai, Shasha and about eight others all piled into the back of his vehicle. *It was surreal, driving all these characters who were stealing my farm to the place where I knew the war vets had tortured people.*

On the way through town, they passed a number of boarded-up shops and businesses. As the centre of one of the country's biggest agricultural districts, Marondera had been full of small businesses dependent on farmers, from spare parts suppliers to cheese shops. Now even Marondera Egg Mart had a sign declaring 'No Eggs'. Nigel resisted the temptation to point out to his companions the effects of the government's ill-planned land reform.

The Land Office was small and they all crowded in behind Chikanda. He took a seat behind the desk and looked at Nigel and Pete with contempt. 'The People don't like white farmers gathering together in groups,' he announced, even though there were only two of them surrounded by ten war vets. He insisted on separating the two white men, placing Pete the other side of a wall. But the wall was only plyboard and did not reach to the ceiling so Pete could hear everything.

'I want to speak to you farmers,' he began. 'We've looked at all the circumstances and you must share your farms.'

As Nigel started to reply, Chikanda shushed him.

'No speaking, you're just a racist!' he shouted.

Funnily enough, I'd never been called a racist even though there were times that I was. Nigel tried to respond but Chikanda lifted his hand and asked him: 'Don't you know the history of Zimbabwe?'

'Well, yes, I do,' replied Nigel.

'But you only know it from the white side.'

At this, the war vets started chanting, 'The whites must go! The whites must go!'

I just sat there putting on a show of bravado and trying to act unconcerned in front of this crowd but you could feel this war going on in people's minds because some of them had worked for me and didn't really feel what was happening was right.

When the chants had subsided, Nigel tried a new tack. He put his arm on Chikanda's shoulder and said, 'What is it you want, my little friend?'

Chikanda was a short, stocky man and bristled at the comment. 'Am I little?' he asked.

'Well, you look little to me, but maybe you're not,' replied Nigel.

The Inspector changed tack. 'Why is Netsai not staying in your house?' he demanded.

'Well, it's impossible she stays there,' began Nigel.

'Aah you see, you are a racist. You whites are all the same.' He almost spat the words.

Nigel shook his head and smiled. *Inside I was feeling very tense for there was this angry crowd and I felt anything could happen any time. I knew the stories of things that had happened in that office. I thought there is no point getting in a rage like they expect from white farmers whose farms had been taken over. The only way I could survive was to wrong-foot them.*

'No, I'm very happy with Netsai moving in, very happy with that,' he said. 'The thing is you don't know my wife, she's got *ma jealous* like you can't believe but I'm not saying I'm not attracted to Netsai.'

He had spoken very seriously. There was a stunned silence.

This Netsai had snarled at me for two days and she was a really ugly lady, small and fat with yellow teeth all over the place, and when she snarled she looked even more ugly. She had been a prostitute with the soldiers so wasn't the most morally upright of ladies. So when I said that, she put on this coy look and said, 'Oh, Mr Hough,' as if flirting with me. At this there was a loud guffaw from behind the ply- board wall, then Pete, who's not the most diplomatic guy, just dissolved into laughter. It was like a release button. Then all the group started laughing and saying, 'Hough and Netsai, Hough is marrying Netsai,' then repeating the story to each other like a biblical tale.

The whole impetus of the meeting collapsed and in the con- fusion Pete and Nigel just left and got into the car and drove back to the farm.

Back at Kendor, they found the wrought-iron gates closed and barricaded. There was no way they were going to get back in. Through the fence they could see that the squatters were already looting the farm. Nigel imagined Aqui queening it over his house. But there was nothing he could do. He knew that they had been lucky to escape with their lives. Time had run out. Now there were no white farmers left in Wenimbi Valley.

*   *   *

Inside the farm, Aqui was in a quandary. *I didn't know them, the war vets that came to the farm that morning when Boss Nigel had gone to Harare. They wanted to intimidate me and get me out so I told them, 'I'm also black and Zimbabwean and also a war vet. I have all my rights. Why are you trying to intimidate me? If I want to stay here I can. I participated a lot in the war and even after the war I carried on and did a lot of work for the party. If I decide to work for the white people that's my choice.'*

When she refused to let them in the gate, they called her a traitor. *I said, 'Don't waste your words,' then the rain started so I let them in to shelter.*

First she had been angry. *I knew our people needed land and thought it was quite right that the government take these farms and land but it should have been properly worked out, not like this. I saw the way these war vets intimidated people, made them scared and wanted everything, even my things. So from the beginning I said, 'I'm not going to let you do anything to the property.' I told them, 'If you start grabbing things from inside the house, that's stealing, that's not land resettlement.' I told them this white person is God's being the same as you and God doesn't want you to do these things, so call off your dogs.*

I don't know how I did it but I was very firm. I felt I was a Zimbabwean too. I even said, 'Some of you here weren't even war vets. Some of you were sell-outs during the war.'

But it was clear that she, alone in her polka-dot apron, could not hold off this gang of squatters with sticks and axes, many of whom were drunk. *It was very dangerous because they were using youths, giving them dagga to smoke to make them crazy. I was very aware that they could turn on me.* To her dismay, apart from Henry, none of Nigel's other workers stood firm. Some fled and others even joined the war vets.

Then I thought, if I joined them, perhaps I could protect the Houghs so the war vets didn't kill them and also save some of their things. I felt bad for Boss Nigel because I could see what he thought

*of me when I was shouting 'Death to whites' and all those things.
But I had to be more enthusiastic than the other war vets so they
wouldn't suspect me. I was used to motivating people from my days
in the war so I ended up leading the chants.*

Once Nigel had gone from the house and she was left alone
with the squatters, Aqui began to wonder about seizing the farm
for herself. As she had suspected, most of the invaders were not
real war vets and some of them were starting to look up to her
as a leader. *Why shouldn't I have it rather than Netsai? I had worked
for the party all those years whereas these people had come from
nowhere. I had signed the list requesting a farm.*

The farm was clearly going to be taken over anyway, which
meant she would be left without a job again. She knew the Houghs
were thinking about moving to Australia and had already applied
for visas so they would probably leave and forget all about her,
just as the Looses had done. With all the whites leaving, there
would be no more jobs for her despite her new cordon bleu
cooking qualification. Her children would have to leave school
without completing their education. *It was nobody's fault; that
was just how things were. Whites might lose their farms but they
got on a plane and left to start a new life some other place, while
blacks lay down and tried to survive on wild fruit.*

Aqui thought about her son Wayne, almost 15 and at boarding
school in Harare, paid for by the Houghs. He was a bright boy
and she had big plans for him to go to college and perhaps
become a doctor or an accountant. Her eldest, Heather, had left
school and longed to go to London and study nursing. Then there
was Vanessa who dreamt of being a top-flight secretary but needed
money to learn shorthand and typing and computer skills. She
did not want them to end up like her. *My dreams hadn't come
true. Maybe this was a way my children's could.*

So she stayed inside the house with Netsai and the war vets,
watching and waiting for her opportunity. She did not think it
would be hard. *They were not clever people. For example, some of*

Nigel and Aqui

them took the big pump that pumped the water for the animals and the house and sold it. How will you farm now? I asked them. They also kept fighting with each other, particularly General Tongogara, Shasha and Netsai who all thought they were in charge. But I cooked them meat from the deep freeze and milk for their tea and mealie meal the Boss had given me so they ended up loving me. In the meantime I managed to lock some of the Houghs' things in the workers' rondavels while I figured out what to do.

For the first few days after the farm had been taken over, Nigel lived in the hope that he could go back in and chase the war vets off because they did not have the right papers. *I also wanted to see what Aqui was doing. I was still more shocked about that than anything.* But in the end his friends Barry Percival and Pete Moore convinced him that to return would be suicidal.

The Houghs had left the farm with literally nothing but the clothes they were wearing and were desperate to retrieve some of their property. The police were unsympathetic to Nigel but Barry's status as a headteacher carried a lot of respect and eventually they agreed to give them two hours in the farmhouse to collect their belongings. However, they would only allow Claire and Barry to go, not Nigel.

Two hours is very little time to pack up a room, let alone a large house of two adults and four children, so they tried to make a list of the most important and needed items. This included family photographs, personal documents, Claire's jewellery, the children's medical records, blankets and the microwave. 'You work out very quickly what's important to you,' said Claire. 'What I really regret is I didn't take things that were of personal value to the children, their toys and little stuffed animals. Even today Emma talks about her little zebra that got left behind. It was their history too and I didn't think about that.'

They arrived at the house to find Netsai lying on a sun-lounger with her feet up, admiring her new farm. Aqui and some of the others were having a braai on the lawn with meat from the freezer and the men had drunk all the beer. Netsai's children were already wearing clothes belonging to the Hough children and playing with their toys. Claire was furious.

By then they had been living in the house for a few days and also the population had come in and looted everything. They'd taken some of our curtains, the meat from the freezer, many things were gone.

It was not easy finding the items they wanted, particularly with the policeman and a group of around ten squatters following Claire around closely. Each time she focused on something and said, 'Those are mine, those are my crystal glasses, my dinner plates, they were wedding presents,' Netsai would claim that the items were hers. Then the policeman would say to Claire, 'Maybe it is yours, maybe it isn't, so you better just leave them here.' Even the new curtains which Claire had only recently hung, the policeman insisted might belong to Netsai.

All the time Aqui was identifying things and saying, 'That's mine, that's mine, I'm the most senior war vet here.'

As fast as Barry and his workers loaded things onto the truck, others would remove them. Time was starting to run out when Barry had an idea. Claire had kept chickens to sell eggs to the local population, and when she had arrived to reclaim her belongings one of the first things the squatters had done was all grab chickens for themselves, fearing she was going to take them. They had tied them in plastic bags with their heads sticking out as left like that a chicken will just sit. The lawn was covered with literally hundreds of these chickens in plastic bags just sitting there. Barry started kicking some of them over so they would flutter about and try to escape, causing everyone to dash about trying to reclaim their chickens. In the meantime he would run and put some more things on the lorry and Claire would try and retrieve a few more possessions.

All the time things were disappearing – guitars, the instrument panel from Nigel's old microlight plane, his father's watch, clothes – many borne off on the heads of former workers who had changed sides pretty quickly. Occasionally Barry noticed Aqui flitting back and forth, handing round beers and grabbing things for herself.

When Claire unlocked the pantry, the one who called himself General Tongogara followed her in and swooped on a bottle labelled vodka. In fact it was Echinacea herb steeped in alcohol, of which she gave the children a spoonful every morning to boost their immunity against illness. He took a huge swig, then spat it out for it tasted foul. 'Aah, I have been poisoned,' he cried, swaggering around, clutching his stomach.

His eyes then lit on the huge deep freeze. 'That is mine,' he announced. This sparked off an argument with Netsai who insisted it was hers. But Tongogara and his sidekicks carried it outside and tied it on top of his little Renault 4.

The most important items such as Claire's jewellery were in the master bedroom. When Netsai realized where they were headed, she had locked the door and refused to open it. A drunken crowd followed Barry along the corridor, bearing Nigel's golf clubs and cricket bats as weapons, as he demanded she open it. Eventually he said he would break the door down. Spitting with rage but clearly not wanting a broken door in her new house, she pulled out the keys from between her breasts.

The bedroom was packed with looted items, many of which she had hidden under the bed. Claire pulled out a children's Bible. 'That's mine!' shouted Netsai trying to snatch it away. Claire opened it up and read out the inscription to her eldest child, 'Dear Jessie'.

The mood lightened when Barry lifted up the bed and pulled out a big box. Inside were 100 condoms Nigel had obtained for handing out to farm-workers. Despite the tension, everyone fell about laughing.

The policeman then said it was time to leave. Outside, they

were greeted by an astonishing scene. The children had been given an enormous blow-up whale for Christmas, which they used to play with in the pool and ride on. General Tongogara had taken a fancy to this and dragged it out of the pool but could not work out how to deflate it. Instead of letting it down, he tried to squash it into his car and drove off with the deep freeze on top and the tail of the whale out one window and the nose out of the other.

Nigel, who was waiting in a car just along the road in case of trouble, could not believe what he was seeing. The ancient Renault 4 chugged past with the warlord and blow-up whale squeezed in together and the whole thing groaning under the weight of the freezer. *That was the last of my farm.*

That evening at the Percivals', he began to think about the future for the first time. Claire had recently started working as a teacher at nearby Peterhouse School, so they would have to scrape by on her salary for a while. They had lost almost everything they owned but they would not starve. There was a nationwide short- age of cooking oil and Nigel had discussed buying some land from his nephew to build a factory.

Compared to a lot of people, things could have been much worse. But I did feel that my faith in human nature had been sorely shaken.

Suddenly his mobile phone rang. 'Mr Hough, Sir,' came the familiar voice. 'It's Aqui.'

Aqui had been haunted all week by the look of bitter betrayal that Nigel had given her as he left the farm. *Of course I felt it was unfair that the Houghs had this big house and I was just a maid. I wished I had more things for my children. But I am what I am, God made me like this even if it's difficult. And after a while I realized it would be wrong to take the farm for I wouldn't feel comfortable with something I didn't work for. I didn't have a clue how to farm.*

Nor did she want the likes of Netsai and General Tongogara to take things to which they had even less right than her. *I knew it was wrong what they were doing and I decided to try and save some of the things of the Houghs. I put them in the roundhouses where I had already put some things aside, like a television. While Madam Claire and Barry were trying to get things out, I took other items that I knew were important to them and I had seen where Netsai had hidden. I had to be careful and suddenly all these war vets came to grab everything so I said, 'No I'm not going to let you, these are my things.' But it wasn't working; they said, 'How do you have all these fancy things?'*

So I opened the deep freeze and asked them, 'Do you want some meat?' and they said, 'Yes,' then I chucked these big ostrich steaks to the far-away hedge so they all ran for it. I gave them lots of bottles of beer from the house to get them drunk for I knew they would kill me if they realized what I was going to do.

Then she picked up the phone.

Postscript

OVER THE WEEKS following the farm invasion, war vets tried to abduct Claire on five different occasions. Groups of around twenty ZANU-PF youths would be waiting for her when she came out of school and in the car park of the supermarket when she finished shopping. She was lucky that each time the school security guards or shop manager intervened. Nigel also found himself surrounded by war vets in his car one day and only escaped by revving up and driving through them. It was so terrifying that the Houghs ended up moving to Harare.

They now live back in Marondera on the campus of the school where Claire teaches. A new baby, Ollie, joined the family in 2004, so there are seven Houghs squashed into the tiny three-bedroom bungalow furnished with the items rescued from the farm by Aqui. It is a far cry from their sprawling farmhouse, and there's a battle every morning for the one minuscule bathroom. But it is a happy home, full of beautiful blond-haired blue-eyed children reading, drawing or playing, and the comforting smell of a chicken roasting – at least until one of the many daily power cuts turns off the oven. Only occasionally does someone go quiet and a far-away look come over their face and you know that they are thinking about the big old farm with its msasa trees and rock groves or Emma's stuffed zebra that now sits on Netsai's dresser.

'I don't like driving down that road past our farm,' admits Claire. 'I try not to look, I feel very bitter. But then when I see Netsai hitching a ride at the bus stop and I'm driving past in my people carrier, I think I'm still much better off. All this land grabbing has not improved their lives; they are still living a life of subsistence. You just feel, What was the point?'

They have arranged visas for Australia but are reluctant to leave their beloved country between the Limpopo and the Zambezi, still hoping that Robert Mugabe will somehow see the error of his ways. 'Now we have a tiny little life,' says Claire. 'I miss the space of the farm and doing my cows and sheep and chickens, but on the campus I feel safe and happy.'

'The thing I am most grateful for is that the children weren't there when the invaders came and so weren't traumatized. They can still have happy memories of the farm.'

In the whole Marondera district there are only five white farmers left out of around 400.

Of the 36 farming families that Nigel is related to in Zimbabwe, not a single one remains on their farm.

'I don't think we will ever get the farms back,' says Nigel, who has various business ventures under way, this time involving crocodiles rather than ostriches, crocodiles being rather less prone to stress. 'I really think it's destructive to mope about the past. The good thing about what has happened is that it makes you focus on what really matters, and that's your relationships with God and family. And of course Aqui. On one side there's still a big cultural divide and our lifestyles are so different. But I feel like a barrier has been broken down. It's no longer just an employer–employee relationship but a friendship.'

Aqui is back living in the shack in Dombotombo, sleeping under the kitchen shelf and sharing the three shoebox-sized rooms with an assortment of her own children, her sister and her sister's new baby. The jit music on her neighbour's radio is as noisy as ever and she can no longer remember the last time the shops had cooking oil, milk, sugar or flour.

Her warm, vivacious personality led to her being talent-spotted and briefly starring in a television soap opera called *Waiters*, set in a restaurant. She played Marjorie, a hard-nosed magazine editor, always threatening to write a bad review of the food.

Like most things in Zimbabwe, the production ran out of money. She is now working for the Houghs part-time, surviving on money sent back from England by her eldest daughter Heather who works in a care home in Southend and longs to study nursing. Aqui still dreams of one day extending the shack.

She insists she wasn't tempted to keep the farm. 'It wasn't mine,' she laughs. 'Anyway I don't want a palace, I just want to be comfortable.'

Although Aqui firmly believes that Nehanda should be avenged and the land returned to the Shona, she is sure that what her old hero Mugabe has done is not the answer. 'There's no point having a farm if you don't know how to farm,' she says. 'Before, when I would get the bus along the Hwedza road to the Houghs' farm, I just would see green the other side, fields of mealie maize, and some nice plump Jersey cows. Instead, now if at all you see maize, it is short and yellow, because it has not been fertilized and not planted at the right time and there are no cows. Mostly the fields are black and burnt.'

Her mother still lives in a hut in Zhakata's Kraal. Nobody has cows or goats any more and the villagers are surviving on baobab pods and ground roots.

Recently the Houghs all went to Sun City in South Africa for a holiday and took Aqui with them. It was the first time that Aqui had ever flown or indeed gone on vacation. 'I went in a big plane with them and stayed in an amazing room with a bathroom as big as my house. We all ate at the same table and they treated me like a sister. It was like a dream come true.'

As a result of Barry Percival's courageous help during the takeover of the Houghs' farm, he and his family became targets of the local ZANU-PF militia. Thugs surrounded his house, chanting and dancing, then abducted him to one of their torture centres in Marondera. The police inspector Julius Chikanda telephoned Nigel and warned, 'We're going to kill your friend.' Nigel was horrified but the ever-resourceful headmaster managed to escape with the help of a local party official whose child was a pupil at his school. A week later Barry and Rosanne Percival and their children left the country for England.

Netsai is still living on Nigel's farm. Her boyfriend Shasha died shortly after the takeover, the third person involved to die mysteriously.

The whereabouts of General Tongogara and his giant blow-up whale are unknown.

EPILOGUE

Great Zimbabwe, November 2005

'LISTEN,' said Shepherd, the guide. 'Can you hear it?'
    We were standing on top of the ruined Hill Complex of
Great Zimbabwe looking out over the Mzilikwe valley. All around
us was a maze of passages and enclosures formed from rectangular
blocks of granite piled row upon row with no mortar to hold
them together yet that had held fast for centuries. Some of the
stones were arranged in chevron patterns, for this was said to be
the King's palace. Down below on the plains I could see a mysterious series of walled circles, the remains of what had once been
the greatest medieval city in sub-Saharan Africa.

Radiocarbon dating and assorted coins, china and glass beads
found in the ruins have revealed that people lived here between
1200 and 1500 but no one really knows who built this place or
why. It is thought that it was once the headquarters of the vast
Monomatapa kingdom, whose kings ruled over all of today's
Zimbabwe, northern South Africa, and large swathes of Mozambique, Malawi, Zambia and Tanzania. The name came from a
Portuguese corruption of the title *Mwana Mutapa* which meant
Lord of the Plundered Lands.

'If you listen well and carefully,' said Shepherd, 'the stones will
speak to you. Some say it is the clicking of the spears of Monomotapa angry at what has befallen his empire.'

I listened hard, my ear pressed against the cold stone as

Shepherd had indicated, wanting to hear, but there was nothing
beyond the rush of blood in my head after the steep climb. No
birds, no wind. Just a stillness as if the land was in waiting. The
rains were late this year and it was a strangely grey day. The
paramount chiefs of the area would be coming up the hill that

night to the Sacred Enclosure to hold a *bira*, a ceremony to ask the ancestors for rain.

Dzimba dza mabwe, houses of stone. It was this place that gave its name to the independence movements and then the country.

I followed Shepherd through a narrow passage between giant scattered boulders into the Ritual Enclosure, a walled circular chamber. On the empty pillars once stood the soapstone birds that became the symbol of the new nation, depicted on its flag and its currency. The long-necked birds with melancholy expressions were thought to represent fish eagles and be messengers of the ancestral spirits. One and a half remained behind; the rest were looted by Europeans, including Rhodes, who kept one on a plinth in his Cape Town residence, but some have now been returned and perch on stands behind glass in a strange black-painted room in the museum. Five came from South Africa, swapped for a collection of 30,000 bees and wasps. One returned recently from Berlin after many travels, for it had been looted by the Russians in 1945 during the city's fall and taken to St Petersburg.

From the Ritual Enclosure, another passage led down to the Acoustic Cave from which the King would call down to the valley to summon one of his queens. The queens dwelt behind the towering walls of the Great Enclosure, a vast elliptical compound with walls 11 metres high and 5 metres thick. Inside stands a large conical tower that featured on the wad of worthless banknotes weighing down my rucksack, its purpose a mystery. Some of the bricks in the base had been broken to form an opening, which Shepherd explained was made by German explorers who thought the tower must contain treasure and drilled into it, only to find it solid.

The ruins are set among aloe trees that look like something left from the time when dinosaurs walked the earth, and the place has the same romantic feel as Machu Picchu. I wandered amid the twisting walls and wondered what had happened to this great empire where more than 10,000 people lived until its collapse at

The Great Enclosure

the end of the fifteenth century. Some believe it was because of the overambitions of its King or battles over succession; others that people left in search of precious salt, or that it had depleted its own resources, forcing the population to move out to create smaller *zimbabwes* like those scattered across the highveld between the Limpopo and the Zambezi.

It was easy to see why, when Portuguese explorers came across Great Zimbabwe in the sixteenth century, they were stunned. The only other stone structures in Africa were the pyramids in Egypt. Black Africans had no tradition of building in stone and the explorers could not believe that the natives they were busy colonizing had possessed such skill and knowledge. They decided that they must have come across the biblical land of Ophir that supplied gold to King Solomon and the Queen of Sheba.

The first to make Great Zimbabwe known to the world, in 1871, was the German archaeologist Karl Mauch who said the walls must have been constructed by Middle Eastern people and thought he had come across the palace of the Queen of Sheba. As proof he cut wood from a door lintel, which he claimed to be cedar imported from Lebanon. It was in fact African sandalwood.

The mystery of the city's origins enabled both black and white to use Great Zimbabwe as propaganda. Right up until independence, the Rhodesian government insisted that it was built not by Africans but Phoenicians or Egyptians. They referred to the soapstone birds as 'Phoenician hawk' and used them on their coins and coat of arms. In 1964, the year before Ian Smith declared UDI, a book was published called *Zimbabwe: Rhodesia's Ancient Greatness*. The author, A.J. Bruwer, asserted that Great Zimbabwe was built by the Phoenicians between the conquests of Alexander the Great. He dedicated his work to the Prime Minister.

Similarly the black nationalists seized on Great Zimbabwe as evidence of a glorious African past to reinforce their right to the land, and named the independence movement after it. Even among themselves, it was useful to boast some connection. In the early days the movement was dominated by members of the Karanga clan such as Leopold Takawira, Josiah Tongogara and Simon Muzenda. Mugabe, who was a Zezuru, gained kudos by encouraging the belief that he was from the influential Mugabe dynasty of chiefs who guard the ruins.

Today in the museum, Mugabe's photograph has been added to the list of great kings of Monomotapa and the chiefs of the Mugabe clan, even though he is no relation.

'His excellency was here in April,' said Shepherd, seeing me looking at the picture. He added that the 81-year-old President had 'bounded like a goat' up the hill which had had me huffing and puffing.

Great Zimbabwe was one of the most beautiful places I have ever visited, yet there were no tourists. In the lodge where I stayed

Overview of the Great Enclosure

the night, I self-consciously took a place at one of the massive tables in a cavernous banqueting hall hewn from a giant rock. My steps echoed across the room. The only other guests were a bemused-looking black couple from Harare who had won a weekend there as a prize. We all giggled as most things we tried to order were 'not available', including toast at breakfast.

In ancient times Great Zimbabwe was one of the wonders of Africa. Modern Zimbabwe is one of its nightmares.

To get to Great Zimbabwe, I had driven through a country that had become a land of wreckage. Victoria Falls, once a bustling resort offering everything from ballooning to bungee jumping over cataracts, was a ghost town. The falls were at their most spectacular and I was showered by the spray, forgetting that my passport was in my belt-purse until I arrived back in London and the immigration official at Heathrow initially refused to accept the waterlogged document. Yet on the walk around the rim of the gorge, I did not see another soul. Outside used to be a row of curio stalls where one had to dodge insistent salesmen holding out carved animals and urging, 'Madam, yes you like hippo?' Now there was just debris: the stalls had been destroyed as part of Operation Murambatswina, Mugabe's 'clean-up' programme. Later, I met the Mayor, a lumbering bear of a man, from the opposition MDC. 'I felt so helpless,' he said, wiping away tears, as he told me of the bulldozing of homes and businesses in his town.

Down the road was Hwange National Park. On my first visit back in 1994, I had seen so many animals – zebra, buffalo, lion, eland – that I stopped counting. This time you could drive for miles without seeing any. Not live, at least. There were corpses of elephants and buffalo whose legs had swollen and burst and they had fallen down dead. This was partly because of the worst drought to hit southern Africa for years. But the real problem was that the park had run out of diesel fuel and pumps to keep the watering holes full.

Bulawayo, the capital of the Ndebele, is still an opposition stronghold. The art gallery was even showing what were clearly protest paintings of Operation Murambatswina, made from pieces of wreckage and with titles like *Inferno*. The city's famous Fifth Street market was a tangle of twisted metal. 'Psst . . . want some tomatoes?' whispered a voice. Traders now sell vegetables as clandestinely as if they were peddling drugs.

While I was there, word came of a dairy farm that had just been invaded out on the Matopos road. In the early days of the land grab dairy farms were protected to safeguard milk production, but not any more. I found a family taut-faced and on edge, serving me tea and freshly made chocolate rice-crispie cakes, and vowing to cling on to the farm started by their Scottish grandmother back in the 1950s. These were the bitter-enders, determined to hang on, knowing their worthless Zim dollars would get them nothing elsewhere. After haranguing the family all day, the truck of invaders from town had gone, but we all knew they would be back. The teenage daughter was in tears and hysterical. Is it worth it, I wondered?

The road to Harare used to pass through prime farmland. Today the fields are blackened and overgrown, the long greenhouses ripped of their roofs and farmsteads stripped of roof tiles and windows. Former white farmers tell me they play 'Spot the cow' on the five-hour drive. I count two and no tractors. Someone explains that the government has set up Provincial Farm Material and Equipment Acquisition Committees, otherwise known as loot committees.

In Harare, the wreckage of Operation Murambatswina was still visible. Most of the estimated 700,000 people who lost their homes in the Pol Pot-style campaign drifted back to rural areas where villagers were already starving. Others had no place to go and ended up living like animals on the dusty ground in shelters fashioned from cardboard. They were surviving on pieces of the rotten potatoes that their children salvaged from the bins. Every so often thugs from the ruling party would come and chase them out, forcing them to find some more rubble to squat on.

Far away in my garden in south-west London stands a scrap-metal giraffe called Elvis that I had bought in March 2005 from one of the curio stalls on Harare's Enterprise Road. The young sculptor sitting among his fantastic scrap-metal zoo of ostriches, elephants and other creatures asked me to give the giraffe his name 'so as not to forget us'. It is a moment I will not forget because just then we heard the wail of sirens and Elvis froze in terror. Moments later the presidential convoy appeared with its motorcycle outriders, ambulances, and trucks full of men in khaki pointing AK-47s, ready to shoot any passer-by that moved.

My heart was sinking as I drove up Enterprise Road again in November, wondering what had happened to Elvis. All that remained of the curio market was some crushed metal that might have once been Elvis's marvellous animals. I asked someone at a nearby shop what had happened and she looked at me in terror, then busied herself in the back.

In the city centre, I was surprised to see flash new BMWs and Volkswagen Beetle convertibles. Their owners were presumably those close to power and thus able to obtain foreign currency at the official rate of 26,000 to the US$, which was a fifth of the market rate of 120,000. So worthless was the currency that brand new signs had sprung up warning of 1 million dollar parking fines rising to 5 million if the car was towed away.

Hiring a car had not been difficult, even if the lady at the Hertz agency at Harare airport (who later admitted that it was no longer really Hertz) did warn, 'This is not a 100 per cent car.' But petrol was so scarce that when it came in people were queuing for three or four days and a full tank was the main prize in the lottery.

I used my US dollars to buy black-market petrol but paid the true cost of this when just outside Masvingo, not far from Great

Zimbabwe, my car slowed to a halt, then lost power altogether. Somewhat fortuitously this occurred just in front of Byword Motors where the receptionist was a grandmotherly white lady called Florence who made me a cup of tea and apologized for lack of biscuits. The mechanic soon emerged to tell me that my fuel pump had seized up because of dirty petrol. There were neither pumps nor filters to be had, so he and his men laboriously cleaned out my blocked ones and sieved the sand from my petrol while Florence told me about losing her farm with its garden that had been her pride and joy. 'I suppose it was a fool's paradise,' she said. She was delighted when I produced a copy of *Homes and Gardens* in which I had been hiding my notes and told me that her favourite magazine *Readers Digest* had been banned in the country ever since running an unflattering piece about Mugabe.

One of her friends dropped by to return the copy of *Pride and Prejudice* that she had borrowed and gossip about the drama competition she was organizing. It seemed odd that amateur dramatics were still going on as we talked of how the country was being reduced to pre-modern times, returning to ploughs and recommissioning steam trains. According to Florence, you could smell Masuingo hospital for miles off because no one had petrol to collect bodies from the mortuary. She, like many I met, was surviving on money sent from her children abroad.

By summer 2006, inflation was above 1200 per cent and according to the government's own Central Statistical Office, a family of five needed 22 million Zimbabwean dollars per month for basic goods and services. Life expectancy for women had fallen to just 34 and cemeteries were running out of space. In November a third of the army was sent home because the government could no longer feed them. The UN described the country as 'going into meltdown'. The first deaths from cholera were reported in Harare and municipality cleaners began finding dead newborn babies people had thrown away because they couldn't afford to feed them.

Yet Mugabe seemed more powerful than ever. His party was re-elected in March 2005 with an increased majority. They had fought on an anti-Blair platform with full-page advertisements in the state media denouncing the British Prime Minister as the source of all Zimbabwe's problems. The election was declared 'seriously flawed' by Britain's Foreign Secretary Jack Straw, and 'free and fair' by observers from Libya, China, North Korea and Iran. The European Union had not been allowed to send observers while a group from the Carter Center of former US President Jimmy Carter, one of the world's most respected monitoring organizations, were turned back at the airport, accused of being 'terrorists'.

Mwana Mutapa, Lord of the Plundered Lands, Mugabe stays in power largely through his web of patronage, particularly to senior military officers. He has surrounded himself more and more with people from his own Zezuru clan and ex-colleagues from the Chimurenga, even those who had once been critics such as Edgar Tekere who had stood against him in 1990 Presidential election and Dzikamai Mavhaire, the man who back in 2000 had dared suggest he retire after the defeat in the referendum. 'You can't be on the outside if you want to survive,' explained one such returnee. To provide jobs for these people, he created a new Senate to which elections were held in November.

With this Senate, Mugabe had even managed to destroy the opposition, which split over whether or not to participate in yet another fraudulent election. Since then the MDC have been tearing themselves apart with accusations that senior members were actually in the pay of the ruling party and given stolen farms by Mugabe. His tentacles are everywhere.

I don't sleep easy in my bed while I am in Zimbabwe. I am there illegally and if I am caught the sentence is two years' imprisonment. I am one of just three foreign journalists to have been named by Mugabe's spokesman George Charamba as an enemy of the state. I have a six-year-old son back home and have heard all about Zimbabwe's overcrowded jails, rife with TB and lice. I do not want to end up in one.

The country might look surprisingly innocuous for somewhere lumped with North Korea and Iran as one of the 'outposts of tyranny' by US Secretary of State Condoleezza Rice. But I have met too many victims and seen too many scars to be under any illusions. This is an extremely repressive regime where people disappear in the night. The state controls the internet and one of the two mobile phone networks and has obtained Chinese technology to intercept the calls on the other. On the few occasions I speak on the phone, we use strange codes such as 'rose gardens' for farms and 'the Yorkshireman' for Mugabe (written backwards, it spells Ebagum).

I have to be careful who I talk to, for I neither want to implicate them, nor be caught. This is getting harder because there are far fewer white faces now than there used to be and spies from the CIO are everywhere. Twice after going into townships, I am told that everyone I spoke to was then visited by secret police.

Nigel books me into a small local lodge just outside Marondera, and only after check-in do I realize that this too has been taken over by war vets. Rather than printing a new menu, they have just written in sadza between the steak and kidney pudding and apple pie. At lunch, perhaps to impress me, Nigel orders the sadza and it comes in thick wads. He tells me that when he was at school this would have been 'kaffir food' that no white would dream of eating.

That night, I walk nervously up the long unlit path to my hut. Inside, the pink-fringed silk lampshades have seen better days, the door does not lock and there is a fat brown centipede in the dirty cracked bath. I hear a car outside and wake with a start imagining it is the CIO. But it turns out to be guests returning from the noisy bar.

My nerves have already been wrecked in Harare, when the electronic gates of the house where I was staying opened for me to drive out one evening, to reveal a road filled with blue flashing lights. That's it, I thought, and froze. Then my amused companion pointed out that they were fire engines.

One day Nigel picks me up to go and see the farm where he grew up. We pass the cracked 'Riversdale' sign and bump along an overgrown track to the old farm buildings.

The squatters think we have come to reclaim it and seem disappointed that we have not. 'We heard the whites were coming back,' says one. An old man pulls out a sheaf of withered-looking tobacco leaves. 'We don't know what to do,' he says. 'We are hungry and no one comes to help us.' The farmhouse has been stripped of all furniture and fittings, and families are squatting among dried faeces, cooking from fires on the floor.

On the way back we pass Nigel's own farm and he slows down.

The ostrich sign is still there though there are no ostriches to be seen. 'Netsai is growing tomatoes now then,' he says. He tells me he keeps finding himself humming the old war song 'Rhodesians Never Die'.

'Do you think you'll ever get the farm back?' I ask.

He thinks for a moment. 'No,' he replies. 'You just have to move on.'

Not everyone has moved on. Later at Nigel's house, Aqui is upset when one of his friends drops by to pick up his child who has been over to play and speaks over her head to me as if she were not there. 'You see things haven't changed at all,' she says. 'They still think they are the masters.' Then, ever ready to give the benefit of the doubt, she adds, 'Maybe he is one of those who lost his farm. And of course there are also blacks like that who won't go near whites, they just hate them.'

When I accompany Aqui back to Dombotombo she takes me to the shack across the road, where 24 people are now living. One large family is sleeping outside around the chicken coop with a few pieces of salvaged furniture – an iron bed and a kitchen cupboard – more victims of Mugabe's demolition. They show me the hole where their house used to be. 'It's like wartime,' says one.

The next morning we leave for her village. It is so poor and the earth is cracking with dryness. 'I have never seen it so bad,' says Aqui, clearly shocked. 'Whose fault is this?' I ask her aunts, 'Do you blame Mugabe?' There is an audible intake of breath. 'You are asking the Unquestionable,' says one woman.

People might not talk about him but there are plenty of rumours. Mugabe is said to be so paranoid that he refuses to open any post. His wife Grace, they say, is under house arrest after she tried to flee dressed as an Arab. Mugabe spends hours each day with a Serbian psychiatrist because he is haunted by the ghosts of General Tongogara and others he has killed.

On several occasions I am chatting with opposition members

when they get telephone calls which they react to with excitement. 'Mugabe is in a heart clinic in South Africa and won't last the night,' they whisper. I know they are clutching at straws for I remember Shepherd telling of Mugabe running up the steep hill of Great Zimbabwe.

Just as the collapse of Great Zimbabwe remains an enigma, so it is a mystery how one man could so wilfully destroy his own country. How could Mugabe, the man who seems at war with the world, be the same man who stunned everyone with his forgiveness and conciliatory speeches after independence? Did he learn too much from Smith's assassins and become an African Macbeth 'in blood/ Stepp'd in so far, that, should I wade no more,/ Returning were as tedious as go o'er'?

But I remember reading how he had warned on taking office: 'The change is not in me ... the transformation really is taking place in the minds of those who once upon a time regarded me as an extremist, a murderer, a psychopath killer. I have remained my true self. What I was I still am.'

I am sad to leave Great Zimbabwe and its houses of stone but I have tarried too long in the country and am fearful of being caught. Shepherd has resisted my attempts to draw him on the country's future. But before I go, he tells me to write something in my notebook. 'We have a saying in Shona – *gomo radonha* – when the King has died the mountain falls,' he says, as if in warning.

CHRONOLOGY

1888   King Lobengula agrees Rudd Concession for Cecil Rhodes to prospect Mashonaland

1889   Queen Victoria grants Rhodes a royal charter to form British South Africa Company to administer Mashonaland and Matabeleland

1890   First Pioneers arrive in Mashonaland and hoist Union flag in Fort Salisbury

1893   Lobengula dies or commits suicide after Jameson's war on the Ndebele

1896–7   First Chimurenga or Shona rebellion against the white settlers

1924   Robert Gabriel Mugabe born in Jesuit mission station of Kutama

1949   Mugabe wins scholarship to Fort Hare University, South Africa, where Nelson Mandela studied. On graduation becomes a teacher in Northern Rhodesia (later Zambia), then Ghana

1957   Ghana becomes first black African colony to gain independence
Joshua Nkomo launches African National Congress (ANC), Rhodesia's first black nationalist party. This is then banned and becomes National Democratic Party (NDP)

1960   Mugabe joins NDP and becomes publicity secretary

1961   Mugabe marries Sally Heyfron, a Ghanaian teacher whom he met while teaching in Ghana
NDP banned and becomes Zimbabwe African Patriotic Union (ZAPU)

1963   ZAPU splits and new group ZANU formed under

Ndabaningi Sithole

Nkomo, Mugabe and Sithole arrested

1964 Ian Douglas Smith becomes Prime Minister as leader of Rhodesian Front

Nyasaland and Northern Rhodesia given independence from Britain as Malawi and Zambia

1965 Smith announces Unilateral Declaration of Independence (UDI) from Britain

1966 Battle of Chinhoyi launches Second Chimurenga

1972 Liberation struggle stepped up to become full-scale war

1974 Mugabe organizes no-confidence movement against Sithole while in jail to become ZANU leader

Black nationalist leaders released, including Mugabe

1979 Lancaster House Conference paves way for black majority rule and independence

1980 First free elections – Mugabe's ZANU wins majority

Rhodesia becomes independent Zimbabwe and Mugabe Prime Minister

1982 Nkomo sacked from government, accused of plotting to overthrow Mugabe, and flees to London

1983–7 Mugabe deploys Fifth Brigade in Matabeleland, killing an estimated 10,000

1987 Unity agreement to merge Nkomo's ZAPU and Mugabe's ZANU

1988 Mugabe wins Africa Prize for his contribution to a 'sustainable end to hunger'

1992 Sally Mugabe dies

1994 Mugabe receives honorary knighthood from Britain's Queen Elizabeth II

1996 Mugabe marries his secretary, Grace Marufu

1999 Launch of Movement for Democratic Change (MDC) under leadership of Morgan Tsvangirai

2000 (12/13 February) Mugabe's new constitution overwhelmingly rejected by voters in Zimbabwe's first referendum

(15 April) First white farmer murdered

(2 June) List of first 800 farms to be seized published

(24–25 June) ZANU-PF wins narrow victory in parliamentary elections after months of intimidating MDC

2002   Mugabe wins presidential elections amid allegations of
massive rigging
Britain, US and EU refuse to accept results
Commonwealth suspends Zimbabwe

2005   (April) ZANU-PF wins increased two-thirds majority in
elections described by opposition and Western governments
as a sham
(June–August) Operation Murambatswina 'Clean up the
Filth' results in the loss of homes and livelihood of more
than 700,000 Zimbabweans
Mugabe awards himself power to confiscate any land with
no right of appeal
(November) MDC splits over decision whether to
participate in elections for a new Senate
Air Zimbabwe grounded because of lack of fuel
(December) United Nations describes country as going into
'meltdown'

GLOSSARY

baas – boss

braai – barbecue

chibuku – beer (also referred to as *whawha* or shake-shake)

dagga – mud mixed with cow dung used for building huts. Can also mean marijuana.

garden – small vegetable plot

guti – thin mist

impis – bands of Zulu warriors

kopje – hill

kraal – Africaans word for enclosure of horses, rattle, or a collection of huts. Probably comes from Portugeuse word curral.

lobola – bride price

mbanje – grass or cannabis

mbira – thumb piano made of a row of metal keys set into a calabash gourd

mhondoro – lion spirit

mombe, mombe – cow

mudzimu – ancestral spirits

munt – originates from *muntu*, word for 'person' (plural is *Bantu*, meaning 'people'), but used derogatively

murungu – white person

muti – herbs from a witchdoctor

nganga or n'anga – traditional healer or spirit medium

panga – machete

piccanin – black child, comes from Portuguese word *pequeno* for 'small'

pungwe – literally 'from darkness to light'; all-night meeting usually involving chanting and singing

sadza – maize porridge

shambok – a whip

shebeen – illegal drinking establishment

spruit – stream

stand – another word for field of crops

situpa – identity card

tokolosh – spirit, kind of goblin

toyi-toying – low rhythmic step dancing often practised by Nelson Mandela. Harare police arrested a group of MDC supporters for toyi-toying in March 2005 under the Miscellaneous Offences Act

UDI – Unilateral Declaration of Independence from Britain, announced by Ian Smith in November 1965

veld – open grassland (lowveld and highveld)

whorwe birds – guinea fowl